# A CELEBRATION
## OF POETS

PENNSYLVANIA
GRADES 7-12
SPRING 2012

creativeCOMMUNICATION
A CELEBRATION OF TODAY'S WRITERS

# A CELEBRATION OF POETS
## PENNSYLVANIA
## GRADES 7-12
## SPRING 2012

AN ANTHOLOGY COMPILED BY CREATIVE COMMUNICATION, INC.

Published by:

A CELEBRATION OF TODAY'S WRITERS

PO BOX 303 • SMITHFIELD, UTAH 84335
TEL. 435-713-4411 • WWW.POETICPOWER.COM

Authors are responsible for the originality of the writing submitted.

ISBN: 978-1-60050-502-7

# FOREWORD

Dear Reader:

Is writing meaningful to your life? The greatest gift that my mother ever gave me was her writing. For over 70 years, she kept a record of every moment that was meaningful in her life. Taking these stories, she created several books which allow me to remember and relive moments in my childhood and the life my mother had as she grew up. She got into the habit of writing and has now left a great legacy.

As a parent, I know that my children bring home samples of their writing from school assignments each week. However, after a few days on the school bulletin board or fridge at home, these slices of their lives often get thrown away.

The books we publish create a legacy for each of these students. Their work is recorded to show friends, family and future generations. We are glad to be part of capturing their thoughts, hopes and dreams.

The students that are published have shared a bit of themselves with us. Thank you for being part of this process, as every writer needs a reader. We hope that by recognizing these students, writing will become a part of their life and bring meaning to others.

Sincerely,

Thomas Worthen, Ph.D.
Editor
Creative Communication

# WRITING CONTESTS!

## Enter our next POETRY contest!
## Enter our next ESSAY contest!

### Why should I enter?
Win prizes and get published! Each year thousands of dollars in prizes are awarded throughout North America. The top writers in each division receive a monetary award and a free book that includes their published poem or essay. Entries of merit are also selected to be published in our anthology.

### Who may enter?
There are four divisions in the poetry contest. The poetry divisions are grades K-3, 4-6, 7-9, and 10-12. There are three divisions in the essay contest. The essay divisions are grades 3-6, 7-9, and 10-12.

### What is needed to enter the contest?
To enter the poetry contest send in one original poem, 21 lines or less. To enter the essay contest send in one original non-fiction essay, 250 words or less, on any topic. Please submit each poem and essay with a title, and the following information clearly printed: the writer's name, current grade, home address (optional), school name, school address, teacher's name and teacher's email address (optional). Contact information will only be used to provide information about the contest. For complete contest information go to www.poeticpower.com.

### How do I enter?
Enter a poem online at:
**www.poeticpower.com**
or
Mail your poem to:
Poetry Contest
PO Box 303
Smithfield UT 84335

Enter an essay online at:
**www.poeticpower.com**
or
Mail your essay to:
Essay Contest
PO Box 303
Smithfield UT 84335

### When is the deadline?
Poetry contest deadlines are August 16th, December 6th and April 9th. Essay contest deadlines are July 19th, October 18th and February 19th. Students can enter one poem and one essay for each spring, summer, and fall contest deadline.

### Are there benefits for my school?
Yes. We award $12,500 each year in grants to help with Language Arts programs. Schools qualify to apply for a grant by having 15 or more accepted entries.

### Are there benefits for my teacher?
Yes. Teachers with five or more students published receive a free anthology that includes their students' writing.

For more information please go to our website at **www.poeticpower.com**, email us at editor@poeticpower.com or call 435-713-4411.

# TABLE OF CONTENTS

# Spring 2012 Poetic Achievement Honor Schools

*Teachers who had fifteen or more poets accepted to be published*

The following schools are recognized as receiving a "Poetic Achievement Award." This award is given to schools who have a large number of entries of which over fifty percent are accepted for publication. With hundreds of schools entering our contest, only a small percent of these schools are honored with this award. The purpose of this award is to recognize schools with excellent Language Arts programs. This award qualifies these schools to receive a complimentary copy of this anthology. In addition, these schools are eligible to apply for a Creative Communication Language Arts Grant. Grants of two hundred and fifty dollars each are awarded to further develop writing in our schools.

**Barack Obama Academy**
**Pittsburgh**
Delacey Green*

**Bellmar Middle School**
**Belle Vernon**
Carol Aten Frow*
Karen Guseman
Todd Yancy

**Bellwood Antis Middle School**
**Bellwood**
Connie Stewart*

**Bishop McCort High School**
**Johnstown**
Lorie Regan*

**Cambria Heights Middle School**
**Patton**
Mrs. Leamer
Tammy Scott*

**Centerville Middle School**
**Lancaster**
Jen Axe*

**Danville Area Middle School**
**Danville**
Donna Heim*

**Donegal Middle School**
**Marietta**
Sheila Ayres*

**Eastern York High School**
**Wrightsville**
Timothy I. Flinchbaugh*

**Easton Area Middle School 7-8**
**Easton**
Mary Paini*

**Elizabeth Forward Middle School**
**Elizabeth**
Lois Leggett*

**Ephrata Middle School**
**Ephrata**
Michael C. Miller*
Debbie Nelms*

**First Philadelphia Charter School for**
**Literacy**
**Philadelphia**
Richard Crain*

**Fred S Engle Middle School**
**West Grove**
Karen Capone*

**Garnet Valley Middle School**
**Glen Mills**
Christina Dean*
Mrs. Ricevuto

**Holicong Middle School**
**Doylestown**
Miss Ambrosini
Monica DeMuro
Jason Hepler*
Mrs. Mandes

**Holy Sepulcher School**
**Butler**
Dorothy A. Johnson*

**Indian Valley Middle School**
**Harleysville**
Laura Fling*
Cindy Vesey

**Kennard Dale High School**
**Fawn Grove**
Mrs. Bowman
Karen Snyder*

**L B Morris Elementary School**
**Jim Thorpe**
Allison Adams*

**Lancaster Mennonite School - Locust Grove**
**Lancaster**
Barbara Josephian
Pat Shelly
Curry Snell*

**Landisville Middle School**
**Landisville**
Diane Anderson*
Scott D. Feifer

**Mifflin County Middle School**
**Lewistown**
Mrs. Dixon*
Bret Monsell
Mrs. Reese*

**Moravian Academy Middle School**
**Bethlehem**
Bud Brennan
Cindy Siegfried

**Motivation High School**
**Philadelphia**
Jessica Coldren*

**Mount Nittany Middle School**
**State College**
Mrs. Dietz
Scott W. Given*
Jennifer Webber

**Neil Armstrong Middle School**
**Bethel Park**
Victoria Donati
Laura Pawlos*

**Northern Lebanon Middle School**
**Fredericksburg**
John Chan*

**Northgate Middle/High School**
**Pittsburgh**
Stephanie Francis*

**Our Lady of Mount Carmel School**
**Doylestown**
Dawn Brooks
Laurina Calabrese
Paula Kin*
Cathy Makoid*
Rosemary Miller*

**Penn Middle School**
    **Jeannette**
        Kelly Podkul*

**Penn-Kidder Campus**
    **Albrightsville**
        Ms. Becker
        Mrs. Berchtold*
        Howard Gregory*
        Jill Klotz
        Angelina O'Rourke*
        Diane Reese*
        Mrs. Tirpak

**Pennbrook Middle School**
    **North Wales**
        Ruth Baltozer
        Scott McGowan*
        Christina Reffner
        Jennifer Seiler*

**Pequea Valley Intermediate School**
    **Kinzers**
        Tammy Andrew*
        Tammy Frank
        Janine Snyder*
        Louwana Weaver*
        Sandy Whiteside*

**Pine-Richland Middle School**
    **Gibsonia**
        Jennifer Hartle Fink*
        Kate Pfeifer*

**Pocono Mountain East Jr High School**
    **Swiftwater**
        Rhonda Brandolino*
        Ms. Nicholene Rolland*

**Sacred Heart Elementary School**
    **Pittsburgh**
        Patricia Faub*

**Saegertown Jr/Sr High School**
    **Saegertown**
        Hannah Keeling*

**Spring Grove Middle School**
    **Spring Grove**
        Korie Young*

**St Luke School**
    **Erie**
        Jacquelyn Shaffer*

**State College High School South**
    **State College**
        Danielle Boyd*
        Kate Hoffman

**Strath Haven Middle School**
    **Wallingford**
        Elaine Shipman*

**Tulpehocken Jr/Sr High School**
    **Bernville**
        Amanda Machonis*

**Valley Forge Middle School**
    **Wayne**
        Melissa Pacitti*

**Villa Maria Academy Lower School**
    **Immaculata**
        Kara Rufo*
        Maureen Wible*

**Wattsburg Area Middle School**
    **Erie**
        Sandra J. Metzler*

**Whitehall High School**
    **Whitehall**
        Jessie Bucchin*

**William Penn Middle School**
    **Yardley**
        Brenda Brown
        Denise Dugan
        Leslie Ettlinger
        Kristilyn Obert*
        Vicki L. Meigs-Kahlenberg*

# Language Arts Grant Recipients 2011-2012

After receiving a "Poetic Achievement Award" schools are encouraged to apply for a Creative Communication Language Arts Grant. The following is a list of schools who received a two hundred and fifty dollar grant for the 2011-2012 school year.

Annapolis Royal Regional Academy, Annapolis Royal, NS
Bear Creek Elementary School, Monument, CO
Bellarmine Preparatory School, Tacoma, WA
Birchwood School, Cleveland, OH
Bluffton Middle School, Bluffton, SC
Brookville Intermediate School, Brookville, OH
Butler High School, Augusta, GA
Carmi-White County High School, Carmi, IL
Classical Studies Academy, Bridgeport, CT
Coffee County Central High School, Manchester, TN
Country Hills Elementary School, Coral Springs, FL
Coyote Valley Elementary School, Middletown, CA
Emmanuel-St Michael Lutheran School, Fort Wayne, IN
Excelsior Academy, Tooele, UT
Great Meadows Middle School, Great Meadows, NJ
Holy Cross High School, Delran, NJ
Kootenay Christian Academy, Cranbrook, BC
LaBrae Middle School, Leavittsburg, OH
Ladoga Elementary School, Ladoga, IN
Mater Dei High School, Evansville, IN
Palmer Catholic Academy, Ponte Vedra Beach, FL
Pine View School, Osprey, FL
Plato High School, Plato, MO
Rivelon Elementary School, Orangeburg, SC
Round Lake High School, Round Lake, MN
Sacred Heart School, Oxford, PA
Shadowlawn Elementary School, Green Cove Springs, FL
Starmount High School, Boonville, NC
Stevensville Middle School, Stevensville, MD
Tadmore Elementary School, Gainesville, GA
Trask River High School, Tillamook, OR
Vacaville Christian Schools, Vacaville, CA
Wattsburg Area Middle School, Erie, PA
William Dunbar Public School, Pickering, ON
Woods Cross High School, Woods Cross, UT

# Grades 10-11-12 Top Ten Winners

*List of Top Ten Winners for Grades 10-12; listed alphabetically*

*Elisa Barguil, Grade 11*
*Townsend Harris High School, NY*

*Cailey Horn, Grade 11*
*Rabun County High School, GA*

*Kevin Maerten, Grade 11*
*Holy Cross High School, NJ*

*Garrett Massey, Grade 11*
*Animas High School, NM*

*Ryan Miller, Grade 12*
*Upper St Clair High School, PA*

*Miranda Paul, Grade 12*
*Menaul School, NM*

*Kimberly Paulsen, Grade 11*
*Viewmont High School, UT*

*Mia Tannoia, Grade 10*
*Bradshaw Christian High School, CA*

*Felicia Thornton, Grade 11*
*Science & Math Institute, WA*

*Emily Wiseberg, Grade 11*
*Collège catholique Franco-Ouest, ON*

*All Top Ten Poems can be read at www.poeticpower.com*

*Note: The Top Ten poems were finalized through an online voting system. Creative Communication's judges first picked out the top poems. These poems were then posted online. The final step involved thousands of students and teachers who registered as the online judges and voted for the Top Ten poems. We hope you enjoy these selections.*

### The Doll's Song

Glass eyes dreaming.
The doll, immobile
is lying on its side.
What kind of dream are you fascinated with?

Broken face staring.
The doll, singing
haunts the room with a dying melody,
the song of love can't be sung either.

The room now silenced.
The doll, forgotten
unable to answer the song's riddle.
Feverish tongue turned cold.

A door shut and locked.
The doll, misplaced
forever lost in the immeasurable darkness.
Still you do not answer.

*Bridget Blosser, Grade 12*
*Central Columbia High School*

### Cherish

Save the babies so that they have chances to bring joy.
Save the scent of springtime lilacs in bloom.
Save childhood as the best time of life.
Don't save sadness,
But save the times of cheer.
Save your loved ones with all your heart.
Save the laughter that blossoms your smile.
Save the comfort under the covers in bed.
Don't save pain,
But save breath of life so dear.
Save the words that have changed your life.
Save the memories that should never fade.
Save the touch of the soft and smooth.
Don't save flaws,
But save the special qualities in you.

*Ann Donatelli, Grade 12*
*Coventry Christian Schools*

### Breaking-Up

This pain inside is killing me.
The one thing that made me happy
Taken, right out from underneath me.
It's amazing what life throws at you.
You never really appreciate what you have until it's gone.
Guess I'll put that fake smile on my face,
So no one knows the true pain I'm feeling.
I guess you could say break-ups are for the best,
But this pain I'm feeling just keeps getting worse.
All I know is,
No matter how bad this pain gets,
I'm not over you.

*David Baker, Grade 11*
*Eastern York High School*

### Mine

Her striking beauty is hypnotizing
My heart melts seeing that radiant smile
Her charming eyes need no criticizing
And her personality makes it worthwhile

The thought of her protrudes my mind each day
Although joyous, I feel a stinging pain
I am reminded of her love this way
Only a shred of hope keeping me sane

Alas! Is this what I've been waiting for?
Her love just another face in the crowd?
Here's the cure, my heart being much too sore
Finally feeling the love I've endowed

That she never leaves my warm arms, I yearn
That we love each other, without adjourn.

*Dominic Civitella, Grade 10*
*Notre Dame High School*

### Lost Girl

If no one told you, then I will
You're the most beautiful thing in this world
But I never saw your face or heard your voice
'Cause you chose to leave me, that was your choice
Sometimes at night, I hear you calling me
Telling me you're coming home
I start to cry when it's all in my mind
And I realize I'm still alone
No one knows where you are
Times for me are becoming hard
Daddy's stressed and he leaves me at night
To meet his friends at the bar
I'm wishing on a star that you will enter my life
And then I will know everything will be all right

*Rondell Calloway, Grade 11*
*Motivation High School*

### Longing

Do you know the power of love? I think I just might.
You constantly fill my thoughts all day and every night.
The ache of being without you, no matter how painful it may be,
Is nothing compared to the euphoria I feel when you gaze at me.

Each moment we spend together, each laugh we share,
Is one I will treasure, no others can compare.
Each time you look at me, each word I hear you speak,
Will be the one that haunts my dreams which remain forever bleak.

My love for you is sincere, stored in the depths of my heart,
You'll realize this one day, I've hoped from the start.
Until that day comes, I must wait an eternity or two
For a lingering dream that may just be about to come true.

*June Xia, Grade 10*
*Strath Haven High School*

## My Mother

My mother's words are so very encouraging
Especially in times of doubt and anxiety,
A simple smile telling me, "You can do this," makes me feel all the better.
My mother is the most incredible woman I know,
She has the sweetest heart and most gentle soul.
My mother always puts others first.
Even when she is the most deserving of all.
My mother sees beauty in all things;
In laughter, in love, in sadness, and in fear.
My mother believes in the power of angels,
Angels everywhere, touching our hearts
And guiding us everywhere we go.
My mother is the most talented listener.
Patience is one of the greatest virtues she possesses,
Not only does my mother listen with an open mind and a tender heart,
But she considers all perspectives, she does all she can to imagine life from another's point of view.
Without my mother I would not be the person I am today.
She is my best friend, she is my guide, she is my support.
I know that God has given me my own guardian angel here on Earth,
This guardian angel is my mother.
With tears in my eyes and a smile on my face, I say to my mother, thank you.

*Rosa Fatica, Grade 12*
*Villa Maria Academy*

## My Love

My Love! You make me fall in love with you daily!
You light the path and my heart!
When I say I love you it means I will do anything for you and will do anything to make you smile.
When I say I love you it means I will ride, die, and fly beside you forever!
It also means that I will support you in whatever it is that you want to do.
The love I have for you is unable to be contained.
I sit for hours just thinking of how I can show you that I love you more and more!
You can never ruin my night because you always brighten up my day.
You are the love of my life and forever you will stay.

*Tiffany Tillman, Grade 11*
*Motivation High School*

## Memoir of the Seasons

In my ignorant youth I believed beautiful trees would die in autumn and come to life again in spring. I found it a tragic tale, to have to pass every year just to be brought back to continue the harsh cycle. Yet, I know now that these trees weren't dying; they were going through hard times and persevering to reap the rewards of another successful season. I know now that I am not dying; I am going through one of the most difficult periods of my life. I'm confident that when it's through, the following moments will not only appear to be brighter, but be more vibrant because I will appreciate them more completely. So, as my tough times roll on with the upcoming autumn season, I will suffer with her. Her beautiful gold and orange tears will fall with mine, and we'll stand dejected together. But my when springtime comes, how we will blossom, and flourish, and thrive.

*Lilia Tkach, Grade 11*
*Neshaminy High School*

## Safe-Keeper

Can't you see all my problems and flaws? Can't you see all the damage I've caused?
I'm not doing my part,
And clearly, it's destroying your heart.
I feel like such an awful disgrace, as I watch the desperate tears streaming down your face.
My chest has never hurt this much, and your little body feels so fragile to my touch.
You're just a child and you still don't know
The great difference between yes and no.
You're too innocent to understand the hardships and stress that one day you'll hold in the palm of your hand.
It doesn't matter to you whether you're on time or late.
The only thing you can comprehend is love and not hate.
You still haven't gone through giving away your selfless heart,
And then getting it back completely mangled and torn apart.
I'm trying my best not to let you down.
I'm supposed to make you smile, not frown.
Everything will be meaningless in the end,
If I can't be what I vowed to be, your role model, your friend.
From this day forth, I want to give you my all.
And I promise to always be here to catch you when you're on the edge about to fall.
I am your sister, but I'm fighting to be something deeper.
I want to be your protection and source of affection. I want to be your safe-keeper.

*Madison Stine, Grade 11*
*Hamburg Area High School*

## Simplicity: That Which We Hold Most Dear

i.   the murky-clear outline of the hills in the morning haze
ii.  the warm tick of an ancient pocket watch against your tear-stained cheek
iii. the utter futility of chasing a firefly, a moonbeam, a dandelion seed
iv.  the soft curve of a amber rose petal in the snow, a last unanswered plea to the early frost
v.   rifling through a bag of juniper spice potpourri, then laughing as you lift out your scent-stained fingers and wave them under your brother's wrinkling nose
vi.  etching your splintering name in white sand in the hopes that the wind will carry it to Narnia, Oz, Terebithia
vii. waking up with a smile on your face and a tune in your head and the doorknob at your fingertips
viii. falling asleep in the summer grass, reveling in the scent of moonlight and midnight, the delicious taste of not-yet-morning dew ever fading upon your lips, your tongue, your cheek
ix.  cracking a spine, flipping a page, breathing in the mustiness of a never(forever)-opened book
x.   raising your hands in praise of God, of life, of beauty, of sickness, of nothing and everything and all that's in between, of darkness and light and shadows and shades of gray; everyone you've ever loved, ever hated, ever known, of the ever-so-simple joys that make life bearable, even beautiful.

*Pratiti Roy, Grade 10*
*State College High School South*

## The Fall

"I'm a falling angel. Yes. You heard me. 'Falling.' I haven't reached the end, but I feel as though if someone doesn't catch me I'll hit rock bottom. Oh, this is okay, right? Wrong! This is not okay. I'm not okay. It's not quick. It's slow and painful. My memories floating upward. I fall down and I look up at those I know, wondering if they can tell if I'm sinking into darkness. Tears sometimes well up in my eyes and I become blinded by my tears, making everything I've ever known disappear. Or am I the one who's become lost?"

"It's hard to tell if someone is falling. Because it's not easily visible to the human eye. But it's still there. Look for the signs. When they suddenly stop smiling, how they seem to be completely out of the group or when they start to pretend that everything is okay when it's not. How could it be? While you're off having fun we're secretly crying in our rooms, because we feel as if we are completely alone in the world. That's how I feel. That's how WE feel. And I'm saying this so you — so everyone knows about us. The fallen angels."

*Julianne Meehan, Grade 11*
*Arts Academy at Benjamin Rush High School*

## Abstracted Empiricism

I painted the most beautiful painting in my head.
I looked and I saw that the light was dead.
The lights are gone momentarily
    to only return with equal metonymy.
Dead silence, the absence of thought.
Thoughts in the shape of a cyclogram,
    doubt throughout.
Wishing sweet nothings in my ear
    from, nonetheless, nothings.
All the polysemic qualities of language
    without the amnesic adage.
Watching the world slowly fade away
    with brilliant mixtures of affinity.
Simplicity within complexity:
    swirling pastels of amber grays,
    violet blues, and charlotte reds.
Tangential beauty, non-sequiturial sketching
    an absence of coherence —
True love tends to forget.

*Cameron P. Kobielski, Grade 12*
*Villa Maria Academy*

## The Brightest Star

Above all else you seem to glow,
But only in darkness do you show.

You light me up as my world starts to fade
Into a dull shadow of black and gray.
An instant smile as I look at you
For your light is the one thing that is true.

I watch as you find your place in the sky
And I begin to wonder how you flew so high.
I envy your beauty, shine, and grace
That cuts through darkness and dances on my face

You shine brighter than anyone
Until you shy away from the morning sun.

*Jennifer Kassis, Grade 10*
*Whitehall High School*

## Children

Children are the face of innocence
They do not mean any harm they inflict
All they are doing is testing boundaries
To see what is right from what is wrong
They may cause sadness once in a while
But most of the time, they bring joy
The world is their playground, and we are just in it
We to them are intimidating figures
Lucky for us, most are pretty openhearted
Their big, gorgeous eyes peer into the souls of others
They look up to role models for aspiration
And never fail to put a smile on people's faces

*Michelle Spivak, Grade 11*
*Central Bucks High School-East*

## The Seashore

In comes the tide, pushing and pullin'
In ride the waves, curling and swollen
During the daytime, while children collect seashells
Sea life is hiding down under the wave swells.
As the waves curl over,
The starfish sinks lower.
When the waves go back out,
It is beautiful, without a doubt.
As the children begin walking home,
They turn to see the last wisp of foam.
In total, when the day is done,
Many people have come and gone:
Their footprints have been washed away
In the midst of the ocean spray.
So also one's life will end
And we know not how or when.
So prepare yourselves for that moment coming
And spend not your life frolicking and running.
Like the waves sweep away the sand;
So will our lives be swept in the end.

*Francisco Shibler, Grade 11*
*St Louis de Montfort Academy*

## Feel How You Want to Feel

What is cold
But perspective?
For one man's cold
Is warmth to another.
Who lives a few hundred miles to the north,
Can man feel warmth?
If he tells himself he is warm,
Does his brain let him think
That his body is not affected by the elements?
Do the elements cease to exist
And what is pain,
But perspective?
Can one tell themselves
That everything is all right
And all will be well?

*Benjamin Purtell, Grade 12*
*West York Area High School*

## A Wonderful Grandpa

My grandpa's name is Mervin Smith
In his younger days, he loved to fish
He would take me to the pond
And show me how to bait a hook
He also taught me how to read a book
He taught me how to plant a garden
Filled with cabbage, tomatoes, and strawberries
We would mow the grass
Then watch birds to let the time pass
Some people just don't understand
That my grandpa is such a wonderful man

*Lauren Smith, Grade 11*
*Eastern York High School*

## I Know

I know…
Misunderstood
But she got married
To a man who understands
Momentarily…

I know…
Ignorance kills all
Some faster than others
We have to seek out knowledge
or risk dying faster and younger…

I know…
What goes around
Comes back around
I know action speaks much louder than sound…

I know…
Before you learn to stand
You'll have to trip and fall
I know true wisdom is to know
That you know nothing at all

*Rashid Sherif, Grade 11*
*Academy Park High School*

## Leave Them Be

Don't try to understand those who don't want to be understood.
Because knowing everything isn't that good.
Some of us want to be left alone.
We hold up walls stronger than stone.
You cannot release those that are condemned.
For they are the ones who choose not to blend.
Let those angels walk by themselves
Because they have went through harder hells
I'm the one who doesn't tell.
I'm the one who is never well.
I'm one of those angels behind a smile
With troubles that bleed on for miles.
I don't want to be understood
Go on with your life as you should.
Because my devils aren't your hells
And there is no reason why I should tell.

*Teedha Leang, Grade 12*
*Arts Academy at Benjamin Rush High School*

## Poetry

When you write it
It takes away the pain
When you read it
You can relate
It draws you in like a black hole
Opening up your soul to the world around you
It keeps you in a trance
With just one sudden glance

*Takwan Hargrove, Grade 10*
*Whitehall High School*

## Notes

There were always notes on the table to read
The words overwritten over top they fell
This reading was only for the clever to tell
I read through some of the notes each day
Just as my wondering eyes walked by, but
When you weren't there, I tried to find out why
When you failed to return for the night
I searched in your words by the dawn
Only notes of where you are going and where you have gone
Upon your night stand, laid a letter of your scent
You wished for meaning, you wished for love in turn
So you went out searching never to return
So notes lay on the table, untouched and uncleaned
All read and understood as clear as a waveless sea
But you're still uncertain, you walk in mystery

Where you are going and where you have gone
Doesn't lay in the notes on the table at all

*Michael Weidman, Grade 12*
*Serra Catholic High School*

## Dovahkiin

Oh sit there young child and let it be told.
A tale, a hero when Nirn was still young.
The earth, still covered in Great Winter's cold,
On peaks sat dragons who shouted in tongues.
The High King was killed, slain by a fierce beast,
And so began a war 'tween man and wyrm.
Praise those who died, in Sovngarde they feast.
A hero, man required, one to stand firm.
And there rose such a hero, stood so tall,
Had body of man and of dragon, soul.
Not born from greatness, never been a thrall.
He bested these wyrms and their souls he stole.
And so begins the legend of the clean
And the pure and the mighty Dovahkiin.

*Korbin Barker, Grade 12*
*Dover Area High School*

## Lifeless

How can the person who can cheer you up,
Be the reason you were down?
When they give you motion sickness
And you're sitting, motionless
When they make you feel like you're drowning
And you're standing on a bridge
When they make you faint
And you haven't moved.
How they make you feel so high
And you've never touched any drug
How they make you feel that you're touching the sky
And you're laying on the ground
When they make your heart flutter
And you're lifeless.

*Nicole Nicholson, Grade 12*
*East Allegheny High School*

### In Dreams Awake

A red glass door with eerie white light
A sign: "Beware the dark birds in flight."
A golden sun drop on a window's sill
A single cloud shuts out the sun's will

A child's flight down an unlit hall,
An important note in a single scrawl
An unopened door that somehow warns
An abandoned castle cut off by thorns

A comet trail that's colored blue
A rainbow rapidly changes hue
A lightning bolt at the peak of day
Seven tombstones lie in the way

A flower stalk strangely, rapidly grows
A sad, lost spirit in a dark forest glows
An empty bedroom haunted by death
Then the dream ends with a single breath

*Katie Borne, Grade 11*
*Commonwealth Connections Academy*

### The Wolf

The wolf walks alone,
With all it has known,
It cries at night,
Never showing it in light,
It doesn't feel happiness,
Never more, always less,
The wolf sees another,
Maybe its brother,
They start to fight,
The wolf with all its might,
The wolf is hurt,
Feeling like dirt,
Its full of fear,
With a fallen tear,
It looks down and prays,
"Please let me stay."
It suddenly feels happiness,
Always more, never less,
The wolf moves on,
Feeling stronger than a bond,
The wolf walks alone.

*Kathleen Michael, Grade 11*
*Farrell Area High School*

### To the One I Never Knew

Sometimes I lay awake in the night,
Wondering what you were like.
Part of me is a part of you,
Even though I never knew you.

You're my unfinished picture,
My puzzle left undone.
Simple retold stories can't fill the void,
But it's all I've ever known.

You were a quiet one, so I'm told.
When you spoke, you had something to say.
You were a middle-class working man,
A bread winner, a husband, a father.

When times were tough,
You adapted and found your way.
As for the rest,
There is nothing more I can say.

So now, years later —
This is to you, the one I never knew.

*Margaret Bien, Grade 12*
*Central Columbia High School*

### Madness

Tranquility at first,
Quenching my thirst,
Finally the turmoil has come to cease,
But not for long is there peace.

Screaming in the halls,
Reverberating in the walls,
Assaulting my ears,
Confirming my fears.

Swirling chaos begins again,
Slowly ruining the sanity of men,
Killing from the inside out,
Destroying me, without a doubt.

I can never go free,
Not with this haunting me,
And even if I escaped today,
My mind has already gone away.

*Susan Gerencser, Grade 11*
*Warwick Sr High School*

### Trying to Write a Poem

I'm trying to write a poem.
Something to inspire
Something to make you think,
And make you want to climb higher.

I've written poems before,
And they've turned out okay,
But for some reason still unknown
I can not write today.

Though I made lines rhyme
Strung together by a thought,
This in no way turned out
How an inspiring poem ought.

Yet still I made this pretty long
So I think I'll end it here.
But take this now as your own proof
That poetry is weird.

*Ashley Vargas, Grade 12*
*PA Cyber Charter School*

### Smart Touch

My hands cradle power.
Infinite information, instant gratification.
The power to move, the power to shake
Is mine.

I am the master of multimedia
Magician of the multitudes.
Slide to unlock.
It's enigmatic energy excites me
And frightens me.

In my hands, The people's hands, is power.

*Erika Cox, Grade 11*
*Upper Perkiomen High School*

### Flutter by, My Butterfly

Flutter by, my butterfly
For summer has gone away.
My dear friend shiver has come out to play.
And at my table she will sit
Until her cousin dark comes visit.
For hurt can't keep away,
How instead I wish you'd stay.
Thus powerless I'm rendered.
Surrender? I will never.
Not until your promises be all filled.
So flutter by butterfly
And leave love where you will.

*Sydney Crago, Grade 12*
*Maplewood Jr/Sr High School*

## The Raindrops Still Remain

The rain has finally stopped,
But the raindrops still remain.
I don't know quite yet
If my shirt will be stained
By the tears I've long forever cried.
But I'm stronger now than I've ever been.

The tears and the pain
Have finally been swept away
By the wind of yesterday.
So tomorrow and the future
Will be brighter
That's why the raindrops still remain.

If I'd have known
Who he was,
I'd have said something to him

The raindrops still remain.
They act as a reminder
That not everything in the past
Is gone forever.
That's why the raindrops still remain.

*Kristi Landis, Grade 11*
*Eastern York High School*

## The Show

Running up, with a rapid slope down.
Staccato signs; controlled shouts,
Soaring up to the sky.
With a soft landing,
On the comfortable, warm ground.

The swish of fabric; the tuning sound.
Squeeze for luck; hug for true trust.
A last glance; all's well.
One soft final hum,
Then with a nod, it begins.

Breathe deep, then a step into the light.
Well-practiced verse, reaching high
With the concluding note.
Loftily floating,
Above the proud beating hands.

Roar of excitement, pulsing to stand.
The rush of joy, overflow,
Worthwhile was the training.
The ultimate moment,
Then the bottomless bow.

*Ellise Chase, Grade 12*
*Villa Maria Academy*

## My Life in Silence

At the river's end, is where she lies
Her gentle eyes seem to stop time
But as my world slows, so does my joy
And I see her body, pale and destroyed
Ice slowing my thickened blood
My body dirty, with laughter and mud
My house of glass is growing dark
The sky is clear, but where are the stars?
Hey, do you remember me?
We met yesterday, underneath the trees
No words were said, but eyes were wide
As bodies limped down the mountainside
I skip what's meant to be undone
My mind wears out, as does the sun
I never got the wake-up call
And now I lie and face my fall
Hey, do you remember me?
We met yesterday, underneath the trees
No words were said, but eyes were wide
As bodies limped down the mountainside

*Dakota Wilson, Grade 10*
*Blue Ridge High School*

## Never Gaze Upon Calculus

When I consider how my time is spent,
in calculus class on this great day,
I become upset and begin to vent.
How did my notebook get so astray?
I shout to the others, "This class is dull!"
But this is a cry that is not hailed,
and I am removed from room to the hall.
My rebellion has completely failed,
What can I get from this cold, distant art?
I am unconcerned with equations.
I prefer something with a heart.
To leave, I would like an invitation.
On calculus, the world should not gaze.
Turn to English, set yourself ablaze.

*Samuel Yastishock, Grade 12*
*Central Columbia High School*

## The World Is Colors

Baby blue is in the sky
Apple red is in a pie
Shiny white is sparkly clean
And the trees are ever green
Bright yellow is in the sun
Dark brown is in dad's old gun
Silver pieces make a tack
And the long night is pitch black
Together all the colors paint
Pictures greater than a saint
A great world with no color
Will never have a rainbow

*Emily Burke, Grade 11*
*Middletown Area High School*

## Waging War

My only sword is dull.
I've even lost my horse.
Should I continue moving forward,
Or should I change my course?
I did not want to fight this war;
The attack was first on me.
And despite my better judgment,
I could not just let it be.
I've been wounded deeply;
Time won't heal the scar.
It's a wonder I survived,
And I'm glad I got this far.
I'm now on the battlefield.
I can feel the light wind blow.
I take one look at my enemy,
And know I must not go.
I advance upon the creature,
While screaming my battle cry.
All that I can say is,
I hope I do not die.

*Shelby Simon, Grade 10*
*Kennard Dale High School*

## Redneck Weather Rope

I have a rope in my backyard,
That tells the weather accurately.
It's called a Redneck Weather Rope,
You can learn how to use it easily.
Here are a few simple facts
That you need to know:
If the rope is white,
It is definitely snow.
If the rope is wet,
It is very rainy.
If the rope is hot,
You know that it is sunny.
If the rope is cool,
It is slightly cloudy.
If the rope is stiff,
It is tremendously cold.
If the rope is moving,
There is a 100% chance if wind.
If the rope is gone,
Hurry, take shelter!

*Mikayla Nester, Grade 10*
*Commonwealth Connections Academy*

**I Run to You**

I run to You to hide.
I run to You to confide.
They've tried to pull me down.
I've cried out to You, Lord,
Alongside You I can abide.

Feels like I'm drowning,
Found I'm so weak.
You've put me on my feet,
Move not Your protection.
Prove Your strength to my enemies.

You know the pain I'm feeling,
And You'll show love is the light of salvation.
Light that leads in the darkened night,
I'm helpless in the fight,
You're the height in the line of sight.

Whenever I'm in Your arms,
Wherever there is, I'm safe.
Wrap me in Your arms,
Entrap me in Your love,
And never let me go.

*Sarah Bucher, Grade 12*
*Home School*


**The Wanderer**

There was once a man cursed to wander the sea
And he often cried out "Why, oh why me?"
His only companions were the man on the moon
And tales of a dish that ran away with a spoon.

The man sailed across the ocean blue
And slayed giant fish that he swore flew.
The only water he had was rain
For the sea water made him collapse in pain.

And the sun did glare down on this man,
Still he said "Kill me, if you can!"
He fell asleep on his boat one night
And awoke the next morning to a lovely sight.

"Land ho!" he cried as he paddled with his hands,
But the sea did not want him on these strange lands,
For the sea had found a man it did cherish,
One who learned to live on a boat and not perish.

They say there once was a man who was cursed to roam the sea
And he often cried out, "Why, oh why me?"
His only companions were the man on the moon
And tales of a dish that ran away with a spoon.

*Josephine Beck, Grade 10*
*Galeton Area School*


**Ripples Unknown**

There are lots of stones for one to choose,
Each with their own unique shape.
They're by the lake, with its greens and blues
Free for anyone to take.

A man comes by and looks at each,
Having a specific plan.
He makes a choice; the air is breached
And it awaits its time to land.

The stone hits the water of the lake
And momentum carries it through.
Its mighty power couldn't be fake
For towards the bottom it flew.

The stone hit the soft, sandy floor;
Its journey quickly complete.
It will stay there, forevermore,
Content at accomplishing its feat.

But what the stone doesn't know
Are the effects of his short flight.
The ripples he created continue to grow
Even after the end of his life.

*Molly Black, Grade 12*
*Christian Life Academy*


**Don't Judge Me**

Don't judge me for what I am not.
Don't judge me for what you think I may be.
I've known you for so long,
But do you even know me?

To question my style: the music I listen to,
The clothes I wear, or the way I worship God!
I am unique and different.

That's the way God made us, right?
In His image, His perfect image.
So don't judge me, or my family,
Or the school I attend or my friend.

Don't judge my life.
It may be easy, but it is wrong.
We have never judged you and have never criticized your lifestyle,
So why judge ours?

Are you jealous?
Cause I'm confused.
Haven't you heard the news?
"Don't judge anyone unless you have walked in their shoes!"

*Erin Estes, Grade 12*
*Villa Maria Academy*

## The Stand

This is it, the final stand,
One-on-one, man-on-man.
Fourth and goal, the relentless struggle,
One last call in this huddle.
The clock's running down, 10 seconds to go.
The offense breaks out, and it's time to show.
Who wants it more? Who came to play?
Who gave their all in every way?
The rain is falling, but a minor detail.
Nothing right now could cause us to fail.
The ball is snapped, and off they go.
This is one shot we cannot blow.
Hand it off, the fullback dive.
I read the play and spring alive.
He takes a leap, one last shot.
We meet mid-flight; make him wish we had not.
For he was stopped, mere inches short.
It is then I feel the love of the sport.
I burst into tears, though filled with glee,
From the sweet, sweet taste of victory.

*Brandon Overmiller, Grade 11*
*Eastern York High School*

## Stand

Life's roller coaster climbs to the top
Then you lose control and suddenly drop.
When you're diving off the cliff at the bend
You wonder if you can stand in the end.
While the sea's currents are swirling around,
It is so difficult to stand your ground.
The world offers relief through drugs and sin,
But these false aids make life harder to win.

Then comes the hopeful message of the dove
That to persevere in life's fight at hand,
You must face it with the courage of love,
You must be fearless with confidence, and
When you've placed your trust in the hope above
With courage and sure strength get up and stand!

*Samantha Beth Keiper, Grade 11*
*Union Valley Christian School*

## Our Angel

Why did you have to go?
You still had such a beautiful glow.
Why do the good die young?
There's a simple reason for this word of tongue.
I miss you, and wish you were still here.
But now you no longer hurt, or live in fear.
I know that you're in a better place.
I long for the day that I will, again, see your face.
They always say "Never say never,"
So I know I will see you again,
And that time will last forever.

*Madison Scarfaro, Grade 10*
*Whitehall High School*

## You Alone

The heavens rip open and Your Majesty
Gallops down in grace.
You alone can save me,
I am awed by Your face.
There is no other who can compare with You;
Chains and people,
They cannot hold You down.

Here You come, You're reaching down.
Oh amazing love,
I feel You all around.
It's captivating,
Just a moments worth of You.
My struggles mean nothing
When You are my joy.

When I need You
You're already there.
And when I don't feel You,
You strengthen my faith
So its harder to tear.

*Sara Schlosser, Grade 11*
*Lancaster Mennonite School*

## Free to Be

As I walked along the crowded road,
I thought to myself, to where do we go?
Like a flock of sheep we amble along
But for what purpose do we walk?
For what purpose do we strive?
Like Drones returning once again to the hive?

Alone I walk and alone I talk
For I am not a sheep;
To myself my knowledge will I keep
For I am not a dog
And I shall let them perish in their fog

Free, free at last I am free!
At last I am free, free to be!

*Zachary Yost, Grade 12*
*Eden Christian Academy - Mt Nebo Campus*

## His Life

He loved to go to the gym,
Say the smelly clothes and muscle milk.
He loved to watch movies,
Say the empty boxes thrown throughout the room.
He liked to hang out with his friends,
Say the many pictures on Facebook and text messages.
He enjoyed motocross,
Say the many trophies and stained gear.
But he disliked going to school,
Say the untouched books and unorganized binders.

*Tanner Moritz, Grade 11*
*Eastern York High School*

### Left or Right

Sometimes you love the one you hate
Other times you hate the one you love
Which one do you choose?
Left or right
The right is filled with black and hatred
Covered with red and love
The left is filled with red and love
Covered with black and hatred
Which one would you choose?
The right is going to fight with you for little things
But love you the whole way
The left is going to love you, but when things go wrong
He won't be there
Which one do you choose?
The right is going to make fun of you
But will stick up for you
The left is not going to make fun of you
But won't stick up for you
Which one would you choose?

*Pooja Patel, Grade 10*
*Whitehall High School*

### The Difficulty of Poetry

Poems…poems…I cannot write a poem.
It is difficult, yet here I sit.
In my chair, waiting for something to come to me.
I wait for some words of inspiration,
Something to change a course,
A new direction, a new sensation.
But still there is nothing.
There is nothing for me to say,
No thought comes to mind, no word spells.
I thought, that if I sit here long enough,
The words would write themselves.
So I look at the white, the blank staring back at me.
I read over the black and soon I realize,
Wait, I have written poetry!

*Rebecca Feveryear, Grade 11*
*Kennard Dale High School*

### Free-write of Simple Abundance

Fish have gills, birds have wings,
demons screech softly while one angel sings,
fear is what angels lack in whole,
love is what life takes as toll,
remembrance is unforgettable,
deja vu is an action that's incredible,
growing up is cake,
the hard part is which path to take,
listen to your mom; the one and only,
for without her you'll be lonely,
mother nature exists in the past,
but with the way we treat her,
how long will she last?

*Andrew Russell, Grade 11*
*Carver High School*

### Whispers of the Fallen

Through a silent forest I walk
Gone are my feelings from numb and shock
Endure them before, I could
But the fault, the lies, never withstood

Whether the blame was ever given
Truly it seems, now I am fallen
And there is nowhere for me to stop
Through this silent forest I walk

Voices come near, so full of forgiveness
This silent forest is no longer a likeness
Heart pounding, my blood rushes
Their calls nothing but empty promises

Branches scratch me, my tears burn
I start to run — run from their concerns —
A coward I may be, though I swore I never would
But the fault, the lies, never withstood

*Victoria Ngo, Grade 10*
*Whitehall High School*

### Children of Mother Nature

My eldest brother is The Angry Sun.
He picks a fight with my sister: The Moon.
They argue about who's the strongest one.
The Wind shrieks because Mother will know soon.
The Cool Moon has the Ocean on her side.
The Fiery Sun has Clouds' sympathies.
She commands the Waves to form torrent Tides.
The Clouds release Rain due to The Sun's pleas.
The Lightning wants to strike the Beach's sand.
The Thunder wants to silent the Wind's cries.
My stem shakes and my petals fall on land.
The Earth quakes and Mother flies to the skies.
Sun sets and their fight is fizzling out.
We're at rest; Mother is out and about.

*Anita Saesing, Grade 12*
*Kennard Dale High School*

### Untitled and Unsung

Let her dance among the sunfish
Allow her to trace your shadow with the sultry air
Watch her as she fades ever so gently
In the summer breeze
But remember her like a storm
Don't run from the thunder
But let the warm June rain embrace you
And when she comes back in the cold September nights
Watch her heart
For it soars
With the heat
Of the dancing
Sunfish

*Allison Bowser, Grade 11*
*Lenape Area Vocational-Technical School*

### Baseball

A batter steps up
Taps his bat on the plate
And all he can wonder is
What is his fate?

The pitcher throws hard
And accurate as well
But the batter cracked the ball
And really hit it well

It is hit towards the short stop
The ball had arrived
The whole game was saved
By the short stop's dive

That was the end
The World Series was played
Better be ready Friday
For the champion's parade

*Kyle Montgomery, Grade 11*
*Lenape Area Vocational-Technical School*

### Slave to the Cross

Following the text to the T,
While you pray your life away.
Living for eternity,
Losing the moments of today.

Pursue the word for life everlasting,
With no doubt in your mind.
Although the Bible is masking,
The truth that you may never find.

There seems to be silence,
No voice to be heard.
No one giving guidance,
Not even one word.

I feel only pity,
For those following the flock.
You live life, but barely,
As time ticks on the clock.

*Garrett Morris, Grade 11*
*Lenape Area Vocational-Technical School*

### Ray Allen

Ray Allen plays ball.
He drains 3's like none other.
He is beautiful.

Ray Allen is great.
He's the best 3-point shooter.
He is amazing.

*Ashley Portillo, Grade 11*
*Kennard Dale High School*

### Beneath Words

Poetry's everlasting meaning flew to the page, and was defined,
It was defined by the concept,
The pen which takes on a whole new life, recreates
A poem thought from within, not only is it art,
It's deeper than a mind can perceive,
Blinded by the inner beauty,
Easily looking with one glimpse
And none after,
A poem neglected by a lack of exception,
Only the seekers will know
What hides between those twisted words,
Once upon a time, written by a genius mind,
Poetry is an overlooked importance,
Like a person who cannot see but only feel,
The problem is, poetry isn't a physical texture,
But a mental connection to the ordinary,
You cannot feel it if you can't see it for what it
Truly is

*Destiny Bonilla, Grade 10*
*Whitehall High School*

### I Miss You

I miss you more than words can say
  With each passing day
I can't believe that you're gone
  Without you, the days are so long
I miss you more than anyone knows
  Now my mood has so many lows
I wish I could see you just once more
  But you're beyond Heaven's Door
I miss you more than people think
  Sometimes I see your face when I blink
I hope you're doing good up there
  You'd better play fair
I miss you more than all the love everywhere
  And for you I will always care
I will never forget you
  And I love you for everything you used to do
I miss you more than words can say
  As I watch the sun come over the bay.

*Troya Hohlfeld, Grade 12*
*Penn Foster High School*

### The Renaissance

Melted now are winter's icy chains.
A new world born beneath our feet
Is christened by the heaven's rain.
Its lush ground cradles us
Through days bright and warm
And holds each person safely
When sunlight turns into storm.
An aura of joy rises up from the floor
As we start to take notice
The chains are no more.

*Hayley Morgans, Grade 10*
*Bloomsburg Area High School*

**The Traveler Who Lost His Way**
The day is icy cold
With the wind nipping at the nose.
The barren ground crunches under his feet
Penetrating the quiet night.
The night suffocates the weary traveler,
The traveler who lost his way.
Nothing can prevent the numbness,
The numbness that creeps,
Creeps through the toes,
Creeps through the nose.
Pervading, persistently pervading.

In a blink of an eye,
Darkness swallows the lone traveler,
The traveler who lost his way.
The only light
Becomes suffused in the darkness.
The night becomes undisturbed
As the crunching slowly ceases.
Wind covers the lone man's tracks,
Concealing his deadened way.
*Kimberly Maasz, Grade 12*
*Villa Maria Academy*

**My Missing Link**
It can start so easily.
It can end so complicated.
It can happen in an instant.
It can build up slowly over a lifetime.
It can be destined.
It cannot be forced.
It can be as simple as a touch.
It can be as complex as a poem.
It can be as sweet as laughter.
And as tart as autumn.
As dreamy as the ocean.
As realistic as death.
It has no rules.
Yet it has limitations.
It is not necessary.
Yet without it, we would all surely perish.
*McKenna Cordier, Grade 10*
*Freeport Sr High School*

**In His Hands**
Everything I own, all of who I am
Is in His hands
Whatever I do, wherever I go
He is with me
Any time of day, morning or night
He watches over me
He is my comfort, and my God
He holds my life
In His hands
*MaggieRose Crawford, Grade 11*
*Greencastle-Antrim High School*

**No More!**
There is nothing you could say or do,
That would make me forget what I know is true.
Your lies dark with roaring deceit!
Its words eating at the truth like a hideous beast.
Spilling with charcoal desires,
Clouded in falsehood, ripping away what it needs to.
Deep emptiness remains behind it.
My tempered mind sustained you, being credulous to its words dripping with guile,
But no more!

Your lies cloy on with me!
When you speak, it is only onyx leaking from your lips.
I will not listen any longer!
You wear a veil of deception,
And in your eyes, I see your rehashed distortion.
You decay into a sea of vile words,
And your words now vivid and ablaze,
I can see who you are.
My tempered mind sustained you;
Being credulous to its blackened words dripping with guile,
But no more!
*Dayanese Alexandra Rodriguez, Grade 10*
*Whitehall High School*

**A Mother's Letter to the World**
Dear World please be gentle with my child,
I was in charge of her life for just a little while.
I was around to mend her wounds and soothe her feelings,
I encouraged her until she got her bearings.
Now all grown up; with my blessing she must go,
into a world of good and evil, that started a long time ago.
Dear World teach her compassion, forgiveness and love boundless,
give her strength to stand up for the weak and spread her kindness.
Give her quiet time to ponder the eternal mystery of life,
never put a price on her heart and soul because of her strife.
Do not coddle her because the test of fire will make her strong,
but allow her wisdom to know when she is wrong.
Teach her that it is far more honorable to fail than to cheat,
teach her to have faith in her own ideas and not accept defeat.
Dear World she will often ask "why" no matter how hard she will theorize,
yet when she gives love, she will learn there is no compromise.
This is a big order I know, but please take care of her each and every day,
because she will make a positive difference on her future pathway.
As the seasons change and the day starts anew,
please be gentle to her Dear World, because my daughter is my gift to you.
*Bridget Fay, Grade 10*
*Villa Joseph Marie High School*

## Emergence

A hundred million miles, stretching on into the skies:
Never saw through the Horiz —
On, so I walked a little while.

You were there with me
Captivating with dangerous eyes,
Your story took me by surprise
As you told it as we reached the sea.

Jump in, you said, embrace the tide
It only hurts if you try to fight
But to not swim hard hurt me more inside.
So I struggled, caught in a wake of pride.

I fought, emerged, dripping on the shore
You looked me up and down some more
Surprise puckered the edge of your sneer
Clarity washed over, and I saw him clear.

If you go with the waves, they'll beat you on the stone.
Better to be cold and dripping, unscathed and alone.

*Julia Wright, Grade 11*
*Avon Grove High School*

## To My Mother

Frequently you're angry,
And frequently you yell,
But when you put a smile on your face,
Everything is well.
Swift and quick you are,
Always ready for a fight,
You are like a viper,
Poised, ready to strike.
Your smile, oh how lovely,
Your face beyond compare,
People wish to be like you,
I'm only halfway there.
The years have been kind to you,
But people, not so much, still you keep on going,
Palm trees after a storm, untouched.
I always have you with me,
I carry you in my heart,
You are like a masterpiece, a da Vinci, fine art.
You are like gold, so precious you are to me,
For without you in my life,
I simply wouldn't be.

*Uchechukwu Iloanusi, Grade 12*
*Upper Saint Clair High School*

## The Beach

The sea is calling
Ocean breezes and sunlight
Waves will never end.

*Jessica Wernig, Grade 11*
*Kennard Dale High School*

## Mirror

The glass slips along the shore,
and a rainbow passes beneath.
A swallow lights upon the branch,
and the blossom cracks the mirror.
The maiden, her beauty, a goddess on Earth,
and her song is an angelic choir.
A long nightingale wing, a pale moon,
and two dots of ink mark the porcelain.
Silk gauze wraps her, hugs her, shields her,
and paints a portrait upon her form.
Cherry blossoms, butterflies, and waterfalls,
and nature, a beauty, upon gold.
She plays, her koto singing,
and the melody lulls the swallow.
Her prince, far above upon the hill,
listens and dreams of the beauty below.
It is sunset, and the prince collects his love,
and they set upon his shimmering steed.
Edo is their goal, and comfort awaits,
and the mirror, behind, becomes red with the setting rays of the sun.

*Arianna Erdman, Grade 10*
*Millersburg Area Sr High School*

## Light of Liberia

The light of Liberia
look into the sky
see what I see
the light of Liberia
staring down at me
she smiles so happily
with pride and grace
the light's named Cianna
with her warm embrace
her shine can be blinding
her temperature is right
I bet you that her light will walk my way at night
nothing can express
my feeling towards her
her light will shine the world
and planets after and before it
Ms. Ci-Ci Brown
brave and strong
let your light shine day and night
throughout Liberia!

*Cianna Brown, Grade 11*
*Motivation High School*

## Senior Year

Senior year flies by
Prom, senior week, graduation
Goodbye Kennard-Dale

*Rachel Fleming, Grade 12*
*Kennard Dale High School*

## The Empty Shore

Walking along the empty shore
Your name carrying on the wind
All the while it's been taunting me
The shore we once had called ours

The waves will take me anywhere
My soul will be telling me otherwise
Because half will always be part yours
And I can never truly leave you behind

The promise of eternity was so easy to see
The thought had once been safe and sound
Though lies had spilled all through our lives
Am I numb to the idea of loving you again?

My hollowed out mind is racing on fire
Catching with the thoughts of you and I
Raging on through the moonless night
Fighting with the chilling fever within

It's not that I can't live without you,
It's just that I hoped I would not have to.
*Ali Matus, Grade 11*
*Lenape Area Vocational-Technical School*

## Snow

Snow.
What a cruel, beautiful thing.
Twirling and swirling around me.
Dusting the trees and ground
Until it's just the snow and me, alone.
What a lonely place to be.
It encloses me,
Surrounds me.
It breaks everything off from us,
Me and the snow that is.
If I would scream
I know no one would hear.
The snow will catch it. And take it.
And never let it go.
How could I escape if no one could hear me scream?
It's just me and the snow. Forever.
What a lonely place to be.
My only friend, the snow,
Melts when I touch it.
What a lonely place just me and the snow.
Now and forever. Alone. Together.
*Ashley McManus, Grade 11*
*Great Valley High School*

## Dark Desire

You, tainted villain,
hold my heart delicately
in your icy palms.
*Calli Wise, Grade 11*
*Carlisle High School*

## Color Guard

Trying to stand still as a statue
Blood pumping through my veins
Concentrating, playing every move in my head
Drum major calls us to attention
Nervousness starts to overwhelm me
Everyone marches on the field; I follow along
A rush of adrenaline runs through my body
I sprint across the football field
Placing my equipment in the right spots
I run back to my opening place and go to the ready
Before I can think, the show begins
Energy escapes me like never before
But, seconds later, the show ends
Brass and winds stop their movement
Drummers throw their sticks up in the air
The pit hold their stance
And the guard holds their ecstatic poses
The audience roars with enthusiasm
Our drum major calls the cadence
Everyone marches off the field
My heart overflows with satisfaction and happiness
*Bridget Hilliar, Grade 11*
*Eastern York High School*

## Clear Choice

Death will be my savior
I do not believe
There is a reason to live
What I say is true
Help me, as my choice becomes clear
Teach me
To end this life.
I have lost my desire
To hope and dream.
I see the light
"Clear Choice" (Backward Version - Positive)
I see the light
To hope and dream.
I have lost my desire
To end this life.
Teach me
Help me, as my choice becomes clear
What I say is true
There is reason to live
I do not believe
Death will be my savior
*Davis Simon, Grade 10*
*Southmoreland Sr High School*

## Raindrops

Raindrops fall
on a summer's day
Falling from the dark
and cloudy sky.
*Michael Bundra, Grade 10*
*Whitehall High School*

**Ashes**

It exhaled after the first half of the forest was put into flames.
It is holding back all it can not to burn down the other half.
It inhales and exhales over and over again until there's an opening space between the tree tops
in which fire could do no harm to the branches, whilst flames launch into the sky.

It's had more than enough.
Almost no sense to hold it in any longer.
Taking things out on the air is nothing near good enough.
It proceeds towards the town, towards the people.
It torches the hearts of others in an attempt to mend its own with the ashes.
This makes sense to it due the lack of care it thought others had.
Now, others' help hurts, their sympathy is sick, and their pity is overtaken by its plumes of isolated pride.

The torching has just begun, the ashes proving dissatisfying
and were not as good as it thought they would be.
The forest and all the inhabitants have been wiped out.
Knowing later in time it'd have nothing left to burn,
the beast shed its first tear as it sizzled on the molten rock before him.
This wasn't what he wanted anymore.

To feel angry and hurt knowing that it denied the trust of others,
it sits in its active volcano as the last of its kind, waiting for the place to blow.
These types of flames when lashed out uncontrollably are only meant to destroy and corrupt.
Although when placed as the centered and controlled source, fire's only result is energy and life.

*Nathaniel Baird, Grade 12*
*Arts Academy at Benjamin Rush High School*

**The Willows**

As I walk along, I see the willows sway. They bring back the memories; bring me back to that day.

At first I was innocent, shy I suppose. Unsure of what would happen if I got too close.
After a while my curiosity grew, so I reached out and you did too.

Closer and more attached we grew, not always speaking but we always knew.
You were my best friend, and I was yours — no matter how absurdly we spent the hours.

Then you changed but why I didn't know; something inside was killing you slow.
Frustrated now, we fought constantly. If only I'd known, but you should have told me.

Then your little secret came out — the rest of your life was a doubt.
Living every day like it was your last, but they all went by far too fast.

Life without you wasn't close to possible, even though it was the most probable.
I had to do something, but nothing could be done so we sat and remembered all of our fun.

And its grip on you tightened, tighter than death.
Literally.

So I walk along, and see the willows sway.
And every day I watch…I watch the willows sway.

*Shannon O'Hara, Grade 10*
*East High School*

## A Late Night Drive

the soft patter of rain
against the windshield
and the
swipe
   swipe
     swipes
of the wipers erase
the blackened skies' efforts
to obscure my vision
headlights
drain the color from signs
and the road becomes a
glazed canvas full of streaks
of reds and greens and whites
bleeding and swirling
while I am swerving
no longer driving on
the road
I am driving through it
*Riannon Caflisch, Grade 12*
*Central Columbia High School*

## Vision of Beauty

Perfect, white teeth between ruby red lips,
Small, delicate frame,
Ocean blue eyes as big as the sky,
A smile for everyone to see.
Vision of beauty.
Broken heart,
Tear-filled blue eyes,
Angry scars on her wrists,
Emotional turmoil.
Feeling not so beautiful now.
*Aubrey Turgeon, Grade 12*
*United Jr/Sr High School*

## Quiet

That achy feeling inside,
It presses down upon me,
And stirs me from the place I hide
To worlds beyond my boredom's sea.
Its fortress hides the brave;
The inner strength masks my fear.
Though only one word would save,
The battle still rages near.
My clumsy courage gains
My voice the victory.
*Megan Miller, Grade 10*
*Faith Builders Christian School*

## These Words Will Float Away

Nothing stays long enough to get down
No one lies long enough to recall
Nothing stays fixed, nothing stays still
Everything's swirling, everyone's rushing
Words float away on a mindless sea
Eyes wander aimlessly for the face they'll never find
Lost forever these words are lost forever
Floating away on wingless skies
They are lost forever to an endless world
Their letters ripped apart, their paper burned to ashes
The tongues born to speak them cut loose from mouths too young to understand
These words will float away on waveless seas
Oceans that run of blood not water will carry them free
Carry them to safety
Safety of other lands, other homes and other lives
These words will float away and be lost
These words will fall from cracked lips and bloodied teeth
These words will fall away from the truth and turn to lies
These words will float away, drift away, fall away
These words live on past us
These words will survive
*Evangeline Esposito, Grade 11*
*Upper Perkiomen High School*

## Put Up a Fight

Life always has a hard course,
But in return many seem to put up a force.
It's a long travel
But in the end it will all unravel.
There are always battles to fight
But at the end of the seemingly never-ending tunnel, there will always be a light.
You just can't give up the war,
Or the battles will come in even more
And even though they may throw you down and leave you feeling hopeless,
Don't give up on yourself and fall,
To get through this life you must stand tall.
There is so much in this life to give,
Like courage or strength.
Without each, there is no reason to live.
The journeys of life are sometimes too much to hold,
Everything has a purpose and will eventually unfold.
And with a little fight, you can make it through.
There is more to this life than you ever knew.
*Maria Tyson, Grade 10*
*Kennard Dale High School*

## Be Real

Stop worrying about what others think.
Be yourself people will judge you regardless of what you do.
Don't follow others be a leader
Show an example for others, a good example.
Be a mentor, help other get through what they can't get through alone.
Be a good friend, don't judge your friend or put them down.
People who put others down need help with themselves.
*Janelli Villafane, Grade 11*
*Motivation High School*

### Dear Tornado

Searching for a home
From day one to the last
Born from those not of its kind
With no place to settle

Inside a wrath is cradled
A monster they call you
Though you own no cruel intents
Spinning, twirling, dancing
In a sea of death threats

But not seen is the soul
Your lingering body holds
Of passion; you yearn, and wish
For a home of your own
Of peace and stability
You are after all
Made of the same as us
Of mother nature and
The elements of stars
Dear, best wishes
And good luck

*Michelle Dang, Grade 10*
*Salisbury Sr High School*

### British Lit Class

Why do sonnets have to rhyme?
These rules are so unfair!
It takes up far too much my time
For what is written there.

Rhymes do not make poetry,
The words within them do.
Format is a luxury;
Rhyme, I think, is too.

These rules were made by silly men
Who are now dead and gone.
It is too late to ask them, then,
What madness they've begun.

Whatever the cause of this and end,
For Lit class, I'll just have to bend.

*Sarah Troxell, Grade 12*
*21st Century Cyber Charter School*

### Storm to Sun

The most fearsome storm
Turns into the brightest sun,
When he comes around.

*Casey Swann, Grade 11*
*Kennard Dale High School*

### My Savior

Jesus, You are my rock, my healer and my best friend.
You are where I find hope when my life seems to be nothing but dead ends.
I look above and stand in complete awe of Your creation,
Knowing that this world is not my final destination.
Though many times I have been led astray, Your will always prevails.
You have never left my side and Your love never fails.
So many times I have looked for happiness in all the wrong places.
It is so easy to get caught up in all of life's races.
However, I have learned that in You is where true joy lies
And following the ways of this world is extremely unwise.
Many people think that alcohol, drugs and money will fix all of life's tribulations
But those things will always come very short of meeting our expectations.
It is only through Jesus that we can be truly free.
There is great power when a child of God gets on their knees,
Humbling themselves before their Savior.
If you truly love God His light will shine through your behavior.
In this world, I know I will have to face hardship and fright.
But Jesus, please help me to keep Your light shining bright.

*Kayla Roberts, Grade 12*
*Keystone National High School*

### With You

If I implored your heart for passion would you crave me in return
Even though flames of betrayal
'Round him chastise with their burn?
Do you feel the same as I do; do you get lost in my eyes?
Do you wonder if we'll make it
Through this vicious hell of lies?
We never knew that one small moment could unveil our destinies
But would you change it, if you could,
Make it so we'd never meet?
For this fervor swirls around us, beating to your pulse, to mine.
And, my Romeo, I'm praying
That I'll have you for all time.
Wash away the smoke that's choking all that we shared from the start.
Let me be the water, cold and sweet,
Upon your broken heart.
Yield, confess I'm Juliet, so that our dreams might still come true.
Even death will never part us;
Just say yes, and I'm with you.

*Bonita Wagner, Grade 10*
*West Perry Sr High School*

### The Student Who Smiled

You see that smile across her face it may be real or really fake.
She hides her emotions deep inside,
Sometimes she wants to hide.
She walks the halls with her head down, it was so hard for her to make a frown.
She acts like nothing's wrong but inside she's like a sad song.
You may be having fun now but will you at the funeral.
All those days of laugh and play
Did you know you were taking her life away.

*Melissa Harkleroad, Grade 10*
*Kennard Dale High School*

## That Day
Each day begins anew
Days go by, people change and grow
Many remember, some forget

I remember that day
Your brown eyes fixated on mine
Your smile, white as the snowiest day, brightened the room
My heart beat
Thump, thump, thump
Your red shoelaces, walked towards me
Spoken words, nervous giggles, shared glances

Unprepared sadness to part,
The crisp air forced bodies to move,
Closer,
Closer,
Feelings poured out like a waterfall
Nervous, excited, giddy
A smile,
A goodbye,
A beginning.

I remember that day when I met you.
*Bridget Kleinhanz, Grade 12*
*Villa Maria Academy*

## Slumberland
I lay my head on the pillow case
and let dreams transport me to another place

Vibrant flowers of purple and blue
Diamond fields so glistening, new
people to talk to about the day
as red and golden bricks pave the way

Arches of color silhouette the sky
Stars at night, twinkling through
clouds well nigh

This is the epitome of paradise
and I never want to leave
But now I must open my eyes
and rub them upon my sleeve
*Morgan ODonnell, Grade 10*
*Whitehall High School*

## Tropical Wonderland
walking on the grainy sand
next to the saltwater beach.
smelling the Caribbean market with their fresh fish.
walking in short pants with 80-degree weather all year round.
flipping open the beach chair all laid back.
taking sight of the beauty of the sun over the horizon.
*Judah Graham, Grade 10*
*Spring Grove Area Sr High School*

## Breaking Barriers
If I were a boy,
My favorite color would be blue
A truck would be my favorite toy
And it would probably be okay if I punched you.

But I'm just a girl
So I should cook and clean
Honestly, that makes me want to hurl
Sophisticated women find me flat out mean.

'Cause I'm quite the opposite of what I should be
I'm a girl who uses a hammer and nail
Most people just sit and laugh at me
And say "You should be a male."

Most people think you should follow the rules,
But it feels too good to prove it wrong to all those fools.
*Kari Schall, Grade 11*
*Lenape Area Vocational-Technical School*

## The Ride
Life's road may throw a curve at you once or twice
The road won't always be smooth, or the car real nice
Friends won't always be at your passenger side
But in the end, it's only about the ride

If you stay on the high road and not on the low
You'll be surprised how much further you'll go
And though by the limits you may not always abide
Just find the right exit and continue your ride

When you come to a dead end and things begin to slow down
Press the gas a few times and then turn back around
The choices are endless and the lanes are wide
But what whatever you do, just enjoy the ride
*Janae Fletcher, Grade 11*
*Woodland Hills Sr High School*

## Mind Mends Form: A Petrarchan Sonnet
In catacomb of bone lay fleshy root.
Darkness weaning; pathed voice of earth's braid,
Where thoughts flaunt shackled hereto coastline wade.
This weak form but a solemn plume of soot;
Mine art o'er these sleepless mobs a mute.
Weary of mine to mind of voice near frayed,
Idle heavens blessed dreaming ere fade;
Halting naught; biting bitter this bare fruit.
But innocence; control to vein I lack.
My mind is but the quaint nest so fertile,
Wherein sweet soul struts its purest mile.
Open wide this sorry state and seal this crack.
My body confines my mind of the key
But herein this soul shall set me a'free.
*Christian Lampart, Grade 12*
*Hempfield High School*

### Ready, Set, Go!

Approaching the starting line, I take a deep breath.
The uneasiness in my stomach begins to settle,
and it is as if the world around me ceases to exist.
I slowly take a step back, and stand motionless
awaiting the piercing sound of the gun.

Boom! Goes the gun, as hundreds set out.
Pushing and elbowing, the journey begins,
striding until one loses his or her breath, or until the end is near.
Everyone is determined to cross first.
Only one can call his or herself the winner.

In the distance one sees the mountain ahead,
and questions, can I make it up such an incline?
The strides become smaller, and the head goes down,
a deep breath is let out, and the climb begins.
The advantage becomes that the remainder of the way is downhill.

The end is near, the rest is a straight shot.
Fans screaming, coach yelling, and a girl on your back,
the pressure is back, it is time for the last kick.
One last breath. Begin the sprint.
I arrive at the finish line, and it suddenly makes sense.
Life really is one big race.

*Aimee Maciak, Grade 12*
*Villa Maria Academy*

### Rush

In the empire state of mind;
rushing never to stop
so fast we become blind.

Never trying to be kind;
shop until you drop
in the empire state of mind.

Everyone's lives intertwined;
always thinking shop, shop, shop
not knowing that we've become blind.

Afraid of being declined;
running to and from the coffee shop
in the empire state of mind.

We tell ourselves to unwind;
but we keep sowing our crop
never to see we've become so blind.

Trying not to fall behind
feeling like our lives have become a spinning top
in the empire state of mind
still spinning, spinning till we've become totally blind.

*Ajiea Hargrave, Grade 11*
*PaCyber School*

### Crooked Reflections

The sidewalk's crooked on the other side
The spindly cracks ride its pebbly sides
Skewed lines etched in the concrete hide
The sidewalk's crooked on the other side

The sidewalk's crooked on the other side
When I scuff over top of its leathery hide
Where logic and fantasy dare collide,
The sidewalk's crooked on the other side

The sidewalk's crooked on the other side
The muck and grass now cross in stride
For in the deep slits they both abide 'cause
The sidewalk's crooked on the other side

The sidewalk's crooked on the other side
As I wallow along on the tilting ride
And water drips down the melting slide
The sidewalk's crooked on the other side

The sidewalk's crooked on the other side
Still slippery where the sweat once dried
For years and years the sun has fried
The sidewalk that's crooked on the other side

*Mary Cooke, Grade 10*
*Mount Lebanon High School*

### Green

There is green spring grass swaying in the wind,
Only to be cut down my men.
There are sweet wildflowers blooming,
Only to be trampled by children.

There are wise trees growing strong,
only to be chopped down by workers.
There is a jubilant grasshopper leaping,
Only to be taken by the curious.

There are shiny leaves falling,
Only to be raked away by the finicky.
There are fresh cucumbers sprouting,
Only to be picked by the hungry.

There are sour apples developing,
Only to be whisked away by farmers.
There is a lazy caterpillar inching along,
Only to be pushed away by the scared.

There is Mother Nature,
And she is looking down,
Upon her sons and her daughters,
With steady green tears falling.

*Gabby Gregory, Grade 10*
*Holy Cross High School*

**Only a Servant...**
A firefighter...
Not a hero
But only a servant
He sits and waits for the bell to ring
Anticipating
To help someone
Not as a hero
But as...
Only a servant
When he rides the trucks
When the sirens wail
It's like falling in love over and over again
But when he goes into a burning building
He may be superman to the person he saves
But...
Underneath that oxygen mask
The face with sweat rolling like bullets
He is not superman
But...
Only a servant
*Cody Butts, Grade 11*
*Eastern York High School*

**Euphoria**
When I see you, the
sky clears up.
Everything becomes
hazy around me.
And when you smile,
everything stops,
pauses for a moment.
My heart bursts into
waves of magenta
swirling into red
shooting stars of salmon
crescents of crimson surrounding
us and only us.
Just for that split second.
*Arianna Guerino, Grade 10*
*Whitehall High School*

**Conquering**
Breaking down the walls,
They're crumbling.
Climbing over the rocks,
I'm stumbling.
Taking my time,
They're passing.
Gaining speed,
I'm passing.
Coming up victorious,
It's happening.
Taking everything I have,
And multiplying.
*Lauren Durniak, Grade 11*
*Greencastle-Antrim High School*

**To Me...Art Is...**
To me...art is life
art is love and dedication...
art is creativity
giving one the ability
to express anything...everything
from thoughts to feelings
leading to actions...real things

Art is the music...
those sounds that I hear
the poems I read
the sculptures I see

Art is the movement of dance
the illustration of emotions...
the photographer's view...freelance...

Art is education
teaching nations...let them grow...
art is that thought stimulator...
giving birth to today's tomorrow...
*Ayanna Davis, Grade 12*
*Imhotep Institute Charter High School*

**I Haven't Seen You in Awhile**
Stop.
You're fading.
Can't you see?
The sun is shining for you,
But you're locked up in your closet.

Stop.
You're changing.
Can't you see?
The clock is ticking so fast,
But you don't seem to care.

Stop.
This isn't you.
Can't you see?
You're better
Than this emptiness you've succumbed to.

Stop.
Don't you miss me?
Can't you see?
I miss you too, but you missed it,
They sold the last train ticket, and
I got on without you.
*Olivia Grazio, Grade 12*
*Central Columbia High School*

**A Secret to Keep**
Come to me,
I'll hold your mind.
Allow me to see,
No longer blind.

Words spoken,
Be not needed.
A silence unbroken,
Remains completed.

From your lips,
You softly speak,
Quick words with a wisp,
As if you have something to keep.

Your breath pushes forward,
The words that keep you blue.
You say like a coward,
"I think I have a crush on you."

You're scared but have no fear.
You think I'll tell, but why would I?
Girl to girl, they will not hear,
For this is kept between you and I.
*Sabrina Marks, Grade 12*
*Nazareth Area High School*

**The Ugly Truth**
Was I that big of a joke to you?
To build me up,
Higher and higher,
Only to remove my pieces
And have everything tumble to the ground
Like a lost Jenga game.
Why could I not see it before,
The ugly side of you?
Your lies were like glass,
Transparent,
Yet I was too blind to see through them.
Maybe I was in denial.
Maybe as your words shook me,
Your actions morphed me,
Ravaging my sense of wrong and right,
My conscience shattering
Like the windshield of a crashed car,
I wasn't really blind to it all.
Maybe I just didn't want to see the real you,
The grotesque being,
That I had so loved.
*Amber Witmer, Grade 11*
*Greencastle-Antrim High School*

### The Kraken

Its angry tendrils reach out of the deep
And it scrapes the sky with its wicked beak.
Our ship could be smashed with one foul sweep
And sink to the bottom of the sea.
Foaming, frothing, the ocean rocks
The ship quakes, barely absorbing the shock.
Now the crew is preparing, not pausing to gawk
At the monster rising out of the sea.
Pure terror darkens the sky
As the Kraken lets out a monstrous cry
We could shoot it with cannons, but it does not die
That monster that lives in the sea.
The captain decides we should quickly retreat
The whole ship is buzzing, every man on his feet
We speed away like we're fleeing from the British fleet
Or that monster that rose from the sea.
As we row like madmen, I hear a shout
The creature has gone, we can come out
Never before had I so feared a bout,
As when the Kraken rose out of the sea.

*Sarah Karasek, Grade 11*
*Berwick Area High School*

### What Is Love?

Love is complicated
How do you capture
A feeling that is indescribable
Who is to say what love truly is?
What is love?
When you are with the girl you love
You feel invincible
You feel warmth inside,
That spreads deeper and deeper into your soul
You feel protective of your love
Because you know if you ever lose her
You'd lose the best thing that ever walked into your life
You treat her with respect and put her first
You make sure she knows that you love her
You don't waste time fighting
Instead you relish in every single moment with each other.
It's getting past the tough moments in life
And building a relationship that will last forever
If you can do that
That is love.

*Jacob Wescott, Grade 10*
*Kennard Dale High School*

### Leaves

Leaves sway in the breeze
Seasons changing everyday
Days are getting short

*Lacy Anderson, Grade 11*
*Kennard Dale High School*

### You

I've seen you before.
That faceless figure in my hazy dreams.
You pull me into the red fog,
And for just a brief time,
I can let the violet swirls envelope me.

At the crossroad of confusion,
Am I walking in reality or running through a sea of hallucinations?
Day and night blend together so smoothly here
In this endless space of oblivion and euphoria.

I wade in temptation.
I hike on the border of obsession.
Running to break the boundaries of time,
I fly across the limits of the sky just to find any relic of you.

It seems so real.
I reach out to touch you,

But I feel nothing.

*Pai Liu, Grade 10*
*South Fayette Township High School*

### The End

Go on without me
To that place you always wanted to see
I still have time, you know
Before I go to that place you want to be.
I still have time to grow
Before I go
But seeing you like this, on your last bed
Makes me want to leave with you, though.
You turn your head
With that expression that I dread
"Don't let me go," you say
With your eyes so bloodshot and red.
I was wishing that I would never see this day
But I guess that I couldn't get around it any other way
You have a sickness that I wish I could mend
But I can't exactly do anything to make it go away.
We were supposed to do something over the weekend
But now I know that it's finally the end
Your eyes have closed and your heart has stopped
Oh God, what can I do? Your life has finally come to an end.

*Deja Hinnant, Grade 10*
*Whitehall High School*

### Dancers in the Sky

Look up and you'll see
Leaps, jumps and twirls in the sky
What a sight to see

*Rachael DeLawder, Grade 12*
*Kennard Dale High School*

## A Fool's Walk

Starting slowly, cautious, cool.
Drifting only to its shade,
A fool, with a guarded fool,
Smiles as its game is played.
The sun sets to coming night
As two together wander off
To its shady, woody light,
Smiling at what some would scoff.
Moonlight shines though passing clouds
Sifting down to forest floor
Strained and dimmed by leafy shroud
Till barely shining anymore.
Happily lost and wholly rapt,
Along the barely-glanced-at paths,
Walks sap in hand with happy sap
And from them both come happy laughs.
Hardly seeing where they go,
Not quite certain of the way.
Know they're lost? Yes, they know.
But they seem happy anyway.

*Christina Heath, Grade 11*
*Pennsylvania Cyber Charter School*

## Growing Up

There's a feeling deep inside of me
When someone acts a different way,
The red burns up and up until
Bam! It can no longer hold.
I lash out at the white carnations
And feel regret afterward.

All night the emotions come out of me
And I begin to think about
The pure ones who took the blame.

I am grateful I am not the same
And act serene like the summer's waves.

*Jessica Kim, Grade 10*
*Whitehall High School*

## The Reality

A dream within a dream
What a curious thought to me.
Has this actually happened to him?
Or is he just crazy?
Some believe he was brilliant.
But who was he really?
A man within a dream?
I think not he is much more than a dream.
His poetry speaks to me
To my deepest depth
But one thing Edgar needs to know
Is we are not just in a dream
But in an endless reality.

*Dillon Wescott, Grade 10*
*Kennard Dale High School*

## My Life

Sometimes in life it's hard to deal with the task at hand
But you know life can never go the way you planned.
I'm a junior in high school; I have to think about college,
Because I want to further my education, past the common knowledge

I'm focused on my mission,
To pay my college tuition before I even finish,
Would that be somethin'?
A problem child that came up with nothin'

Now I feel I have the power to express myself,
Truly test myself and come out on top with a lot of wealth.
I'm ready to pave my own road,
And make new tracks in fresh snow.

No more being the follower and waiter,
I'll do my own thing, I'm my own savior.

*Cade Costigan, Grade 11*
*Lenape Area Vocational-Technical School*

## Yellow Dress

I remember the yellow sundress with tiny red and blue flowers on it.
You wore it constantly.
You told me you would live in that dress if Mom would let you.
And I remember you always smiled when you wore it.

But then the ticking grew faster, and the time bomb of angst inside you burst.
You threw out the yellow dress and started wearing ripped jeans.
Now you never smile.

A few days ago, I found that old yellow dress in the basement among the dust and memories.
I looked at it, I caressed the cotton, and I thought of my sweet little sister.
I wondered where she went.
But when I look at you, I realize you threw her out
Alongside that yellow sundress with tiny red and blue flowers on it.

*Cory Taggart, Grade 11*
*Fox Chapel Area Sr High School*

## Streets

I live in these harsh streets not aware of my surroundings.
I stay indoors, I sleep, I dream,
I strive for change of the oppression of living here.
I don't see a place for me I see faces among millions,
Wanting to reach out and scream this is my story what's yours?
Waking up from a dream I think what if that was a real
Decision based on me or of someone else.
Living the same beat of the morning like the
Golden sun as it takes turns with the glowing silver moon in the abyss of twilight.
Nonetheless I walk among them as a single hole in sociality
Where the weak remain at low and the high reaches the top.
We need to change and not seek the comfort of these streets.
Will we ever change…?

*Andra Ware, Grade 11*
*Motivation High School*

## Stuffed Animal

On the bus, on the plane,
in the car, in the train,
regardless of where he is,
he is always the same.
Soft and sweet with a twinkling eye,
he was always there, he was the dependable guy.
He would listen to secrets;
he would dry off her tears.
He never judged what he heard,
with his ever-listening ears.
Now years have passed and he sits in the back,
he watches his girl leave,
he watches as she packs.
He's left in the dark,
barely leaving a mark.
Just trivial plaything to his only love,
soon she will be gone,
gone to up above.
So there he will sit,
for years and years,
waiting for someone new so he can dry her tears.

*Emily Beale, Grade 11*
*Avon Grove High School*

## I Thought I Saw You Today

I thought I saw you today but I knew it wasn't true,
but of course what else is new.
You're not here but yet you are,
I can't believe it's been ten years and we've made it this far.
I suffer in silence, alone, and scared,
while others quietly stare.
While others are lost deep inside their dreams,
I lay sleeplessly listening to the silent screams.
I open my eyes hoping for a miracle,
but yet no sign of anything spiritual.
At night I lay crying in a big bed of tears,
after all these years I can no longer hide my fears.
Dad you are always with me at my side,
for there is nowhere to hide.
I thought of you today and every day before that too.
But of course what else is new.

*Amber Goss, Grade 11*
*Mifflin County High School*

## Love

Your eyes are like the sunset.
The way you smile drives me crazy.
The way you laugh at my little antics.
The way you brighten my world.
The way we make each other happy.
No matter what we make each other smile.

My world would be nothing without you.
Baby, I love everything about you.

*Cody Leightley, Grade 11*
*Lenape Area Vocational-Technical School*

## Unanswered

10 o' clock at night, I lay in bed,
10 o' clock at night, you put the gun to your head.
What were you thinking?
Fast forward 12 hours, the doctors say there's no hope,
It's a short, slippery slope.
What were you thinking?
An hour, a day, a week goes by.
I can't stop the tears from Mom's eyes.
What were you thinking?
2 months have gone, almost too slow.
Your friends, your family, all trying to get back in the flow.
What were you thinking?
You had so many of us who care,
Yet you wouldn't give us a chance, it's so unfair.
What were you thinking?
I won't see your smiling face,
At graduation, or birthdays, not a single trace.
What were you thinking?
Out of all the questions that remain,
There is one, unanswered, that drives me insane;
What were you thinking?

*Kristin Bomboy, Grade 10*
*Northwest Area Jr-Sr High School*

## I'll Never Let You

they don't see you, all they see is scars.
they look right past you, they don't even know who you are.
you feel invisible now, fading into the background.
you're feeling alone, like no one wants you around.
it's a struggle everyday to feel happy in any way.
you can't do it anymore, you're ready to quit.
but keep your head up, even though the rain may pour,
pull yourself together when you can't take anymore.
keep your chin up, keep it held high,
stop second-guessing, stop letting time pass by.
gather your strength, its time to break out of your shell,
just be yourself and give the haters something good to tell!
just hold on, because i promise to be your rock.
i'll always have a ready ear if you ever need to talk.
know that someone cares and that i'll always catch you,
so if you ever try to fall, just know i'll never let you!

*Tabitha King, Grade 12*
*West Middlesex High School*

## Mockingbirds

It's a sin to kill a mockingbird,
They only repeat the lies they've heard,
The innocence they keep is strong,
It's a shame to say they once got along.

The new things they tell are endless lies,
Neither of them can hold alibis,
Like rain and fire they were once the same,
But it all ended the night the last storm came.

*Gianna Chase, Grade 10*
*Holy Cross High School*

**Sudan: The Bronze City of Symphony**
The tall, graceful statues of ebony
That line the bronze city of symphony
I look below from the clouds above
Staring at the beautiful country I love
But even with all the flaws
The uneven protection of laws
All the genocide and war,
What did you do it for?
Why did you murder and kill?
Did you do it for the thrill?
No real Muslim would kill innocent people
We would rather be peaceful.
Omar Al-Bashir, President, and whom the people fear,
Why did you hurt your own people?
The tall, graceful statues of ebony
That lined what was the bronze city of symphony.
To allow them to starve until they resemble twigs,
While you feast like a king, you filthy pig!
These are my people and I will not rest,
Until your arms are behind your back in a People's Arrest!
I may be a sea away, but I will be back, and forever I will stay.
*Dina Abdel-Rahman, Grade 12*
*Truman High School*

**If I Were an Angel**
If I were an angel I would protect the ones I love,
keeping them safe as I watch from above.
I would be there when hurt was too much to bear,
letting them feel the love of someone who cares.
A voice of evil teases the mind of a helpless man
confusing him with emotions he wishes to ban.
I would chase away the evil which tries to hide
and create hope and courage to fill him inside.
The heart of a girl who does nothing but love
is trampled on and gets only a push and a shove.
I would write her an encouraging letter
to say her loving heart deserves better.
If I were an angel I would make all things right,
no tears or hurt would be in sight.
I would do my best to change the pace,
and make this world a far better place.
*Alexandra Baughman, Grade 12*
*Greencastle-Antrim High School*

**Childhood Lost**
Every night she weeps over a lost childhood
Over the lost mannerisms and toys
The innocence and cootie-ridden boys
When pretend-play was real life
When being tucked in at eight o' clock was a highlight
When nap time was torture and she played with her food
When she thought she wouldn't grow up too soon
And so every night she weeps over a childhood lost
She'd give anything for it back, no matter the cost
*Laura Felix, Grade 10*
*Upper Dauphin Area High School*

**Winter**
Winter, a time where natures freezes still.

When you hear the occasional clatter and smash
Of icicles striking the ice covered floor of the forest.
When you hear Zephyr blow through the frozen limbs of the trees
And make them wince in pain.

A time where death runs rampant through the forest
Like an icy mist.
You hear the faint thundering of Jupiter's anger
When trees fail to stand.
You hear the pain and death in the trees,
Like they are crying out for help.

Just like the trees
Our life eventually comes to an end.
But that end only matters if we face it unprepared.
*Ethan Koons, Grade 12*
*Greencastle-Antrim High School*

**End of Junior Year**
Goodbyes ring out to all knowledge or any want of it.
We say adieu to those who force this learning upon us and
Farewell to the nights of constant study and coffee.
I send a lovely "Adios!" to the textbooks in history class.

Hello to warmth, and all things wonderful.
Greetings to the darkening of skin.
Aloha to my friends across the country.
Welcome wonders and wishes upon a star.

"Life is made up of meetings and partings,
That is the way of it," said Kermit the frog.
Now we gladly part with knowledge
And meet our three months of atrophy.
*Heather Waddell, Grade 12*
*Brockway Area Jr/Sr High School*

**Monica Rose**
My sister and I are close in age
We love each other with each passing day
Whether in the same room or at the same place
We always greet each other with a smiling face
We rarely bicker but if we do
In less than five minutes our battle is through
Close in age and closer in heart
We're closer now than we were from the start
She's more than a sister
She's more like a friend
I know she will be here with me to defend
The laughs we share and memories made
Are thoughts in my mind that are often replayed
I know siblings are usually not close
But my older sister, mentor, and friend is Monica Rose
*Kourtney Martin, Grade 11*
*Greencastle-Antrim High School*

**Never Let Me Go**
Water is flowing, thoughts are rushing,
memories are filling my brain,
birds are chirping, the sun is blazing,
sitting in this field gazing at the sky,
the scenery is beautiful,
our thoughts run wild, as we hold each other's hands while we're sitting down, talking about,
all the times we've shared, me thinking, why does this boy care so much for me?
there is a gust of wind going through the air,
it makes my hair go all crazy, it's all in my face,
you move it away gently, you lean in to kiss me,
the kiss was ever so soft, like kissing a teddy bear,
it showed me the sense you care,
you whisper in my ear, I love you, don't you ever leave me or I'll be nothing without you,
I say I think you'll be just fine, you were someone when I met you, the guy I fell in love with, isn't that right?
you say yes, but you made me the person who I am today,
I love you I say,
we held each other so tightly in that field that entire day,
as nightfall began we decided it was getting late so we begin to walk,
you wouldn't let me go,
you held me so close the whole way home,
you whispered in my ear never let me go.

*Lizzy Zalus, Grade 10*
*Deer Lakes Jr-Sr High School*

**The Search**
I feel that I am one thousand stars away
Searching for a place or idea
That has vanished with the trees.

Where can I afford weakness?
Be a little brighter? Feel a little deeper?
I forget that the flowers in pictures are really out there.

There were seashells in the desert —
I found one with my hand, cleaned out the dust,
And looked up at the biggest sky there has ever been.

I felt alone as I sat and stared up above
Saw the stars so far away —
The stars that will never know me.

I seek out those who desire greatness
With only inside competition.
Those who ought to be remembered.

I have ghosts of my own,
Scars of my own,
But I wish to be free.

I don't know this world enough to judge,
But I will find no perfect place —
Only a strong, calm soul.

*Elizabeth Shackney, Grade 11*
*The Ellis School*

**We Are the People**
We are the people
The people with hearts so big
Expectation so indescribable
Arms wide open to success

We are the people
The people with songs in our mouths
Hands spread wide out
Legs running toward open doors

We are the people
The people who never stop caring
With ears that never cease hearing
That run from those who aren't daring

We are the people
The people willing to put the talk to action
Who aren't afraid of transaction
Who'd rather help than hurt
Who believe in faith, love and trust

We are the people
Who know life isn't as easy as it seems
Who know that peace doesn't come with ease

We are the people

*Oyindamola Busari, Grade 10*
*Penn Wood High School - Cypress Street Campus*

## The Waiting Game

Applications, essays, and a final grade,
These are a few of my favorite things.
Patience, prayers, and nerves frayed,
Preparing for next year is what this brings.

Decision letters determine fate,
An acceptance letter is what I await.
Anxious seniors with a high heart rate,
As they open their soon-to-be fate.

Dressers, desks, and a new lamp,
These are a few of my favorite things.
Endless opportunities that allow a revamp
Of memories that high school brings.

Even if it was not the number one,
College life has just begun.
But when all is said and one,
We overcame the waiting game.

*Maddy Reichel, Grade 12*
*Villa Maria Academy*

## Like No Other

My pencil is like no other
It is a source of my artistic talent
From my pencil flows limitless imagination
My pencil is like no other
It has the ability to bring ideas to life
With my pencil anything is possible
My pencil is like no other
The unknown can become known
A moment in life can be captured
My pencil is like no other

*Kayla Dick, Grade 10*
*Kennard Dale High School*

## The Cat

I saw a cat perched in a tree,
And quickly saw what it would see,
To be a bird, both fair and wise,
To quickly meet a cruel demise.
The cat did pounce with righteous fire,
To smite that bird perched on the briar,
And as I watched, bird's head in breach
My ears then heard a mighty "Screech!"
And as I watched the hawk descend
I knew the cat would meet its end.

*Joshua Butcher, Grade 11*
*Greencastle-Antrim High School*

## Memories in White

Watch as her little hands skip across the ivory keys
Coaxing a gentle, tinkling melody from the piano
As they follow behind the aged hands of her white-haired grandmother.

Laugh as she breaks the perfect whiteness of a sea of snow
With her fleecy ashen coat
As she forms an angel in the soft, cool powder.

Gaze as she glides down the aisle in her pearly dress
As the sweet, sleepy scent of pure white roses
Drifts delicately throughout the marble-walled chapel.

Listen as she sings a quiet lullaby
To her fair haired daughter as she dozes off
Swaddled safely in warm, cloud-like blankets of wool.

And smile as her old hands lead her granddaughter's
In a graceful stroll across those same white keys
That they learned to dance upon so many years ago.

*Ryan Miller, Grade 12*
*Upper St Clair High School*

## The Reason for the Clouds

Clouds
Out of reach
Infinite in their shape and numbers,
Unaltered by the hands of man.

Dreams
Your true desires
Infinite in their possibilities and numbers,
Unaltered by the hands of man.

The clouds remind us of dreams
As the sun shines through, the beauty of our dreams are brought to light
The darkness of a storm symbolizes setbacks, lightning danger, thunder confidence
Midwinter snowfall hints at the reward of a goal reached, transcendental beauty.

When the power of man tries to break you
Look no further than the clouds
They show the course of your dreams
The reason you should never give up on them.

*Ian Dorman, Grade 11*
*Central Mountain High School*

## My Life in Terms of Surfing

My perfectionism is like the perfection of your stance.
My dedication is like the practice surfing takes.
My weeks are filled with early mornings like the break of the first waves.
My strength is like the "get-back-up" attitude of surfers.
My journey is like the long treacherous walk to the beach with your board.
My personality is like surfboard: strong, supportive, unbreakable.
My opinion is like the break of the waves: rough, clear.
My life is like surfing.

*Grace Morrison, Grade 11*
*Eastern York High School*

## Corn

The brownish fields are marred by death and time.
No longer are they plants of green sublime.
They snap and crackle as the winds decree,
And never show the gold that lay beneath.
This corn, odd mutant form which comes from grass
Must fall and die from winter's icy blasts.
Before it gives its life to freezing cold,
It forms an ear which yieldeth wealth untold.
A combine passes 'twixt the withered rows
And gathers grain before the hungry snows
Can blight the golden grains with rot and mold
And leave them useless bits that can't be sold.
The mighty farmer labors through the day.
He never can afford a slight delay.
The duty falls to him to feed the earth,
With fields of corn with massive length and girth.

*Nathan Hykes, Grade 12*
*Greencastle-Antrim High School*

## The Maze of Life

I travel to the distant edge of Earth
To see the brightness of the Sun in day,
To see the very reason of my birth,
And wish there be a much easier way.
If only, there were someone to save me;
If only, there could be someone like you;
In darkness, you're the light that I can see;
For you're the only one I know who's true.
But light of Sun and Earth will just vary;
And nothing can ever remain the same,
Except you, and your undying beauty;
Which makes everything else seem like a game.
At last I have you there to save me from,
This maze of life and its tedious drum.

*Kunal Lobo, Grade 10*
*Avon Grove High School*

## Sorrow

The rain pounds on the ground
while the glass crashes with the sound
natural disaster takes its place
while all the color drains from your face
bars that keep you hidden behind doors
the horror that makes you
drop to the floor
why are we still
carrying our flesh
why do we keep
going through this mess
instead of love; we hate
but after hate
there's death
what a misfortune
the living can only dread

*Denasia Thompson, Grade 12*
*Coatesville Area Sr High School*

## Surreal

Reciprocity is a tricky realm.
Sense impressions are nothing,
but ideas.
Even the greatest minds
have difficulty.

Let the world color
the table nasa
passing lodge on Sass
and a founder's hall
brushing powdered leaves.

What is the meaning?
I don't know, I don't know
Trinity Cemetery, the frosted
grass eerily creeps.

Two lanes for a unicycle,
which to choose?
I don't know, I don't know.

We are going up, the end
is near. I know heaven
is real, but my life is so
surreal.

*Rebecca Sweny, Grade 12*
*Villa Maria Academy*

## Winter's Close of Day

Gasp.
One breath in, quick.
The icy, metallic shock
like lightning to the skin.

Patter, patter,
red toes and heels exposed
wash away white from the canvas,
creating a negative image:
white scattered in the dark above,
dark splattered in white below.

Step, jump, run,
into the house out of the cold.
Fiery warmth, sweeping forward,
to gnaw on tingling toes.

Was it worth it?
Worth a blanket of cold,
slowly thawing away, to dance in the night,
through the crystalline white,
under a chandelier of light
in the darkened sky —
winter's close of day.

*Jennifer Torrance, Grade 12*
*Villa Maria Academy*

### Ode to Japanese Maple Tree

I was paid twenty dollars an hour
From a neighbor
To clean out the garden of weeds.
When I arrived,
I noticed red fire,
Burning bright
In the molten lava of the day.
Constricted like a boa's prey,
Green vines strangling,
Tight as nooses in the gallows
Around a stump
Clinging to life.
I shoveled, cut,
Ripped away vegetation.
I am a creator,
A builder of perfection.
Red fire roars bright with green blood.
A jungle of green
Comes to be no more
Than a no-man's-land
Of red fire.

*Austin Pollock, Grade 10*
*Plymouth-Whitemarsh High School*

### On Stage

Walking out on stage can set me free—
It has the power to transform me
into someone without a worry,
someone without a care.
I can be me and not feel scared.

In front of the lights,
performing the songs,
I know that on stage I can't go wrong.

The stage sets me free and
gives inspiration—

To dream, to act, to sing,
to give motivation.

*Morgan Strickler, Grade 11*
*Eastern York High School*

### The Boy

His life living in fear
No accomplishment, nothing to bear
No feelings or emotions but hate
No future no life not even faith.
Mind and heart trapped inside a vault
Why is he like this?
Nobody knows probably not his fault.
Mom and Dad nowhere in sight.
Brother somewhere living a better life.
He's alone, but why?

*Derick Mom, Grade 11*
*Motivation High School*

### A Thousand Songs

When everything turns to nothing
And the sky is falling down
I'll take you by the hand
And spin you all around

I'll plant a kiss upon your lips
With a melody in my head,
I'll sing to you a thousand songs
To make you smile again

When the world has turned its back on you
You've got nowhere else to turn
You'll look above and see the sky
And watch those faint lights burn

I'll tap you on the shoulder
And help you see the light
I'll smile for you and dry your tears
Until your world is bright

*Jaime Swank, Grade 10*
*Council Rock High School South*

### A Million Cries

One lay down under,
A million cry

A million left out to rot,
No one asks why

Madagascar to Zambia
Poverty and famines all around

A million cries,
but no help to be found

Your mountains high
Your valleys deep

A million cries
Mother,
Will no one hear you weep?

*Tejwant Gomanie, Grade 10*
*Whitehall High School*

### Walking Along the Beach

As I walk along the beach
My feet imprint in the sand
As I walk along the beach
I begin to wonder who I am
As I walk along the beach
I look behind me
As I walk along the beach
I realize that no matter who I am
I will always leave an imprint on the world

*Leah Kordaz, Grade 11*
*Kennard Dale High School*

### Just a Feeling

Love is just a feeling,
Something in your heart.
Sometimes it's sweet,
And other times it's tart.

Sometimes it makes you happy,
Other times just worse,
Some days it's a blessing,
Others it's a curse.

Love can be true,
It can also be a lie.
It can make you smile,
Or just break down and cry.

Love can stay forever,
Or leave just like it came.
But when it finally does…
There's only yourself you blame.

*Brittany Muckel, Grade 11*
*Eastern York High School*

### Crazy with You, Crazier Without You

I'm in love with the way you smile
And I'm in love with the way you hold me
I'm afraid for ever losing you
Because I couldn't live without you
This happiness is what I'm falling in
As long as you're here, I'll be fine
On you I will always rely
But the truth is, I'm crazy with you
And crazier without you

*Taylor Clark, Grade 11*
*Kennard-Dale High School*

# Grades 7-8-9
# Top Ten Winners

*List of Top Ten Winners for Grades 7-9; listed alphabetically*

*Keelan Apthorpe, Grade 8*
*St Anne Catholic School, TX*

*Kelly Brown, Grade 8*
*Fairbanks Middle School, OH*

*Natalie Ciepiela, Grade 7*
*Landisville Middle School, PA*

*Golda Dopp, Grade 9*
*Davis High School, UT*

*Madeline Elliott, Grade 7*
*Holly Middle School, MI*

*Lydia Heydlauff, Grade 8*
*Gilbert Middle School, IA*

*Mariella Jorge, Grade 8*
*Madrona Middle School, CA*

*Kaitlin Kilby, Grade 8*
*North Kirkwood Middle School, MO*

*Maryann Mathai, Grade 8*
*Windy Ridge School, FL*

*Jacob Nelson, Grade 8*
*Leesville Road Middle School, NC*

*All Top Ten Poems can be read at www.poeticpower.com*

*Note: The Top Ten poems were finalized through an online voting system. Creative Communication's judges first picked out the top poems. These poems were then posted online. The final step involved thousands of students and teachers who registered as the online judges and voted for the Top Ten poems. We hope you enjoy these selections.*

### Snowboarding

I love snowboarding in the winter time
Jumping on the lift with all of my friends
When we reach the top we hope it's prime
People on the mountain wear the new trends

Snowboarding is the best in November
Great to come down the slopes in winter pow
Killington is a memory I will remember forever
When my friends and I hit jumps we say ow!

I have a cool Solomon snowboard
I have thirty-two boots size eleven
It is also an amazing park board
My boots fit me nice and feel like heaven

You must keep up with the latest fashion
I love snowboarding and boarding is my passion
*Robert Turnbull III, Grade 8*
*Pocono Mountain East Jr High School*

### Don't Worry

Your smile as beautiful as the sun
But forever lost within pretty lies
Knowing life is just a crazy rerun
Over and over, same pain in your eyes

Hiding the broken, hiding the deep scars
Tears that are shed are never to be seen
Hurt by names, a prisoner behind bars
Hide from the lies, people can be so mean

The world seems so big, while you feel so small
You're in a crowd yet still feeling alone
Scared of the world, yet don't fear, just stand tall
Look around and see, you're not on your own

Forever you, in the dark be the light
You're perfect so don't worry, it's alright
*Brianna Lavin, Grade 8*
*Pocono Mountain East Jr High School*

### Not What It Seems

They all think it is simple
Never realizing the troubles endured
They think you don't have to try
As if you will always be a really smart guy
One day it will just happen
It comes as a feeling of understanding
From there, your questions will forever grow
What you will think of next, you will never know
It is like you are always running
You understand something and it only leads to more questions
Questions might even come in your dreams
Being considered smart is not what it seems
*Jacob Frye, Grade 8*
*Penn Middle School*

### Philadelphia

Sometimes I hear the
Things they say about this place,
And I just don't understand.

Philadelphia!
The things it has to offer!
The art and the science!

Hush. Don't not say the
Foul words you wish to say
Against my only home.

California may
Have beaches and palm trees,
But they don't feel my love.

Why disturb the cycle,
The mill of people who pass
Every day in this place?

Philadelphia.
You see what you make of it.
I see a palace, yes.

Philadelphia.
You are my Alabama,
Home, sweet home, I love you.
*Caroline Wozniak, Grade 8*
*French International School of Philadelphia*

### Ode to My Grandma

Ode to the memory of her gentle hands,
Sweeping my hair back,
As she sang me to sleep.

Ode to the memory of her fingers,
Weaving a needle,
As she teaches me how to sew.

Ode to the memory of her frail body,
Sitting across from me.
As she tells me the story of a boy who lost his grandma,
But was comforted by the fact, that she was watching over him.

I remember the day when I was dressed in all black,
As she lay in front of me.
I was too young to understand,
But old enough to feel sorrow.

Ode to the bracelet,
Silver as the moon,
With dangling hearts, that jingle like bells.
For I remember being told,
"She wanted you to have this."
*Britt Lovett, Grade 8*
*Shipley School*

### Crystal Water
Water
Turns to crystals
As the bright sun shines down;
Waves start to crash on the shore line
Midday.
*Sarah Andres, Grade 8*
*St. Luke School*

### Insects
Scary things,
Small, colorful, helpful,
Shapes and sizes vary,
Will camouflage themselves for protection,
Insects can be helpful and destructive.
*Matthew Macri, Grade 7*
*Holy Sepulcher School*

### Mountains
Mountains
Stand tall,
Towering over others,
Snow covered on top,
Hills.
*Rachel Cox, Grade 7*
*Easton Area Middle School 7-8*

### Easter
Very colorful,
Children decorating eggs,
Flowers start to bloom,
The sun shines very brightly,
Easter is the most colorful holiday.
*Mark Benkart, Grade 7*
*Holy Sepulcher School*

### In the Wind
Look, there
Like ghosts traipsing
Through the crisp autumn air
Leaves descend from their wooden homes
Sadly.
*Taylor Liegl, Grade 8*
*St. Luke School*

### Why Ninjas Wear Black
There once was a ninja named Mack,
who tried to stand out from the pack.
He only wore white,
was killed in the night,
and that is why ninjas wear black.
*Jannah Martin, Grade 8*
*Ephrata Middle School*

### Love
I see you walking there
So beautifully, with the wind flowing through your hair
You stop to stare
I look away, pretending not to care
Your eyes sparkle as they meet mine
I also stare, so gentle and kind
You sit down on a bench and call me over
I come and sit, with my head on your shoulder
I start to smile and blush really red
As you gently touch and pet my head
You are so sweet to me
Letting me know that love is our main key
You brush the hair from my cheek behind my ear
Letting me know that a kiss is near
I turn away because I know it will happen too
As you come closer and whisper, "I love you"
I turn back to see you sitting there
We both seem to feel the love in the air
We come closer and closer, until our lips finally meet
And we both smile because this is a memory we will both forever keep
*Colleen Lang, Grade 7*
*St Luke the Evangelist School*

### Things I've Learned from the Words He's Said
Some people can say that love is blind;
It throws you around in a million different directions and still,
You can't see where you're going half the time.
Mr. Right; he's the best thing you'll never find,
So you settle for second best when the best is right there and still,
Some people can say that love is blind.
So you get back in the "old grind;"
Think you finally have it all, but still,
You can't see where you're going half the time.
Through the labyrinths of lies you find
That all was always in your hands and you knew it all along and still,
Some people can say that love is blind.
You always try to keep an open mind
He's standing right there! And still,
You can't see where you're going half the time.
He's not one in a million, there's none of that kind;
But he was forever yours, and he held you and said the words:
"Still some people can say that love is blind;
You can't see where you're going half the time."
*Hayley Sturgis, Grade 9*
*Tamaqua Area Sr High School*

### Mystical Creatures
Mystical creatures
not yet seen by human eye
they have wings as white as winter snow
a mighty horn perched on top its head, displayed like a gold prize just won
gracefully gliding across the sea of clouds, it brings joy and happiness to all below
though most people think they're just a tall tale that only children believe,
I believe because seeing is not always believing.
*Kaitlin Decker, Grade 7*
*Pennwood Middle School*

### Black Rose

Sadness is like a black rose,
all alone
in a field of colors.
The only one different,
the only one acting as itself,
not afraid to show its
true
feelings.
The black represents the empty
inside it.
The loneliness,
the mist from the air,
rolling off in dew form,
makes it seem as if it were crying.
The thorns on the stem
represent the piercing in your heart.
The aftereffect
of the pain.
When you add these all together,
you get a rose.
A black rose.

*Charis Gatoura, Grade 7*
*Tulpehocken Jr/Sr High School*

### Last Antarctica

Like a desert, cold and bitter
Covered in a blanket woven from snow
There is a place where no man lives
And has species no one knows

Where Penguins and polar bears roam
The Earth's lowest altitude
The continent with no single country
But meets all lines of longitude

Now that research is being done
And camps are being set up
All of my cuddly friends are taking off
I sit in my tent, drinking hot tea from a cup

Alas for all of this
Here I am back
I must leave for a meeting
So, start up the Cadillac

Farewell friends…

*Eric Rhodes, Grade 7*
*Pennbrook Middle School*

### Love

Love is like gossip
It's spread around and distorted.
So it stands to reason that
No one ever really grasps the concept.

*Madisyn Breiner, Grade 8*
*Northern Lebanon Middle School*

### It Found Me

It waits there beside me
All day and all night
Waiting to attack
I'm nervous I'm scared
I'm frightened all the time
I don't know what to do
I want to leave
I want to go
But I can't
So I stay
I stay until the break of dawn
Then I leave
I run off when it's not around
Now I'm all alone
I have nothing
I have no home
Nowhere to go
No one to love anymore
No friends to share laughs with
But worst part is
It found me

*Stacy Martin, Grade 7*
*Tulpehocken Jr/Sr High School*

### Who Knows

Only the wind knows
When it's going to blow
Making trees swing and sway
And only the rain knows
When it will pour
Only the sun knows
When it's going to shine
As if it only had a few more moments
And only the snow knows
When it will fall
Covering everything in white
Weathermen can only hazard a guess
So fly with me
When the wind carries me away
Stand and kiss me
In the pouring rain
Run alongside me
And shine just the same
Throw snowballs at me
When everything freezes over
And be mine

*Hannah Steinmetz, Grade 8*
*Penn Middle School*

### Summer

When the sun is beating down
You will want to stay cool
So take a dip in the pool
But be sure not to drown

*Ryan Kavanagh, Grade 7*
*Arcola Intermediate School*

### Red

Red.
The color of fire,
the blazing flame,
a cause of death.
Red.
The color of roses,
a beautiful flower,
with a delightful scent.
Red.
The color of a lady bug,
a little bug,
that's so sweet and cute.
A color of so many meanings.
Red.

*Gabby McGillin, Grade 7*
*Strath Haven Middle School*

### End of Day

There's a cabin in the wood,
And it's built quite snug and good;
And I really think we should
   All live there.

There's a mockin' bird a-singin'
While its way a-homeward wingin'
And an owl is tightly clingin'
   To an old dead limb.

'Tis a quiet, peaceful way
To end another day
That is running away
   From the night.

*Darren North, Grade 7*
*Rockhaven Christian School*

### Hold On

Hold on to hope
Even if it's all you have left

Hold on to peace
Even if the world around you is crumbling

Hold on to love
Even if you feel like it won't help

Hold on to faith
Even if the going gets tough

Hold on to life
Even when it knocks you down

*Sarah Groff, Grade 7*
*Pequea Valley Intermediate School*

### Birds

Birds
Nature's song
Singing, flying high
Peaceful sounds, joyous noise
Artists
*Natalie Folks, Grade 7*
*Easton Area Middle School 7-8*

### Rain

Such pain,
Falls from sky,
Till morning is nigh,
There are many clouds around,
While it falls onto the ground.
*Matthew Rechenberg, Grade 7*
*Holy Sepulcher School*

### Spring

New flowers,
World starts anew,
Pretty, young, beautiful, green,
Always trying to rebuild again,
Spring brings color and new life.
*Harrison Brown, Grade 8*
*Holy Sepulcher School*

### Spring

Longer days,
Lots of sunshine,
The animals wander around,
Beautiful flowers start to bloom,
I love the season of spring!
*Allie Megahan, Grade 8*
*Holy Sepulcher School*

### Spring

Snow thaws,
Days get longer,
Seeing imprints of paws,
The sun's light is stronger,
New growth is seen all around.
*Rachel Roos, Grade 8*
*Holy Sepulcher School*

### Jesus

He's alive,
Died for us,
Rose in three days,
He hung on the cross,
He saved us from all sin.
*Helen Kanaitis, Grade 7*
*Holy Sepulcher School*

### Something Blue

A girl's wedding is something that she looks forward to her whole life,
From single, to engaged, to now being a wife.
As a young girl she dances to the tune "Chapel of Love,"
And imagines her entrance decorated with flowers and doves.
Something old, something new, something borrowed, something blue,
Her dress will be beautiful and elegant too.
The moment that she has been waiting for her whole life is about to come true,
In just a few moments she will be saying "I do."
Her father escorts her down the aisle,
As she sees her fiancé standing there with a big smile.
As she enters the reception full of fun and dance,
She cannot help but to give her yummy cake a quick glance.
She throws her bouquet up in the air,
As all of the hopeful young girls stare.
As the clock strikes midnight and the dancing is done,
She is not sad, but happy because she knows that she has found the one.
Years from now as she remembers the day she walked down the aisle,
She will look back on that magical day and smile.
Just like Romeo and Juliet,
She found her one true love,
One glance at him and she was set.
*Christina Motz, Grade 7*
*St Luke the Evangelist School*

### You

You walk around with a smug look
Watching with your beady eyes and saying that we don't deserve to be here
Thinking you are supreme

You laugh at compassion
You gloat over your misdeeds
Thinking you are the most superlative

You make fun of the lonely
You don't know how much it hurts
But you still think you are superior

We know that you are ruthless, cruel, and arrogant
But we keep our heads held high
And ignore the fact that you are without a soul
*Sam Gamberg, Grade 7*
*Welsh Valley Middle School*

### I Love You

i love you for your patience. Your kindness and faith in me
inspires me to move on with life through all its curves and bends
i love you for your gentleness when we both disagree
pointing out what you dislike without hurting me or my feelings
i love you for your faith and kindness to me that soothes my weary soul
i love you for your friendship that you give me without saying anything
i love you for your thoughtful ways that set my spirit free
i love you for caring in me, that makes my life seem whole
i love you for what you are and how you make me feel
i love you for the boost you give me when I'm sad so often without praise
*Emily Karl, Grade 8*
*Ephrata Middle School*

### A Day at the Beach

Here at last,
Ready to have a blast.
I lay by the ocean
Listening to the commotion.
Then I hear the seagulls fly
Way up in the clear, blue sky.
I feel the warm sand beneath me
And hear the waves rolling in the sea.
The fiery sun
Is baking me like a bun
Tanning my skin
As the volleyball team scores a win.
I see the other side very sad
Stomping their feet and looking mad.
The sun now sets,
I have to go.
Will I be back?
Oh, I don't know.
*Abby Luensmann, Grade 7*
*Bellwood Antis Middle School*

### The Beach

Seeing the ocean dance,
Umbrellas opened wide.
Swimmer's going deep in the blue ocean

Little kids running about
With excitement, hopes, and dreams.
Making sand castles,
And flying kites

Hearing the ocean waves,
And the boats roaring past.

Walking along the water,
As the sun is setting,
With my feet getting wet,
Sand sticking to the wetness.
Feeling rough and cold.
*Bobbi Lynn Erisman, Grade 7*
*William Penn Middle School*

### Love Against War

Let us be free
If love is just love
Then war is just war.
Trade guns for love,
and fire with doves.
Love mends the broken
And listens to the unspoken.
Bringing on peace,
let the hate decrease.
Saving souls through all salvation,
Let us be free.
*Rachel Scott, Grade 9*
*Pennbrook Middle School*

### Do Things Over

If I could do things over
I think I'd start with me
and be a better person
that I always try to be

If I could do things over
I'd try to make things right
and try to mend them
with a little insight

If I could do things over
I'd be sure to smile
and be happy and caring
no one has been that way in a while

If I could do things over
I'd make sure to be
the person that's inside
that I want everyone to see
*Anna Hays, Grade 8*
*Penn Middle School*

### Perfection

Perfection is a word
So strong
A noun not used often.
All think they are perfect,
but scars and bumps
proven not.
Scars I say,
but internal I mean.
Deep in the tissues of
the heart,
brain,
and soul,
lay scars.
So if you or someone
Else says you're perfect,
Prove them wrong because
everybody makes mistakes,
You're not perfect,
neither is anyone else.
*Kayla Jaquay, Grade 7*
*William M Meredith School*

### Gone for Now

We're still together, even if you're not here.
Far away we'll meet again some day.
I loved you, and you love me.
Death is life and life is death.
Together we'll be. Family is forever.
One thing I loved is gone.
The memories I cherish.
Still together but far away for now.
*Kylie Kuhn, Grade 7*
*Armstrong Middle School*

### A Walk

I look both ways
To my content
No cars coming
We walk

The bridge is long
Tedious and unforgiving
The sun beats down on my scorched skin
We walk

I stop to rest
A drink to quench my thirst
Its tangy juice sits in my mouth
We walk

Out of the corner of my eye I see
A paradise, lush and green
I move swiftly on the concrete
We walk

Our time is up to return to my life
It felt like a dream
But my sister is waiting
Her classes are over
We walk
*Ethan Van Metre, Grade 7*
*Strath Haven Middle School*

### The Dark Man

The dark man follows you
Stalking you in dim light
But disappears when bright
Making you turn twice

The dark man follows you
You hear footsteps
Sensing someone coming behind you
Inches within your grasp

The dark man follows you
But, when the moon goes down
And the sun is up like a lone star in the sky
The light burning through his eyes

He disappears
When light is shown to your front
He lurks back,
Silently anew

The dark man follows you
Overwhelmed with fright
You turn around swiftly
To find him all around you
The shadows follow you
*Sean DeBiase, Grade 8*
*Penn Middle School*

## Hold On

Hold on to the good things in life
Hold on to what you believe in
Even if people say it's not true
Hold on to the love you have for someone
Even if it's not going to last
Hold on to the memories
Even if they're over
Hold on to the future
Even if it's not going to come
Hold on to the life you're living
Even if you're at your worst

*Brianna Ross, Grade 7*
*Pequea Valley Intermediate School*

## Mom

Why won't you let me have one?
I know I'm responsible to get one.
You say I'm not old enough.
I won't spend all day on it.
If you only let me have one.
It would mean the world to me.
It wouldn't be a crime.
If you would only say yes,
I would be so happy.
Mom,
If you only got me this one thing.

*Grace Sonney, Grade 8*
*Wattsburg Area Middle School*

## Things a Zombie Knows

moans and groans
yells and screams
and craving brains
but they don't like it when it rains
underground
uptown
in a cemetery
but you can't find them in a
library
we will never know why they're mad
we just know they are bad

*Dante Martinez, Grade 7*
*Easton Area Middle School 7-8*

## Gymnastics

Like a cheetah running so fast
Off my hands, I turn to go back
My feet hit the floor
I'm ready to soar
Like a bird with open wings
I go as high as the sky
Like a plane taking off
There's no turning back
Everyone cheers!

*McKenna Mayers, Grade 7*
*Bellwood Antis Middle School*

## I Am

I am ready for the game of my life.
I wonder what the huge crowd under the lights will be like.
I hear the crowd screaming in my head.
I see every fan cheering for my team.
I want to win this and be national champs.
I am ready for the game of my life.

I pretend to run into the end zone and score that game-winning touchdown.
I feel every fan running onto the field at me.
I touch the game-winning football and feel that smooth pigskin.
I worry about coming out on the bad end.
I cry, imagining us losing and the other team celebrating.
I am ready for the game of my life.

I understand there must be one winner.
I say we're not going to lose, no matter what.
I dream about holding that championship trophy.
I try to do everything I can to win this game.
I hope that we will win this championship game.
I am ready for the game of my life.

*Brandon Hooper, Grade 7*
*Pequea Valley Intermediate School*

## Mourning

If you have ever mourned,
You know it is a feeling that you will never forget,
It forces you to create a realization of the world you live in,
When all your life you have pushed it aside to save your sanity.
Always constructing a barrier of ignorance between what you want to be true,
And what is true.
Mourning is the battering ram that undoes and unfastens the gate.
It happens so fast that you become a shell of shock.
And then the floodgates drown your heart with sorrow.
Then, it hits you,
A revelation.
Strangely, you feel peace.
Almost as if the person was shrouding your view of the world,
And that now you come to see it in a new way.
A lonelier way.

*John Bogert, Grade 7*
*Pennbrook Middle School*

## Sisterhood Is Like…

Sisterhood is like…
Sisterhood is like cupcakes…it's sweet.
Sisterhood is like fashion…it changes each year.
Sisterhood is like books…you will always learn from it.
Sisterhood is like music…it plays a certain tone.
Sisterhood is like the sun…it shines through the clouds on a rainy day.
Sisterhood is like flowers…it brings beauty and color into your life.
Sisterhood is like a joke…it makes you laugh until you cry.
Sisterhood is like a roller coaster…it brings on the fright and excitement.
Sisterhood is like ice cream…there's always more flavors to try.
Sisterhood is like a butterfly…it brings a bright smile to your face when you're feeling down.

*Michelle Gehman, Grade 8*
*Ephrata Middle School*

### The Dark

The light flickers off
All alone in the dark
Blind to what is around me
Afraid of what lies ahead
But too afraid to turn back
My heart beats faster and faster
My palms become clammy
I look around in panic
I'm caught in the middle
A light flickers on
I'm home again

*Sarah Swinderman, Grade 8*
*Pine-Richland Middle School*

### Show Jumping

Show jumping
Is satisfaction, confidence
Respect and care
A world of extremes
A legendary performance
Is a superior performance
A jumper's dream
Inspiration to win
At a glance it is strong and sophisticated
Elegant and enduring.

*Kara Humphreys, Grade 8*
*Unami Middle School*

### What a Big Brother Knows

Takes care of chores
Gets paid more
Likes to play sports
And wear baggy shorts
Gets the newspaper
Says hi to neighbors
They go to school
Then play at the pool
They like to have fun
I know because I am one.

*Jaylin Millin, Grade 7*
*Easton Area Middle School 7-8*

### The Champion

The champion never falls,
The champion doesn't break,
He does not run away from fear,
The victory he only hears,
People respect his great achievements,
For they could never do the same,
The champion is never left in shame,
He can do what they cannot,
He is the champion,
Greatest of the great

*Jared Jordan, Grade 8*
*Danville Area Middle School*

### The Girl on Fire

A revolution she did not mean to start
Two boys that loved her with all their hearts
This twisted plot begins to unfold
A huge decision that could tear her apart

The berries were a vital part, her actions too bold
So he watched her every move, his eyes so cold
This uprising needed to be put to rest
If he was not pleased, consequences would be as he foretold

So he gave her only so much time and put her to the test
She tried to succeed, but her performance was not her best
The tyrant was displeased and the effects were dire
Sparks were flying, she needed to lead, but was under a lot of stress

They wanted to make her their leader, someone everyone could admire
Everything began to pick up and terrible things transpired
Too many people suffered, so many citizens disappeared, and there were a few misfires
So she became the Mockingjay and returned as the girl on fire

*Emily Reichard, Grade 8*
*Penn-Kidder Campus*

### Girls

Can all the girls please stand up with me for this?

When I was younger I used to love Wonder Woman for her powers, but now that I'm older,
I realize that she means much more than that.
I have something to say to all the girls in the world…
We are here for a reason…
We can be here for anything and everything…
We can be here to share our love like magnet to a refrigerator…inseparable
We can be here to be beautiful like a rose…blooming
We can be here to be smart like a phone…genius
We can be here to be strong like the gravity…forceful
We can be here to work for our rights like MLK…dreaming
We can be here to show that we are just as good as men,
Even if it is a man's world…change
If you don't know or understand why we are here,
Don't be mad, because you are here for a reason…

We are all like Wonder Woman in our own way…
The world is full of wonderful girls.

*Kimberly Campagna, Grade 8*
*First Philadelphia Charter School for Literacy*

### Life

As the grass grows high
The vines wrap around the crumbling house that once was filled with life
As you grow closer to the fallen-down trees and the dried-up lakes
You hear water…it sounds as luscious as silk
And when you come close to it you see life all around you
Trees with apples and leaves, peaches, plums and pears,
And even some trees dripping with sap
It is…it is life.

*Isaac Dieguez, Grade 7*
*Pennbrook Middle School*

**April**
The tap of the leather.
The crack of the bat.
Screams from the crowd.
The sound of fireworks.
The glorious weather.

Fresh cut Evergreen grass.
Bright blank chalk races down the foul line.
The azure of the sky brightens up the day.
The sun heats up the day, like a campfire at night.
One of the most gorgeous things in sight.

Fans cheer as they see their favorite players.
The two teams are ready.
The wild ride to October is not steady.
You will not need any layers.
Baseball is back!
*Rob Betza, Grade 8*
*Pine-Richland Middle School*

**The Magic of Reading**
At the beginning of a book you come upon
A golden door with a handle of brass.
Grasping the knob to open it up,
You're pulled inside another world.
A place where imagination roams free
A time where wonders come true.
You fight alongside the heroes, side by side
And keep up with the rivalry against the villains.
Discovering a magical power on the way,
And finally defeating evil.
You thank the writer for the time of your life.
But knowing
That little golden door
Is always unlocked
To bring you back to this
Other
*World.*
*Helen Qi, Grade 7*
*Strath Haven Middle School*

**The Trees of Love**
The ground, soft and damp,
Receding beneath my feet,
The tree's leaves rustle as the wind blows,
The scent of the air that makes my heart beat,
The stars in the sky shining dully,
The moon's bright light shines where they meet,
The trees that twist together and spread far apart,
The smell of its bark so sweet,
Its branches rise high, curving and arching,
In the distance I hear a dog barking,
Yet nothing disturbs me in this special place,
Where the love that was shared is shown.
*Lauren Pankiewicz, Grade 8*
*Bellmar Middle School*

**My Room**
Piles and piles of clothes
Sitting on my bed.
My books sitting on the dusty old shelves
Just waiting for me to open
Them up and read.

My covers all messy
With my fluffy puffy pillows on the bed.
My white beautiful curtains
Coming all the way down to the floor.
The sound of my alarm clock
Going on then off.

My room.
The smell of vanilla.
The sunlight coming in to brighten the mood.
My haven.
My responsibility.
*Kelly Peters, Grade 7*
*William Penn Middle School*

**If I Were in Charge of the World\***
If I were in charge of the world
I'd remove all homework-related concepts,
Paperwork of any kind,
And mechanisms that have no importance.

If I were in charge of the world
There'd be clearer night skies,
Bluer waters,
And healthier wildlife.

If I were in charge of the world
You wouldn't have to do chores,
You wouldn't have to write essays,
You wouldn't have to be alone,
Or have no one to talk to.

If I were in charge of the world.
*Katherine Alvaro, Grade 7*
*Pequea Valley Intermediate School*
*\*Patterned after "If I Were in Charge of the World" by Judith Viorst*

**Life Is Like…**
Life is like gambling
you never know what kind of cards you're going to get
you need to take risks to succeed
sometimes the odds are down on you
but you come back
sometimes you're on top of the world
and the next moment you lose it all
always changing, always growing
but if you play your cards just right
anything is possible
*Alex Modrzecki, Grade 8*
*Ephrata Middle School*

### Decision

Two paths, two ways to go
What they lead to I do not know
I know there will be no turning back
What's done is done and that's a fact
I ask which road I should walk
But the decision is mine to make
I must determine which course to take
What's waiting at the end I cannot tell
But hopefully, the end will turn out well

*Katrina Bernaus, Grade 7*
*Strath Haven Middle School*

### Granddad

Go go go!
Awww
The sounds of Sunday
In your company
Are always the same
When Sunday ends
It is a shame
But I can't wait for the next one
See you in a week!

*Travis DeBruyn, Grade 7*
*Strath Haven Middle School*

### Spring Flowers

The fresh scent of flowers
has filled the air
like perfume
that is being sprayed everywhere.
The colors can be seen
from far away,
they are bright
like the sun
showing off to everyone.

*Kaitlin Sutton, Grade 8*
*Lake-Lehman Jr High School*

### Can't Sleep

Sleeping in my bed
With my pillow under my head
I cannot sleep
I hear a beep
I wish my alarm was dead

*Maggie Burns, Grade 7*
*Easton Area Middle School 7-8*

### Life

Crash! Here's a gift sent from heaven,
A gift that you should enjoy
A gift given for a specific purpose
An emotional, colorful phase,
Full of dark and bright colors too,
A gift sent from heaven just for you!

*Kimberly Herndon, Grade 7*
*Garnet Valley Middle School*

### In the Rain

I wish I knew all of Earth's wonders.
Never to be doubted, and never put down under,
but I know that wonders in my mind, will enlighten the sky like thunder.

I wish I could be a desert cactus standing tall.
Much too dry for tears to slowly fall,
but I know that I can brighten the day, spreading glee to all.

I wish I were a falling raindrop.
I'm falling but still remaining on top,
but I know I am at the top of the world in my mind, and my falling path will never stop.

I wish I could somehow take away all pain.
Nothing to lose, but therefore nothing to gain,
but I know I will be hurt, and this will keep me sane.

I wish to be a movie star,
Basking in the fame,
but I'm just a lonely commoner, being discouraged in the rain.

*Tyler Broen, Grade 8*
*Pine-Richland Middle School*

### Spring

The crisp, clear, colorful sky has no clouds,
The air has a sweet smell like gooey chocolate chip cookies.
Buzzing bumblebees fly carelessly from flower to flower.
Fresh flowers have a fragrance as sweet as honey,
Young kids are gentle giants in the emerald-green grass.
The sun is brightly shining over meadows of gorgeous daisies,
I know what time of the year it is, it's finally spring!
Children's lively laughter rings in my ears like church bells.
A gentle breeze licks the back of my neck,
A slight chill then catches me, and drags me back.
Beautiful butterflies that are every color of the rainbow gracefully flutter by.
Birds chirp loudly from high in a light pink cherry blossom tree.
Light rain showers fertilize the newborn flowers.
Spring is now here!

*Nicole Barbacane, Grade 7*
*William Penn Middle School*

### Don't Waste Your Life

The world keeps spinning
Whether you spend it well
Or just throw it away
There's no one to depend on, You're all on your own
Change your mind, And make mistakes
Do something you love, Or like someone you hate
Live on a farm, Or write your own book
Do something wild, And have fun in your life
Then grow up mature, And do a little more
Get married, And start a family
So spend your life well, and don't throw it away
You choose which road, So choose the right way
No one to blame, except for yourself, On how you decide to live your dash.

*Shaylie Reynold, Grade 8*
*Spring Grove Middle School*

### A "Hunger Games" Decima

In District 12, my heart does lie.
The people try to keep their lives
while dodging tracker jacker hives.
I hunt with Gale under the sky,
we await the day we will die.
But maybe we'll live another day,
hoping Effie Trinket won't say
your name when she pulls the white slip,
and you won't take that awful trip
to the Capitol, I dare say.

*Leslea Rodig, Grade 7*
*Tulpehocken Jr/Sr High School*

### Totally Different — Kind Of

So there's this kid
He's a totally different person
As he writes the same poem
He puts a different verse in
Maybe it's time to show 'em

That we aren't so different after all
We normally do things the same way
Even though we were born on the same day
In our own way we're still totally different

*Jake Myers, Grade 7*
*Big Spring Middle School*

### Rain

The rain is pouring.
Rain is pouring softly, quickly.
Pouring softly, quickly the rain goes.
The rain goes pitter patter.
Goes pitter patter, the raindrops splatter.
The raindrops splatter on the streets.
On the streets raindrops fly down.
Raindrops fly down on people's faces.
On people's faces the raindrop falls.
The raindrop falls onto the lake.

*Laura Daher, Grade 7*
*Salisbury Middle School*

### What a Dancer Knows

What a dancer knows.
When to flip,
How to move their hips,
Put their foot behind their head,
Then they go to bed,
They come back later to dance some more,
They can balance on their feet,
While the lights create heat.
A dancer may dance for hours at a time,
But soon their dance bell will chime.

*Carly Hill, Grade 7*
*Easton Area Middle School 7-8*

### Snow Crypt

Alone, lost
I'm now nothing.
This harsh, cold demon from the sky stole you.
It poisoned you and there wasn't a cure
Watching you sit in that sad confinement
Growing weaker and weaker
I would sing to you, to see your smile
I was foolish
The piano was like an organ playing at a funeral
It was your birthday and I wanted to take you outside.
We reached a small garden full of beautiful blue flowers
You started to get cold and wrapped your arms around my neck, whispering
"I love you."
Your body went limp and your eyes went lifeless
You couldn't have…you were gone.
I screamed as loud as I could
How could you leave me!? You couldn't just fade away!
That's when I noticed you weren't really gone
Your spirit lives on.
My sister, if we ever meet again
I would very much like to play with you

*Marissa Donapel, Grade 8*
*First Philadelphia Charter School for Literacy*

### Life

Life is a mystery, clues constantly found.
Life is a candy shop, many choices to be made.
Life is a game with no time-outs.
Life is a one man huddle.
Life is a lay-up from the three point line.
Life is a roller coaster, hills going up and down.
Life is a glass bottle, one mess-up could shatter you.
Life is a game of follow the leader, you can be a follower or you can be a leader.
Life is trying to walk for the first time, it is complicated.
Life is a bed, you can be lazy or do something with yourself.
Life is practice, it could make you perfect.
Life is an amusement park, many things to do.
Life is living, live your life while you have the chance.

Don't sit back and waste time.
Go do something with your life while you still have the time.

*Eric Anderson, Grade 8*
*First Philadelphia Preparatory Charter School for Literacy*

### The Fishermen

The day starts when the fisherman turns the key on his boat.
The engine sputters to a start.
The captain puts it into gear.
It starts to slowly cruise out of the bay.
Waves rolling off the bow and wake forming in the stern.
The fisherman gets his gear ready and is determined not to walk away empty-handed.
The fisherman pulling in the trophy of the day.
The day is ending while the boat is drifting into the slip.
The fishermen takes his fish and goes home happy and satisfied.

*David Ruta, Grade 8*
*Fred S Engle Middle School*

### To Help

I know you're upset as everyone can see,
I just try to help
But you won't let me,
I try to ask questions
But you just shout,
Can you ever tell me
What you're crying about,
Is this a secret that you can never tell
I'm only you're friend
You don't have to yell,
I just tried to help

*Paige Dornhoefer, Grade 8*
*Wattsburg Area Middle School*

### Love

love can        not be
heard, seen     and has
no scent. love is like a
swirling rose, pulling
you in deeper, and
deeper into the
center, once
you realize
you see
your
love

*Andrea Montijo, Grade 8*
*Saegertown Jr/Sr High School*

### On Fire

My heart is in flames,
Burning me, and causing me pain,
It sets my life to misery,
I fall, into a dark pit,
Full of venom and hate,
I thrash around,
As it lights fire,
Remembering all the hate and pain,
Where I lose my memory,
Of love and comfort,
I've erupted into flames.

*Jennifer Chai, Grade 7*
*Upper Merion Middle School*

### Summer

Summer floats
into my yard with flowers
dancing into the new environment.
Her creators zoom from one flower
to another flower.
Summer is darting rays as
bright as the colors of the rainbow.
But, Summer gets dragged away when
Fall crawls in, and tries to get the spotlight.

*Emily Hammer, Grade 7*
*Garnet Valley Middle School*

### Oh Those Wildwood Days

Down in New Jersey is a place well known,
Snooki calls it a home and the Situation roams.
Visit for a day, a week, a month or two,
The people here don't mind, you'll get the clue.
Morey's Pier is a blast and the famous wooden roller coaster is fast.
Sun-tanning by day and board-walking by night.
The cool ocean breeze is perfect for an afternoon of kites.
Lying with your head in the sand and your toes in the water.
Little boys laughing and playing catch with their fathers.
The arcade is like a day at the fair,
Winning stuffed animals and throwing money without care.
Shorts and flip-flops all around, surfing shops scatter the town.
Bobby Rydell gets inspired,
And colorful fireworks are fired.
Every day's a holiday and every night is a Saturday night.
Get some friends and rent a surrey, or look out your window at the Ferris wheel lights.
"Watch the tramcar please" gets stuck in your head, hear the seagulls while laying in bed.
Gateway 26 is a lifetime of fun rolled into one,
Eating on top of Stewart's, sipping root beer that's as cold as the bitter winter.
This is only a fraction of the experience,
And all I can say is, "Whoa those Wildwood days, wild wild Wildwood days!"

*Kylie Stephens, Grade 7*
*Pennbrook Middle School*

### The Mighty Dragons

Are they real or not?
Was that bird you saw way up high really a bird,
or was it a dragon keeping watch from above?
Was that rainbow really a rainbow,
or the newborn sun reflecting off its scales?
We do not know any of these answers but what if they were real?
Would we have the guts to climb upon one's back,
or would we hide in fright from their very appearance?
For they could easily crush bone with one mighty swipe of a forepaw.
Would a band of humans claim one for themselves?
Would they use that for good or evil?
Would their sapphire blue be the last thing you saw before you left this world?
Or would it be the best thing you have seen saving you from certain death?
Or would there be both sides?
Would they collide and create a new kind of war?

*Celine Vogelsong, Grade 8*
*Spring Grove Middle School*

### Home

Another day in this horrid place
I don't know how much more I can take
Praying every day and night that I might see my loved ones once again
Wishing these tears could build a bridge leading home
This tour is torturing
Knowing every day could be the last
Taking this risk for freedom
But knowing it's worth something
So here I am hanging my boots for the final time
The torture is over, I'm going home

*Jared Shank, Grade 7*
*Cambria Heights Middle School*

**Nothing More, Nothing Less**
I fell to my knees unfed.
All I saw was the color red,
This head high above my arms and shoulders was driving me to the edge.
I couldn't bear this energy; I needed to jump this ledge.
I feared I was a slippery slope; I threw in the towel and lost all hope.
Death then welcomed me to his two-way kingdom.
Death sat there and waited patiently with his phantom.
Death appeared in a ghostly shadow and shook my hand;
His hand was rough and coarse like sand. He had a head but no face.
He then read my life story and called me a disgrace.
He said to me with a dull sullen tone, "You must come with me."
"But Death, you must answer this one question before we flee."
I tried my best to not look him in the eye as if he was Medusa.
He then glared and scowled at me as if I was the biggest loser.
"Fine, make it quick," he grumbled.
"Do you ever feel sympathy?" I questioned as the lightening flashed and thunder rumbled.
Lonesome death then spoke and said, "No, I feel nothing. I am death, nothing more, nothing less."
I snapped out of the dream, and now I must confess
That the gnawing jaws of death almost had me,
But I locked all my doors and luckily death forgot the key.

*John Mackey, Grade 8*
*Saucon Valley Middle School*

**Peace**
The grass was green, and the trees swayed in the distance, it felt like nothing could be seen, but by me and me alone. Next to the wood were the colorful flowers, and animals that did roam. I knew they felt safe here, and I knew this was their home.

The sky was clear, blue and bright. It could always be like this I thought, if they'd leave it alone. I'll treasure these moments though. For now though the place is peaceful and perfect, it's nothing but sunlight. It was warm, it was right, and nature agreed too. And I'll know forever, that this is true.

It sounded close to silence but, even if faint I could hear birds singing, and the sound of hooves crunching leaves, as mothers lurked nearby while their young ran and played. The tree leaves ruffled as the wind blew by. So if I said it was silence, it would be a lie.

This place, it makes me feel safe and right and if it was my choice, I would be here day and night. It's peaceful, it's calm, it's safe, it's warm.

Although sometimes I question, will this place stay warm? Will it ever not be safe? Will one day it not be calm? What if someday it's destroyed, changed and won't be the same? Will it always be…peaceful? Right now I hope it will stay this way, always safe and always…peaceful.
Peaceful,
Peaceful.

*Laura Gombocz, Grade 7*
*Saucon Valley Middle School*

**I Come From**
I come from a family that will never give up and will keep going when things in life get hard.
I come from a mother who was strong, loving, and caring, but most importantly trusted in God no matter what!
I come from a father who has loved and cared for me and who has taught me to be a good leader.
I come from a school that has given me knowledge, strength, and courage in myself and in God.
I come from a church who teaches me to love Christ, and I know that they are there for me no matter what.
I come from a great and powerful God who has given me the family and friends I have.
He also has given me this life, which I absolutely LOVE, and the strength to push on.

*Cayla Murphy, Grade 7*
*Conestoga Christian School*

### Spring

Cherry blossoms,
Busy, working bees,
Jesus Christ saves mankind,
Life begins to grow anew,
Loving families come to celebrate tradition.
*Jordann Versaw, Grade 8*
*Holy Sepulcher School*

### Orchards

Attractive flowers,
Flood through fields,
All colors except black,
Inhabit deserts and tropical islands,
Grow petals that blend with nature.
*Rachael Versaw, Grade 8*
*Holy Sepulcher School*

### Trees

Blooming, swaying,
Buds newly formed,
Green is coming back,
Fruit is starting to grow,
The trees are growing green leaves.
*Rachel Cherry, Grade 8*
*Holy Sepulcher School*

### Flower

it is beautiful
the way the sun shines on it
pretty as can be
*Anna Mineo, Grade 7*
*Easton Area Middle School 7-8*

### Man's Best Friend

A big furry friend
Runs down the road after you
With a black wet nose
*Jed Bartos, Grade 7*
*St Luke School*

### Wandering World

Trees dance in the wind
Waterfalls splashing on rocks
Flowers blooming in the spring
*Jeanette Smith, Grade 7*
*Pequea Valley Intermediate School*

### Fall's Beautiful Trees

the colorful leaves falling
slowly to the soft green ground
in the fall night sky
*Darrian Peace, Grade 7*
*Pequea Valley Intermediate School*

### Going to See The Phantom of the Opera

I stand in the midst of an enormous crowd.
All I see are the backs of total strangers, all dressed for the upcoming show.
Everyone around me has smiles that don't fade, as if their mouths are glued there.

I look up at the pitch black sky with no stars to keep it company.
It's almost as if the bright lights and signs around me
want all the attention to themselves as they light up the night

I'm surrounded by the buzz of conversation,
the horns of cars screaming into the night,
the street corner musicians playing softly.
Soon though, loud musical voices will fill the air.

Are all of the people around me as anxious as I?
Can they barely contain the excitement of seeing a Broadway show?
Will the show be the best of my life, or leave me sadly disappointed?
These are the questions that race around my head as I find my seat in the theater.

As the lights grow dim and *The Phantom* is about to start, my anxiety is overwhelming.
After the months of anticipation, it's hard to believe that this moment is finally here.
I feel so elated and joyful as the actors begin to perform.

I can't believe this day is finally here.
I can't believe it,
I cant believe it,
I can't believe it.
*Kayleigh Boyle, Grade 7*
*Saucon Valley Middle School*

### In the Night

As I'm running, I see deceased tortured bodies that surround me.
Black fuzz balls scurry in between my feet. In the night…

Spotlights chase my shadows as I break free from the pain.
As of now my only friend left is the moonlit night. In the night…

The yells of guards follow the footsteps that have been imprinted into the ground.
I can still hear the screams of the terminal prisoners that have been left behind.
Although I still keep running. In the night…

Why must this happen?
Why do they choose to beat, imprison, and kill the people like me?
When will the maze game end and the light that denies the darkness begin?
In the night…

I am scared. I am tired, but nothing will stop me from escaping this hell trap.
I feel happiness and excitement as I finally see the last unguarded pathway to light.
As the sharp rocks poke holes in my feet, which would usually cause agonizing pain,
The adrenaline rushes through my veins distorting the pain so I never stop.
In the night…

I must escape!
I will escape!!
I have escaped!!!
*Brendan Gertz, Grade 7*
*Saucon Valley Middle School*

### The Battlefield

Alone I stand with no one by my side;
A single warrior with just my shield.
Without a friend, I can but only hide.
It is just me on this great battlefield.
I look ahead to see what I must face.
My demons are looking me in the eye.
I need a comrade to help me erase
These troubles that alone I can't defy.
I fight, I try, but I just cannot win
When I am like a wolf without its pack.
I need some help, a friend, a pal, my kin,
To help me face my fears and to attack.
No one joins me, I guess I'm on my own.
I'll just have to take on this world alone.

*Emily Bohannon, Grade 9*
*East High School*

### I Wanna See

I wanna see the day I graduate
I wanna see me go off to college
I wanna see me get a job
I wanna see me meet a nice guy
I wanna see me get married
I wanna see me have a child
And I wanna see that child grow up
I wanna see my child be successful
I wanna see me help people or
maybe change someone's life
I wanna see a lot of things
But most of all I wanna see
me live a happy life.

*Victoria Yost, Grade 8*
*Spring Grove Middle School*

### Sadness

Sadness is blue
It smells like dying flowers
It tastes like salty tears
It sounds like a crying baby
It feels like you're getting rained on
It looks like an ocean
Sadness is an empty heart

*Noah Frantz, Grade 8*
*Saegertown Jr/Sr High School*

### The Summer

Summer
Hot, wonderful
Tanning, swimming, sleeping
Pools, drinks, flip-flops, vacations
Running, walking, sweating
Fun, beautiful
Summer

*Corey Robinson, Grade 7*
*Garnet Valley Middle School*

### Lost Smile*

We were once united.
Over generations,
we had shared friendship
and smiled upon one another with kindness.

Now,
we are not one community,
There are Christians, called 'righteous', and deemed worthy of life in this country,
and there are Jews, called 'filthy', and blamed for difficulties we all suffer through.

We, the Jews, are forced to crowd into unsanitary ghettos
until the day comes
when soldiers break down our doors,
wrestle us from our homes,
and as we are herded into cattle cars,
they still smile upon us.
But I am certain
that the gesture has no kindness.

*Frankie Kavalir, Grade 8*
*Jefferson Middle School*
*\*Dedicated to all who suffered during the Holocaust*

### The Night

The Night
My mom picked me up from soccer, crying.
Clear droplets streaming down her puffy cheeks.
Her sad face, red as a tomato.
Her wavy brown hair all scrunched and wet.
The Night
The doctors found a purple, plump lump.
You lost all your perfect, brown hair all around it.
You couldn't even bark, nor make a simple, small step.
The Night
They found you had cancer, spreading throughout your young, furry body.
My dad screaming "NO!" in my tiny, ringing ear.
Him rejecting the painful medicine, to make you never wake up.
The Night
My dad made a horrifying decision.
We held on tight, gripping your weak, skinny paw.
Your eyes shutting forever, leaving my family and I behind.
Memories of you little kept in my head forever, late at dark.
The Night

*Brynna Haupt, Grade 7*
*Schuylkill Valley Middle School*

### Dawn Foxes

The foxes have disappeared.
And those who saw the foxes have disappeared.
Those who saw the foxes by the hundreds,
And how they clawed the silent tundra into blizzards with their paws,
Their threatening eyes open, clawing at dawn.
Those who saw the foxes have disappeared.
And the foxes have disappeared.

*Vikram Sundar, Grade 7*
*Garnet Valley Middle School*

## My Life Has Been Wasted Without You

I am sorry for not being in your life all these years,
for causing many of your precious tears.
I act as if you do not exist,
And if you did,
I act as if you wouldn't be missed.
I act like I do not care,
And to you it is not fair.
I have lost many chances at a bond with you,
And as your life advances, you become less fond of me,
that is completely true.
I hope you forgive me for not being a good person to you,
And if I could, I would like to relive the moments
That I wasted without you.

*Mikayla DeLuca, Grade 9*
*Coventry Christian Schools*

## You're Gone

You left me a month ago on the 9th of January
Alone without words to speak. Confused and lost
You were my friend, my best buddy and my grandmother
You meant the world to me, Sometimes I got mad
But I loved you and now you're gone
You left me without a good-bye or a see ya later
I miss you and I need you
These emotions hit me harder day to day
Without you I'm lost and alone with no one to talk to
You were my everything and still are my everything
You're gone but never forgotten
I will forever love you
Good-bye and see you later

*Aaliyah Lee, Grade 8*
*First Philadelphia Charter School for Literacy*

## A Mother's Love

A mother's love is always sweet.
A mother's love is also warm,
like the feeling of summer.
It's nothing better than your
mother's love oh how tender.
It's such a nice feeling in
knowing you have your mother's cozy love.

*Alexis Murray, Grade 8*
*Hardy Williams Academy Charter School*

## The Sense of Blue

Swimming in the deep blue sea, peaceful and cold
The water surrounds, under the baby-blue sky
Pushing on, to reach home
I see bluebells blooming under the sun falling
The blueberry sky, will rise once again

*Chelsea Riggins, Grade 7*
*Pequea Valley Intermediate School*

## Mishaps

Misconception, the effect of mishearing,
Leads to miscommunicating and misinforming
Thus causing misunderstanding
Which consequently results in mistruth
Becoming misjudgments
That are misguidedly mishandled
Turning to mischaracterization.

The outcome is mistakenly mislabeling
And thereby misfiring
Tactless statements; which is mistreatment
Of one who is misperceived;
Mistaken.

The result is misshapen views of oneself; misbelieving
In the vile allegations one hears, misplaced
Happiness; and misery.

Before long, that someone is missing,
Lost; misallying and mistrusting
Death; who misguides so that times of ecstasy are misremembered;
Ending in misadventure and misacting
When Death's repugnant lips are met under the mistletoe.

*Caitlin Friel, Grade 9*
*Holicong Middle School*

## The Ocean and Me

I approach the water
Sand creeping into every little crevice of my feet
The wind mussing my hair
Blowing the copper locks
Into my eyes
Sticking to the makeup on my face

I finally get to the water
The water whispers to me
As it crashes forward
Pulls back into the body that it tried to escape
Like a child pulling away from its mother
And the mother pulling it back

Then everything inside of me clicks
As I dip my toes into the freezing water
I feel complete
As I reunite with the part of me
That I must leave every year

Soul to body
Peanut butter to jelly
The ocean and me

*Lizzie McIlhenney, Grade 9*
*Penn Manor High School*

## Our World
Bombs burst on the battlefield
As women and children cry
Our world burning

Earthquakes rattle
Buildings and souls alike
Our world shaking

Tsunamis kill thousands per second
Engulfing everything once loved
Our world drowning

Then, a faint glimmer of hope
A white dove flies against a blackened sky
Our world enchanted

Battle lines are erased
Sworn enemies act as brother and sister
Our world forgetting

Strangers help each other
Flowers bloom, the world says thanks
Our world healing

Hate and difference evaporate
As love and forgiveness envelop the earth
Our world in peace.
*Elise Barberra, Grade 7*
*Indian Valley Middle School*

## Past and Future
Not that long ago
Maybe thirty years or so

There were people all around the streets
Running around moving their feet

Portions were slighter
And people were lighter

Now today is a different story
Now our lives are not so hunky-dory

We have our electronics and TV
Not really taking care of you and me

Eating much more
Portions soar

Attempts are being made
To help this kind of life fade

If we want to be more fit
We need to get out there and MOVE it
*Isabel Cardi, Grade 7*
*Strath Haven Middle School*

## Dreaming of the Beach
The warm, relaxing, cozy, soft sand
The blue waves rumbling
The fresh-smelling breeze
Smelling like the beach

Wishing I was there
Feeling like I'm in heaven
It's the best place to be…
The beach

I keep on dreaming and dreaming
it is like I'm there
Seeing the blue waves
And the warm, relaxing, cozy, soft sand

I just want to be there
*Taylor Karan, Grade 8*
*Penn Middle School*

## The Work of an Artist
The etching of a pencil
Scraping fiercely against the paper.
Avoiding the unnecessary stencil,
This is the work of an artist.

As the piece is nearly finished,
The hard work coming to a close,
The pencil is diminished,
As the artist's hand froze.

Admiring the piece he worked to complete,
Staring at the finished masterpiece,
The artist did stand still.
And again, lifting the pencil,

To continue the work of an artist.
*Kiersten Marshall, Grade 8*
*Danville Area Middle School*

## Flyin' By
As I blade down the streets,
I stare in pure shock,
At my newly done feat,
While still beating the clock.

I had flown down the streets
Sending leaves to the air,
As I went faster and faster,
Like I just didn't care.

The crowds still were cheering
They had seen me whiz past,
But not that much else,
I had just been too fast.
*Joselyn Schlosser, Grade 7*
*Pennbrook Middle School*

## Joining Forces
Heard from miles away,
Thumping as hearts pound,
Begging for love day after day,
But to us it's a deafened sound.

The faces of the innocent,
Who know nothing but to cry.
The faces hidden behind dirt,
Can't clean because the rivers are dry.

Their lives could be fearless,
Full of hope, passion and love.
But our hearts must resemble,
The sign of peace; the dove.

Keep the dreaming in hope,
Until your colors come alive
The world can be a better place,
As long as we strive.

Together as a world,
Taking different courses.
Together as a world,
Everyone joining forces.
*Shannon Sweeney, Grade 7*
*Indian Valley Middle School*

## Poverty
Unclean water little food
Stomach's hungry
Desperate mood
Sickness and disease
Affecting my health
Lack of medicine
Lack of wealth

No home no roof
Not even a bed
To rest upon my weary head

Working hard to get a job
Bring home some money
To stop the sob

New hope, new life,
Something good
To stop my hunger
I have food
Not much for a day
But I can see
A new life ahead of me
Poverty no more
*Ben Yerk, Grade 7*
*Indian Valley Middle School*

### Dear Professor

Dear Professor Wade,
Please give me a good grade.
I stayed up all night
to make this just right.
If you think it is bad,
then I will be sad,
because all I have said
came straight from my head.
I hope you like this great work of art
because if you don't, it'll break my heart.

P.S. On second thought,
grade as you ought.

*Karch Helsel, Grade 9*
*Bishop McCort High School*

### Writer's Block

I have the writer's block.
I don't know what to write.
I think and think about what to type,
But my mind is just white.
Should it have a twist of fate?
Or suspense to give readers fright?
I can't really think clearly
With a writer's block in sight.

But my mind is really clever,
A little irony in the thought.
And so I write a poem
About writer's block.

*Michael Ord, Grade 7*
*Landisville Middle School*

### Shadows Are Like Rumors

Shadows are like rumors.
They stick like a bad tumor.
They follow you around,
During a stroll around town.

They shrink and grow.
They never let go.
At home they may go away,
But they are back another day.

Once they start they are hard to stop.
They will never fully disappear,
Because shadows are like rumors.

*Hope Kiehl, Grade 7*
*Landisville Middle School*

### Dreams

We all have those dreams
Where we wish to be the best
Only few achieve

*Brianna Wallace, Grade 8*
*E T Richardson Middle School*

### The Sunrise in the Morning

From summer to Christmas Day
The sun of hope hangs high in the sky
Proud and shining its light of love, a new day begins
The inheritance of the earth, the new generation
The passing on of the duties of mankind
The changing of the guard at the dawn
High tide on the coasts of the world
Phases of the moon begin anew
The sea foams and bubbles with anticipation
Of the new day of humanity, a day of peace
This was an age of unrest
An age of dissension, desolation, and hurt
But the bonds and shackles of malevolence
Break at the hands of renewal worldwide
The final shadows of night give way to the starlight
The sunrise in the morning ushers a new life
A fresh breath of clean air, a new day for all
We shall maintain a vigil o'er the fires of tranquility 'til the dying embers fade
Though it may not last long or even come to pass
The sun will one day rise, this chapter of discord will finally end
The sun will rise in the morning, whenever the morning may be

*Jonathan Engel, Grade 8*
*Independence Middle School*

### Inner Battle

From my brow drops another bead of sweat
Another one takes a shot that I'll never forget
Shadows shroud the battlefield
Only I am left without a shield
The bullets zip by, one hitting my ear
In that moment, I can't help but shed a tear
I fall to the ground and pray
It's faint, but I hear someone on my side say that it'll be okay
I can barely speak, but I manage to reply, "Just not today"
I just wish I could leave this awful place, but for now I'm forced to stay
I wince as I feel another strike
They'll never understand what it feels like
Soon they are all ascending
Even I can tell it'll soon be ending
Another one takes aim
I have no one but myself to blame

*Zachary Rhine, Grade 8*
*Ephrata Middle School*

### The Fire

She is surrounded by towering walls of flames.
She feels the heat beating on her face, torturing her skin.
The smoke shrouds her vision, fills her lungs.
Her lips become cracked, her throat dry.
The only moisture that the flames do not devour are her silent, glistening tears.
She cries out for help, but she is alone in the battle.
She tries to run, but she has nowhere to go.
She slowly becomes one with the fire, a pile of ashes, silent and forgotten.

*Monica Shope, Grade 8*
*Pine-Richland Middle School*

## The World

What is this place that we call a world,
it's evil, corrupt, mad,
the truth is lies,
I see it in their eyes,
you can trust no one,
so many criminals,
their finger prints everywhere,
it's not a safe place,
you always get hurt,
from far away, it's beautiful,
but up close you see,
now ask yourself,
is this the way He wanted it to be?

*Owen Stover, Grade 8*
*Northern Lebanon Middle School*

## fear of flames

remember the people
see the smoke
hear the screams
hear the sirens
see the flames
see people running
remember the flames
breathing very hard
breathing but only smoke filling my lungs
burning building
try to forget
remember what happened
will try to forget

*Erika Allen, Grade 8*
*Wattsburg Area Middle School*

## Love

Love keeps my heart together,
It will last forever.
I want to be with you,
My words are true.
I will come to you,
If you come to me too.
If you need me,
Right there I will be.
If you say you love me,
Then our love is true.
Then I shall kiss you,
To be loved by chu.

*Israel Wells, Grade 7*
*Northgate Middle/High School*

## Spring

Leaves sprouting,
Flowers so colorful,
Animals no longer sleeping,
Spring is the best season ever.

*Mikaela Connolly, Grade 8*
*Holy Sepulcher School*

## Louder She Screams

Louder and louder she screams
As she is calling out to us

Trying and trying to warn us
Through cries of pain and struggle

She can't protect us anymore from the hot blazing rays of sun burning through us
And the crashing violent waves that descend upon us

"Do you hear me?" she yells
"Am I here?" she cries

"What about me?"
"What about all I give?"

"Stop what you are doing to me now!"
"Stop!"

"I'm your home, your life, and your Earth."
"Take care of me."

*Elizabeth Latella, Grade 7*
*Grey Nun Academy*

## When I Am Young Then Old

When I am young I will eat unhealthy and with my fingers
When I am old I will eat healthy and with silverware

When I am young I will be bored all of the time
When I am old I will be able to do what I want

When I am young I will make dumb decisions
When I am old I will make better decisions

Whey I am young I will go out and have fun
When I am old I will stay home to be with my family

When I am young I will have my whole life ahead of me to make my goals
When I am old I will have less time to make my goals

When I am young I will meet new people
When I am old I will stay with my friends and family that I know

*Faith Welling, Grade 8*
*Trinity Middle School*

## Dance

Feeling free like a bird,
Jumping high like a kangaroo,
Dancing is one of my passions.
Toes pointing, legs leaping,
I soar through the air.
Spinning, a fast, exhilarating rush of energy boomed through my body.
Dashing across stage, I feel like I can do anything.
Dance, my passion.

*Katherine Eckhoff, Grade 7*
*Garnet Valley Middle School*

### Hope

The wind is screaming with sadness.
There are no storm clouds and yet it still rained
The chairs filled with mourning family members
One by one, happy memories are remembered then forgotten
It seemed as if Noah needed to build a second ark —
When things seemed at their worst
And there was no hope of forgetting what had happened
I was feeling all alone with no one there for me
Mother found a cute little puppy all alone
With a collar that read "Hope" —
Time was running away faster then I could imagine
Life was stuck in fast-forward
Every moment became easier because I had hope
But soon enough the puppy became a dog
Like I became a woman —
When mother and I were looking through old pictures
We came across one that seemed to be impossible
I held mother close in my arms
In the picture was the same cute little puppy
With a collar that read "Hope"

*Zach Brink, Grade 8*
*Valley Forge Middle School*

### Ease Her

We disregard nature in the worst manner.
We destroy, mine, and slaughter her!
She will take her cruel vengeance on us one day.
And we will be sorry for our horrible mistakes.

We need her to let us live,
But we in no way repay her for her refuge
A straggling few care for her and much less aid her.
Countless care but fall short of taking action;
Those who do are cast out and punished

But I worry about her as should you
Mother Nature is our source of life and well being
Why should we take her for granted?
She has done nothing to hurt us.

We know what will come if we do not act to save her
So why wait?
Act now to be free of the sure horror to come,
Mother Nature needs us now more than ever…

*Jonathan Downs, Grade 7*
*Pennbrook Middle School*

### Someday

Someday I won't have to be in sorrow.
Someday we won't be mad.
Someday you will miss me like I missed you.
Someday we will find love.
Someday you will love me.
Someday I might not love you.

*Weston Fetterolf, Grade 7*
*Pequea Valley Intermediate School*

### If I Were an Animal

If I were an animal
A monkey is what I would be
I would swing through the jungle
And socialize in the banana tree
Or maybe I would be a lion,
My roar would be so great
That it nearly summons
Every creature
In the tri-state
Although,
A hippopotamus seems cool
If I was one
I would hang out
By the water hole
And lounge around
With all the animals
I'm still not sure which animal I would want to be
They all seem interesting
But I think the best thing to be
Would have to be me

*Sarah McNutt, Grade 9*
*State College High School South*

### The Last Ride

Passed another year, still nothing to fear.
All the gifts open but one,
None could match the one that would come,
None being nearly as fun.
A Mercury Marine engine,
A Boston Whaler hull.
Would make any one's day fantastic,
Never made a single one dull.
After a week he got his license,
While the lakes kept calling him.
He planned to go for a ride,
It's too bad it ended dim.
As a wave came upon the ship,
Too big to keep afloat.
Still the waves just kept bombarding,
Devouring the boat.
As dawn rose to a brisk morning,
One life hung by a thread.
It's too bad he was so young,
For he was the one found dead.

*Allan Edgarton, Grade 8*
*Valley Forge Middle School*

### What I'd Cook for My Teacher

If I could cook for my teacher,
I would start with worm salad
Bee stinger casserole will be the next thing I add
Served for drinks will be salt water soda
Our wonderful dessert will be sea snail cupcakes
I hope she doesn't put me in the oven to bake.

*Megan Meissner, Grade 7*
*Fort Couch Middle School*

### School

Kids are passing out
But at the end we are free
Right now learning sucks
*Kaung Ko, Grade 7*
*Easton Area Middle School 7-8*

### Spring

Warm air greets us now
Pink pedals fly all around
Listen, there's no sound
*Alexandria Austin, Grade 7*
*Easton Area Middle School 7-8*

### Sun

The sun, it shines bright
As it lights up the day break
It sets into night
*Samantha Chaffier, Grade 7*
*Easton Area Middle School 7-8*

### Newt

Little tail wiggles
As water ripples across
A tiny blue pond.
*Adam Williams, Grade 7*
*St Luke School*

### The Beautiful Bright Stars

Stars shine so brightly
Up above the winter skies
Glowing in my eyes.
*Krista Kitts, Grade 8*
*St Luke School*

### Eruption

The big volcano
Erupts with the color red
And lands on the ground.
*Jason Constable, Grade 8*
*St Luke School*

### Moon

Bright and beautiful
Rises in the dark and cold
Shining in the night
*Giancarlo Bedoya, Grade 7*
*Easton Area Middle School 7-8*

### Wolves

Hair as black as night
Give some people a great fright
Silent as midnight.
*Nicholas Machinski, Grade 7*
*St Luke School*

### A Journey Back in Time

I traveled back in time on the twenty-third of August, 2011
To a picturesque place my mom refers to as "heaven."
The car trip was a total of fourteen hours long;
Breathtaking scenery as we went along.
Rigid-edged mountains and tree-lined highways,
The sun set over the rolling hills, ending the day.
Finally, we arrived at Lake Michigan, our destination,
To stay several nights on Mackinac Island…a dream vacation.
There is an absence of cars: no auto noise, and exhaust-free air.
Most visitors travel by foot to get from here to there.
Our "taxi," a horse-drawn carriage, passed a lush landscaped park
To the Grand Hotel, one of the island's main landmarks.
A real brass key opened our hotel door.
We could not wait until the next day to experience more.
By the time we got used to the island and getting around,
Sadly, our time was up, we needed to be homebound.
After writing this poem, I am drawn back to visit again,
To see this quaint, historic, pre-automobile place. I just do not know when.
*Luke Crawford, Grade 7*
*St Luke the Evangelist School*

### Summer

For almost four months you provide me with warmth,
a mother covering her child with a blanket,
allowing me to go swimming in the cool blue water
when it is too hot to stay in the sun.

Strolling the shore as my flip flops flick sand on the back of my legs
while your hot sun bakes the Earth.
The summery weather brightens my day,
boasting beautiful, white flowers.

You gracefully give me the pleasure of no school,
until September comes around again banging on the door and you're gone.
But your warmth is still there,
like a present on Christmas morning, silently waiting to be revealed.
*Cassandra Pennie, Grade 7*
*Pennwood Middle School*

### The World I Live In

All I know is that this is not reality,
As I lay here taking a deep breath of the daisies all around me.
How I got here, I do not know,
But the way I feel here I do not want to go.

Suddenly, I hear bombs exploding and children crying.
When I look around the field of daisies is gone, and I see people dying.
I close my eyes so I don't see,
But the images follow me into my dreams.

I run away from the pain,
But I trip over misfortune.
This dream is so insane,
But then I realize this is just the world I live in.
*Victoria Batten, Grade 9*
*Renaissance Academy*

### Sunday Race Mornings

You wake up in the motor home
Walkout to the smell of diesel
From the bulldozer and water truck
There's dew on the dirt and the mist on the grass
The bacon and egg sandwiches cooking
As riders work on their bikes.
You hear bikes roar and when practice
Starts you see bikes soar.
People crash and get slashed
And in the end you might
See some trash.

*Cody Sanders, Grade 8*
*Northern Lebanon Middle School*

### Season's Senses

Senses fill the air in every season,
listen to the light rustle of autumn leaves,
taste the softness of light winter snow,
smell the beauty of bright spring flowers, and
feel the warmth of summer's bright glow.

With each season there is a sense.
a sense of warmth,
a sense of cold,
a sense of new, and
a sense of old.

*Tara Shaffer, Grade 9*
*Bishop McCort High School*

### Pictures

Pictures express one's feelings and thoughts;
They show a story of the good and distraught.

They depict the happiness in a young one's soul;
Some show the scene of a couple on a stroll.

They may show the lost and hungry in the world;
Or maybe just a small puppy, tightly curled.

Pictures are words frozen in time;
Even if they aren't so sublime.

*Frankie Illuzzi, Grade 9*
*Bishop McCort High School*

### Tumbled

There once was a girl from Hope
She always loved to jump rope
She hopped with a swish
She flopped like a fish
And tumbled her way down the slope

*Mackenzie Brubaker, Grade 7*
*Lancaster Mennonite School - Locust Grove*

### My True Love

If I could even tell you how I feel,
You would drown in the words that don't exist.
You are the one, who helped my heart to heal,
You are my love, I will never resist.
Always on my mind, all day and all night,
In my heart you'll never be forgotten.
You are the sun in my eyes at daylight,
I have you, I must be spoiled rotten!
Can't go a day without being with you,
Thinking about always and forever,
We must belong together, just us two.
I can't think of us apart, no! Never!
The thought of leaving you breaks my soft heart,
Our love is a masterpiece of art.

*Kayla Price, Grade 8*
*Pocono Mountain East Jr High School*

### Do You Hear What I Hear?

To be or not to be, that is the question,
To hear, oh what I hear, here is my suggestion.
The crash of the waves along the shore,
Sometimes so fierce like a lion's roar.
The clash of two hockey sticks attacking one ball.
Or, the rain pelting and wind that howls it call.
These are the sounds that give me comfort like a mother's embrace.
I have more sounds that make me smile,
My cell phone ringing because I have been waiting a while.
The rhythmic music and how I feel its beat.
My kitty purring as she finds her comfortable seat.
The giggles and laughter shared only between friends,
Secrets kept and promises to the end.
These are the sounds that make me who I am.

*Patricia Hart, Grade 8*
*Centerville Middle School*

### Little Man

It means sad, handsome, and love
It is the number 66
It is like a sad life of a great kid
Who tries to make people happy
Even though he is never welcomed

People should not go through what I have
It is the memory of last year
It is the memory of my dad
It is the memory of my family

My name is Liam
It means to do good, be a good influence to others,
And remember the great people in my life.

*Liam Tuohey, Grade 7*
*Prospect Park School*

### Attack of the Wolf King

Three wolves, one sheep
Two black, one gray
Sheep scared, crying loud
Wolf growls, moving close
Bites leg
Sheep bleeding, limping bad
Sheep tries to run
King kills wolf
One black, one gray
Sheep crawls silently
Two wolves fight
One bites, one claws
Sheep gets away
King wins
One gray, all alone
One king

*Joseph Goudy, Grade 7*
*Garnet Valley Middle School*

### Lifetime

In this lifetime
Many things go wrong
People commit crimes
But that's not me
I want my time
To be spent wisely
Friends on each side
A space for a jeep
To meet a guy
That I
Could spend a lifetime with
I want to be worth
At least a dime
In this lifetime many things go wrong
But in the end
We all die.

*Nikki Small, Grade 8*
*Spring Grove Middle School*

### Achoo

Sneezing and stuffed,
Eyes sting and annoy.
You scratch till you puffed,
But the enemy has a better ploy.

Medicine can help,
But the villain's still not at bay.
There has to be something,
To make these allergies go away.

I go through the tissues,
One by one.
When the pollen subsides,
My life is more fun.

*Kevin Dineen, Grade 7*
*Our Lady of Mount Carmel School*

### Recycling

Cans, jars, glass bottles
Getting thrown in the street,
Not being very good role models
Change the environment
Start to RECYCLE
The earth will be clean…
If you do
If you don't we will be surrounded by goo
It has been improving
But not enough to stop the pollution killing
Making you unhealthy and dirty
And feeling like you're drowning
With can, jars, and glass bottles surround
Start to RECYCLE
Plants are dying and animals too
We are next if we don't start
I need it and so do you
If we don't start sooner or later
It may be too late to start anew
RECYCLE NOW!

*Michael Bealer, Grade 7*
*Indian Valley Middle School*

### The Woodland

Towering trees stand up like giants
From the forest floor below,
Flute-like voices of the wood thrush
And the cawing of a crow.
Showy trilliums, lady's slippers,
Growing by a moss-gown'd log,
Gurgling water in a streamlet,
Murmurs through the morning fog.
Stepping lightly to the water
Is a buck with well-trained ear,
Watching for the slightest movement
Or a sign that triggers fear.
Flying swiftly through the forest
Is a hawk on rounded wings,
Chasing prey with heart aflutter
And so shrill the hawk's scream rings.
Oh, I love my wild woodland
Where the pine and hemlock grow,
To the city, hot and crowded,
I would never want to go!

*Randall Peachey, Grade 8*
*Rockhaven Christian School*

### Softball

Field, Sand
Batting, Throwing,
Fielding
Intense, Exhilarating, Exciting
Heart Racing
Love It

*Alexis Jenkins, Grade 7*
*Easton Area Middle School 7-8*

### Constellations

Up in the sky, all so high,
Are the stars
I've seen every night.

Without fright,
I pull my eyes open.
They're filled to the brim,
My lashes twinkle to the rim,
Reflecting the star's
Bright light.

Very vast is the space
That holds our world together.
United as one, we are all connected.
In one way or another,
We are born from our mothers,
And raised as people,
As love, as life.

Our connection may be severed,
As butter to a knife,
And that day will come.
We'll know it by watching
The stars.

*Sophia Trettel, Grade 8*
*Spring Grove Middle School*

### Reasons

The reason I love reading
Is because it's a whole new world
A whole new life for me
A whole new someone to love me

The reason I love writing
Is because I create the whole new world
The whole new life
The whole new someone to love

The reason I love daydreaming
Is because I can make anything happen
Any adventure begin
Any dream come true

The reason I love telling you this
Is seeing you listen
Seeing you smile
Seeing your eyes light up

The reason I love who I am
Is because this is my world
This is my life
This is me

*Laura Condon, Grade 8*
*Sacred Heart Elementary School*

### My First Love

When I first met you, I thought you were cute
When we first talked, I suddenly went mute
When we're together, we're both very shy
We knew we liked one another, our hearts couldn't lie
You're cute, you're gentle, you're sweet
You make my heart skip a beat
The bond between us was unbreakable
It was beautiful, it was incredible
It didn't start this way
It happened just one day
You smiled at me
And I saw you differently
Unexpected, what you did to my heart
But I knew that this was the best part
Your smile, your laugh, they brighten my day
They make me smile in every way
And if only they could feel it too
The happiness I feel with you
They'd know our love is true
Out of the other guys, there was no need to shove
I knew from the start that you where my first love

*Ashley Manjarrez, Grade 9*
*Golden Valley High School*

### Beach

Walking on a warm blanket of golden sand,
I pick a little up and let it sift through my hand.
A blue boarder stretches out as far as my eye can see
Outlining the pink horizon sky
It feels as if it is just the ocean and me.
The aroma of coconuts fills the air
The wind blows the scent through my hair
The protracted pace of the crashing waves peacefully relaxes me
The calming sensation tells me to come
I start taking brisk steps. One. Two. Three
As I come closer, I feel something covering my toes
I wiggle them and keep my eyes closed
The cool sensation takes away the heat
When it leaves I am like a child waiting for Santa Claus
I just stand and anticipate the next time we meet.

*Maria McFarland, Grade 8*
*Bellwood-Antis Middle School*

### Take a Moment to Realize

How many people would like to go swimming later?
Count
Under the ocean sea
Deep, blue, quietly swimming free
I see a dolphin! It is so beautiful, calm, flowing.
So deep down
I could stay there
Forever, in the sea with the beauty
Crystal clear
Takes away all stress, worries, fear, brings peace.

*Lindsey Price, Grade 8*
*Saegertown Jr/Sr High School*

### Starfish

Sleeping and sticking to a rock
Free to play and swim with my flock
Warm soothing boring days
I have once again landed near the dock

So many ways for me to enjoy my days
Every day the tide brings me new ways
I wonder where I next may land
The waves will bring a brand-new way

I get washed upon the warm sand
I get poked by strange hands
The brightly colored fish wish they could follow me
The clear teal sea reaches out her hand to bring me in from land

Among my travels I have seen the wonders of the sea
I am the luckiest one, I am so free
I get to lay around all day and catch some Zs
We are the best animals of the sea, how can you disagree

*Monique Jervier, Grade 8*
*Penn-Kidder Campus*

### Have You Ever Seen the Sky So Blue

Have you ever seen the sky so blue?
Reflecting like a star on the midnight moon
Or the sun that hides behind the clouds
Playing hide and seek with the ground.

Have you ever seen the sky so bright?
Glistening with such an eager delight
For all the days it had things to do
Have you ever seen the sky so blue?

Have you ever felt so much love in the air?
With so much trust, and so little despair
The days have been long and will end soon
Have you ever seen the sky so blue?

Remember the sun that shined through the clouds
And the birds were an opera singing "tweet" all around
For the hope that it will come back soon
Have you ever seen the sky so blue?

*Grace Morschauser, Grade 7*
*William Penn Middle School*

### Ode to Mud

Produced from the magic of dirt and water,
A brown stinky mess, like melted ice cream.
Little kids play, pigs roll, and cars splash.
This brown stinky mess is easily the most putrid doodad on Earth.
Giant rain boots wading through mini bacteria-filled puddles,
Bacteria-filled cities that scream with every splash.
The simplest, most joy-filled, yet annoying ever Mud.
Mud is a world of its own hidden in our own world.

*Gabby Mosch, Grade 8*
*Centerville Middle School*

## Tennis

As I approach the court people fill the bleachers one by one.
I can hear my heart beat
as every second I step or speak.
Not even out of breath
and there is always one drip of sweat falling upon my body
and forming a puddle at my feet.

It's like a pail of water has just been drenched on my head.
I hold back every nerve I possibly can
I hear a faint of the whistle blow, telling me the games have begun.
I stand in my hot spot.
Waiting…for the ball, it's just me and my racquet
S-M-A-C-K!…
I made it!

Clock has ticked again, ticking every move I make
the ball gets closer and closer
I Grrrrrrunt!
Bam I make the win!
I blank out_____and resume into reality
making the move the whistle blows at the perfect time.
Glad to know the games have ended
until another year!

*Jamie Dougherty, Grade 7*
*William Penn Middle School*

## The Forest

Dawn arrives and the forest awakens.
Light floods in through gaps in the trees.
Rivers rumble back to life.
Soldiers are fresh and ready.
Battle begins.

Noon hits and the forest is alive.
Dozens of animals in action around every plant.
Rivers reach maximum speeds.
Soldiers enter battle mode.
War wages on.

Dusk strikes and the forest grows weary.
Animals exhausted after the tedious day of work.
Rivers abolish the weak.
Soldiers are tired of fighting.
Motivation is lost.

Night arrives and the forest dies.
The sun is shot out of the sky.
Rivers lay their dead to rest.
Remaining soldiers quit.
War concludes.

*Jake Miscio, Grade 9*
*Holicong Middle School*

## Our World

If I were to see the world
What would I see
Would I see all the creatures living in harmony
Or would I see all the war, destruction, and hate that seethes

If I were to hear the world
What would I hear
Would I hear it cry out for "help"
Or would I hear it scream and yell and tell me to leave

Whether or not I can hear or see it
There is something genuine I can do
To help the world we all live on
Maybe pick up some trash or plant some trees

*Samantha Witherow, Grade 8*
*Wattsburg Area Middle School*

## Water Dances

Water dances
He twirls and twists
Jumps and glides
He waltzes smoothly to the rhythm of a small stream
Or mambos wildly like a crashing river
He merengues to the beat of the thunder
And creates a romantic rumba to the wind
He sambas to an eruption
He shakes and shakes and shakes
But no matter what water dances
Every droplet cha-chas
Saying "catch me if you can" with his flirtatious smile
Even tangoing sternly on the shore
And for the finale he may even put out the fire with a spicy salsa

*Cassie Surmacz, Grade 8*
*Penn Middle School*

## Life

We wonder what life should be,
It's actually beyond what we see,
we want to understand all we are able,
we all write our own life's fable,
our own story, our own destiny,
nobody else can see our own glee,
when we know another person's love,
it feels like an angel coming from the above,
we don't know how to explain it,
but it feels like a fire in your heart was lit,
when we feel down and low,
ourselves we do not show,
life is a journey, not a simple task,
to be loved, is all that humans ask.

*Tyler Himmelberger, Grade 9*
*Conrad Weiser High School*

## Love

Love is a book filled with joy and sadness
Love can make you feel alive and complete
Sometimes it makes you feel lots of madness
Like when you're with someone, and they will cheat
You can fall in love or be fooled by it
If you're fooled you won't know anything else
When he is gone, you will have a big fit
When it's true, you will hear the sound of bells
He'll love you a lot and hold you so tight
It will make you feel so perfect and cute
That is when you know he is in the right
He might be able to wear the wedding suit
Love can sometimes lead to a deep heartache
But that's only if you make a mistake

*Monica Albarran, Grade 8*
*Pocono Mountain East Jr High School*

## Love Flowers

Love, is like a flower
Blossoming in the sun
Growing, with every hour
Just waiting, for the one.
But with every passin' moment,
The flower slowly withers.
There's no way to control it,
It cracks, with bleeding slivers
The flower eventually fades and dies,
After all the slivers have ceased,
And over the ground, those petals lie,
With many a fold and crease.
Love, like flowers and fireworks alike,
Are at first bright and blossomed, but then fade into the night.

*Bernard Karlowicz, Grade 8*
*Lake-Lehman Jr High School*

## Middle School

The day goes by in an endless blur
Teachers talking, students listening
I reach my locker and its metal tranquility
I'm tempted to lie down and surrender to slumber
But…
I carry on, dragging myself to my next class
My head drifts toward the cold, hard desk
I hear my name ring out
My head snaps up
I realize everyone's watching, all eyes on me
I've been asked a question for everyone but me to hear
I sigh, and the teacher asks again
I answer, only to drift back down to the cold hard desk and…
Sleep

*Sarah Myers, Grade 7*
*Strath Haven Middle School*

## Nature's Beauty

Wisps of wind, and radiant sunrises
Bright neon flowers grow, but don't bloom yet.
In the dead of night, an owl arises
It soars and spies a spider's silky net
Woven with thread, almost sharp as a knife.
It glistens and twinkles in the moonlight.
A quiet, still world, yet bursting with life.
Nature is exquisite, even at night.
The brilliant sun shows and wakes all the land
Scattering light far as the eye can see
Some creatures learn to fly, others to stand
A heartwarming sight, filled with such beauty.
This nature can be forgotten at times
But we can remember, sometimes in rhymes.

*Megan Smale, Grade 8*
*Pocono Mountain East Jr High School*

## The Football King

Here I sit in a smelly locker room.
Awaiting my team's undetermined fate.
I am choking on the odors that loom.
And hoping that I do not suffocate.
I strap on my helmet and tie my cleats.
Then we rush out the door onto the field.
I can hardly stand the blistering heat.
I need a powerful sun blocking shield.
The offensive line practices the blocking.
The quarterback warms up his throwing arm.
The sun's heat rays show no signs of stopping.
The opposing team shows no signs of harm.
I stretch out my legs and pull my hamstring.
That is the downfall of the football king.

*Tyler Van Grouw, Grade 8*
*Pocono Mountain East Jr High School*

## Too Scared to Tell

Someone I like I am too scared to tell
I've liked this guy since the very first sight
His looks can put me under a deep spell
With a smile so cute, and eyes so bright.
His laughter is always adorable
He's sweet and kind and fun to be around
To tell him how I feel I'm unable,
But in my every thought it's him I found.
I wish I could see him every day now
Because somehow he's always on my mind
Maybe I will tell him someday, somehow
It is him in my heart that you will find.
Although I'm not sure if it is true love
But when he's near my heart flies like a dove

*Samantha Rose Perez, Grade 8*
*Pocono Mountain East Jr High School*

## I'm From

I am from a mixture of cultures,
All united together in one
With just a simple "I do"
A word of joy and bond forever
Playing with Barbie dolls with all accessories

Running on the field with the wind
Playing manhunt with a little bike
Racing for blow pops stuck in my hair
With magazine in my hand a smirk comes around
Laughter around the three Stooges in a box of entertainment
From wishing for one day to be tall and rich

I am from a woman of humor and no mistakes
Warmth in her heart
Hard work and all
I am from a mom
With pride and joy
The mom I will love forever

*Veronica Colozza, Grade 7*
*William Penn Middle School*

## Campfire Thoughts

In the forest, the trees whisper my name
As we gather around a crackling fire
I feel like I am in some evil game
With all of nature trying to conspire

I love the wilderness in the day
When all is happy and bright
But when the light goes away
Scary calls sound through the night

The leaves are luminous and glowing
The bushes show silhouettes of creatures
But surely it is only my mind showing
All of the forest's terrifying features

In the morning, I know everything will be fine
Nothing bad will arise
Even though I feel a prickling up my spine
That tonight I will get a nasty surprise!

*Sarah Riegel, Grade 8*
*Daniel Boone Middle School*

## Brownies

Brownies are warm,
When they're out people swarm,
One by one each brownie is gone,
So I bake many and have a sale on my lawn,
It's so sad to see them go,
I'll make some more,
And put on a show.

*Olivia Nieves, Grade 7*
*Pennbrook Middle School*

## I Am From

I am from homemade paella and steaming tea
And a crazy laughing family
From rosy red cheeks in the cold
And a little Polish nose

I am from never ending trails and cliff jumping
And music drifting through the walls
From hard work and an artistic hand
And dreams reaching a new land

I am from summer sunlight playing on water
And flip-flop tans and painted toes
From running with my half family
And icing my bruised knees

I am from a smiling father and loving mother
And traditional maple treats
From imagination taking flight
And making your own beat

*Hannah Rodriguez, Grade 8*
*Ephrata Middle School*

## Million Dollar Hit

It's my turn, I go up to the plate,
I'm so nervous I might nearly faint.
The pitcher pitches the ball,
The first one was kind of dull.
Then I remember everything I need to know.
The other team is my foe.
The ball is pitched, I hear the crack.
Now I try to make the lap.
Around the bases as fast as I can go.
I take a look at the ball, before I knew it I was almost home.
The ball was in someone's glove.
Then the girl on third gives me a shove.
I fall over, but the ref didn't see.
I get back up overflowing with glee.
The ball is in the infield, I have to run faster.
This game has been such a disaster.
We only need one more run to beat the other team.
Sliding into home as it seemed,
We won the game two to three.

*Tawni Feeney, Grade 7*
*Bellmar Middle School*

## Sun and Rain

Sun
Bright, hot
Shining, smiling, blinding
Sky, streaks, clouds, thunderclouds
Falling, crying, splashing
Cold, dark
Rain

*Rachel Steckbeck, Grade 8*
*Lancaster Mennonite School - Locust Grove*

### And Yet...

The air, suffocating, thick and heavy,
All eyes staring, just staring.
I take the first step, small. Timid.
Agonizingly slow. The palpable air.
And yet...

I can't. The pressure is pushing, shoving me to my knees.
The eyes, simply watching
Me.

A deep, shaking breath,
Inhaling the thick, sweaty air.
Another step. Small.

The weight, the pressure.
Unbearable. I can't.
I take another, fearful step.
My heart beating, pounding in my chest.
The eyes. All just looking, burning holes into
Me. And yet...

Another step, bigger.
The pressure fills the air.
If I breathe, if I step again,
Then what?

*Julian Brubaker, Grade 8*
*Lancaster Mennonite School - Locust Grove*

### Hearing Your Heartbeat

The moment is finally here.
Working into a roar, the crowd starts to cheer.
I am boxed between faces of children and adults,
when they are suddenly brought to a halt.

The announcer was like a beating heart,
rarely missing a beat.
Hearing their names makes me gleam with excitement,
hoping to see them.
But I am shortly stopped by some taller fans,
who rudely tend to stand.

Trying to catch a glimpse, I squirm around the obstruction.

The lights danced like ballerinas,
not knowing where to land next.
Suspenseful fog throttled the noses of the impatient crowd,
screaming for their attention.
And then you see them.

At that second, I was taken back to my younger days,
begging my father to see the famous Globetrotters.
And now this day, I'm finally here.
Although I may wish to embrace and surround them,
the most I can do is cheer.

*Marissa Panasiti, Grade 8*
*Bellwood Antis Middle School*

### Fury

Stepping into the sweltering kitchen,
The heat lashes out at me.

My glasses fog up, and the noodles seethe in pain
as they cook in the boiling water.
The rice cooker hisses.
The oil from the pan smarts your arm, in a red haze of revenge.

The pots bang together, the cabinets slam closed.
Seasonings shriek as the pan sizzles them.

The oven timer buzzes alarmingly,
The fiber-filled celery snaps and crackles
when the knife ruthlessly takes its life.
The chef clangs the decorated porcelain plates,
The steaming gourmet meal scalds my tongue.

I sit frustrated and uncomfortable on the hard, cold plastic chair,
and yearning peace,
I gaze out the window into the promisingly peaceful world.
Yet, to my despair,
the sun blinds and burns my eyes.

I ask myself,
Is this a kitchen of fury?
Or a world of fury?

*Noah Lee, Grade 7*
*Good Hope Middle School*

### Peanut Butter Sandwiches

I love the taste; it's always great.
It looks charming on any plate.
How to make it?
Bit by bit.

First is the toast;
you need this the most.
Pop it into a toaster oven,
and out comes crunchy toast that tastes like heaven.

Ding, ding, ding! The toast is ready!
But be careful! The toast is piping, so you might get unsteady!
Carefully place the two slices onto a plate.
Oh, it's going to taste great!

Mm, the peppy, pure, peanut butter is next.
Scrape it on so there are no more white specks!
The heat makes it melt and it gets all creamy,
so hurry up while the bread is still steamy!

Slap together the two slices of toast.
Together, I know you'll want them the most.
Cut them diagonally with a spreading knife,
and eating this will make you become full of life!

*Sarina Chow, Grade 8*
*Pine-Richland Middle School*

### Beautifully

It is not just your beauty that I resent,
It is the peaceful nature that you represent.
You are a divine angel, floating from above,
Meant to send down your gentle love.
And once again, you escape away,
From the cruel, harsh world of today.
I wish that I could be so tame, yet free,
So that I may live in peace eternally.
I hope one day to be more like you,
Because you are all that is pure and true.
*Michaela Lucas, Grade 7*
*Moshannon Valley Jr/Sr High School*

### Popcorn!

Waiting for each kernel to pop,
Watching the microwave closely,
Sitting patiently, when will it stop?
Listen for the ding that means it's done,
Leaving the room for even a moment,
May result in burning more than one.
Take it out while it is still hot,
With butter and salt is the best.
Make sure to check for any burnt spots,
And enjoy your popcorn with a movie.
*Emily Nonnenberg, Grade 7*
*Redeemer Lutheran School*

### March

Skates in
on a rainbow,
bringing the birth of new plants.
Skipping around
on new springtime grass,
attracting rain showers
like a magnet.
Then it zips out of the way
weaving a new path for
April to arrive.
*Cameron Saunders, Grade 7*
*Garnet Valley Middle School*

### Love

Like a symphony,
We will be together for an eternity,
The kiss,
You would always miss,
The chocolate "Dove,"
Our sweet love,
Never to go away,
You're always here to stay,
All mine,
To the end of time.
*Kalie Darby, Grade 8*
*Danville Area Middle School*

### Bright Midnight of Life

Life is like a kaleidoscope, filled with colors.
One mirror shows the parties, happy families and marriages –
Death, illness and betrayal lie away on the other.

One mirror shows a bright majestic ball of light,
shining its warmth down, not a bit of dismay.
Opposite is a blood red crescent,
Casting threatening shadows as the darkness beckons to you.

Which mirror shows,
when passion, bliss, or love consumes you?
Or what about when,
the grief, misery and sorrow won't escape your head?

What happens when you twist the kaleidoscope,
And catch a glimpse of what your life could have become?
Or the consequences of twisting it again,
and gasping in disbelief at the reality that it truly is.

What about the swirls of color?
The bright, fluorescent yellows and whites leap into precious day.
Meanwhile the blacks and deep blues linger in the sky.

And forever will these opposites clash, more so in the future than today.
One can only dream of the paradise, where light will devour darkness –
instead of just becoming entangled.
*Autumn Hause, Grade 8*
*Richland Sr High School*

### Happiness

Happiness is a wonderful thing.
Although sometimes without it, your life can be a bird with a broken wing.

Everything is sad and grey.
Even when you hope and pray,
You can find no happiness in life,
As if your heart has been stabbed with a knife.

Nothing satisfies your persnickety mind,
Always concentrated on what one cannot find.

When you find yourself in this kind of phase,
You must see past the thick, unending haze.
Life could be a lot worse,
At least you're not under an eternal curse.

So think about all the good things that came your way.
Did someone say something that would have made your day,
If you would have been a bit more gay?

Although it may be a hard and difficult thing,
You need to learn to just let go and not cling.
But most of all how to mend a broken wing.
*Amanda Grube, Grade 7*
*Landisville Middle School*

### The Dancer
The crowd is clapping
You feel like the star.
You just stand smiling
Attitude divine.
When you dance you
Feel so free.
Like the sky is the limit.
People comment on how
Beautiful.
You are as graceful as a
Fish in water —
As peaceful as a bird in air.
Nobody can take away the beauty
Of a dancer.
As the music begins the
Sensation has just begun.
*Alexus Miller, Grade 7*
*Bellwood Antis Middle School*

### Dirt Biking
Turning off the railroad track
Not even thinking of turning back
Approaching the forty-five degree hill
Anticipating the great thrill
I began to feel scared
As I started up unprepared
I wasn't ready for the other side
A steep hill like a water slide
As I saw the hill below
I thought my stomach just might blow
I thought I may end up like some before
Crashing and feeling like I hit the floor
Instead I went down sliding
It had my teeth grinding
I was happy I didn't crash
And decided in a flash to go home in a dash
*Ryan Kerns, Grade 7*
*Bellwood - Antis Middle School*

### I Miss You
I can't believe you're gone.
My face is drowned in tears.
I know you're in a better place,
Though it's been painful through the years.
I hope the day when I too, am gone,
I'll get to see your face.
For time is moving slowly,
And I'm beginning to waste.
I wish I could join you now,
But that's not the way it is.
Wait for me, I plead.
So I can join you.
Wherever that may be.
I miss you.

*Lianna Ketcham, Grade 8*
*Saegertown Jr/Sr High School*

### A Gift from My Dad
A special gift from my dad,
I miss him so very bad.
The gift is little, shiny, and gold.
It stands on my shelf, unique and bold.

My dad lives in Havertown.
He flies around the world.
He's been in the air, upside-down.
and in little planes that whirl.

I think the divorce was for the best.
All the time, my parents would fight.
A strong, scared feeling in my chest,
would keep me awake the whole night.

My gift represents love,
from my dad far away.
I guess getting divorced,
has a huge price to pay.
*Erica Storey, Grade 7*
*J R Fugett Middle School*

### Spring Cleaning
Hurry! Hurry! Just follow directions.
Hurry! Hurry! Don't ask questions.
Hurry! Hurry! No time for leaning.
Hurry! Hurry! This is spring cleaning.

Hurry! Hurry! Plant the flowers.
No! No! It won't take hours.
Hurry! Hurry! No time for dreaming.
Hurry! Hurry! This is spring cleaning.

Hurry! Hurry! Sweep the floor.
Hurry! Hurry! Wash the door.
Hurry! Hurry! No time for screaming.
Hurry! Hurry! This is spring cleaning.

Relax! Relax! The day is done.
Relax! Relax! Time for fun.
Relax! Relax! Everything is gleaming.
Relax! Relax! That was spring cleaning.
*Kurt Walker, Grade 9*
*Bishop McCort High School*

### Beauty of the Morning Weather
Imagine walking in the morning
over the cold, wet ground.
As the birds start flying
and kids start running on the playground.
Then they all start crying
when the rain comes around.
After the rain, a rainbow starts soaring
and you could smell the flowers all around.
*Miranda Henry, Grade 8*
*Saegertown Jr/Sr High School*

### One!
Darkness
Silence
Sadness
People dying
Children crying
As the world suffers
Everyone watches
Standing still
Feeling hopeless
It starts with…

One
One person
One mind
One heart
Lead the world to change!
Have you done your part?
Give the world your heart
Use your voice
Spread the love
It starts with
One
*Cameron O'Donnell, Grade 7*
*Indian Valley Middle School*

### Sweet Victory
My team was down by two in the game.
My team needed a sudden flame.
As my team ran the play "sideline"
Joey Padula stood behind the 3 point line.
When Nevin Wood passed the ball to him
Joey shot the ball right through the rim.
While the other team left with a frown
Joey felt like a king with a crown.
Bellwood-Antis just won the states
Now they are honored with increasing rates.
What makes this victory even sweeter?
Bellwood won with a buzzer beater.
*Jarrett Taneyhill, Grade 7*
*Bellwood Antis Middle School*

### Need to Know
I can talk about you nonstop.
About the good and the bad moments.
The times you go out of your way,
So we can see each other.
But you need to let it out.
They need to know!
Soon I'll have to leave,
We could have so many more moments!
Are you ashamed?
Embarrassed?
I love you more than anything.
They need to know.
*Samantha Phillips, Grade 7*
*Schuylkill Valley Middle School*

## Long Lasting Love

Your love is soft like sweetly singing birds,
Nothing in the world makes me feel better.
I feel safe with all your romantic words,
Full of jumping joy from your love letter.

You make my heart and soul beat all the days,
Loving you is not that hard for me to do.
Your love makes me smile in so many ways,
I will never ever stop loving you.

Your personality keeps me going,
The way you look makes me wish on a star.
The way you see love is softly showing,
Nor did I think we would go this far.

I always think about the times we spend,
If you are not with me my life would end!
*Brianana Wooten, Grade 8*
*Pocono Mountain East Jr High School*

## Masquerade Beauty

Looking through the revealing, shiny glass
Shows a face full of powder and is gold.
Without powder means being as dull as brass
And facing those looks, so why be that bold?

Removing mask of beauty; recovered
Elegance that would never be a shame.
Unmatched purity and wit has hovered,
With other shadowed beauties that missed fame.

Defects stay and continue to succeed;
Ruining a mind with imperfection.
To look for grace was not quite guaranteed,
When fake comes first in every direction.

Concealer in hand, one thing comes to call…
Does this youth know who is fairest of all?
*Christina Kazanas, Grade 8*
*Pocono Mountain East Jr High School*

## Blinded

I thought NOTHING could bring me back.
I was infuriated and alone;
Hatred and anger tangled and clogged my throat.

As I was blinded by anguish, resentment, and rage,
My stubbornness chained me to the pain.
I was soaked from head to toe in frustration.

But one LIGHT stood.
It was full of power, life, authority, and vigor.
She wrapped arms of love around me,
And I found hope.
*Maya Dula, Grade 7*
*Lancaster Mennonite School - Lancaster*

## Happiness

When you feel unhappiness,
Eat something sweet,
Sing a song,
Laugh loudly,
Shout and smile.

Just let's feel happy
Do not put yourself in a box
That makes you unhappy

If you are angry,
Look at nature
It will make you calm

Cry, when you are sad
Laugh, when you are happy
Everything is for you
The world did not push you out
God is always with you
*Rachel Seo, Grade 8*
*Lancaster Mennonite School - Locust Grove*

## The Beauty of Friends

Friends are like an apple tree
They grow with you forever
Friends are always there for you
They never leave your side
Friends are like sugar
They can be so sweet
Friends are like candy
They can be so sour

Friends are who we hang out with
They are who we are always with
Friends are the ones who will stick up for you
They are always there
Friends are like family
They know everything about you
Friends are the ones who keep secrets
They are like your diary that no one knows of
Friends will always see the silver lining in you when you're down
They will be there for you...forever and always
*Alexandra Zecca, Grade 7*
*Garnet Valley Middle School*

## Smile

Smiling makes you happy.
It helps you when you're sad.
When you get one from a friend it helps you when you're mad.
Smiling is a gift.
So give it when you can.
You can smile to a friend who needs a helping hand.
Smiling is the only gift that you can give for free.
So why no give to your friends and family.
*Shawn Fisher, Grade 7*
*Strath Haven Middle School*

## Nightmares

There was a girl, her hair so red,
Who was lying in a little bed.
As she starts to sleep, she clutches a toy bear,
For when she closes her eyes, she is filled with dread.

She runs and runs, through a thick forest, without care,
With dark mud and sticks through her long, red hair.
As she runs, the sky above her turns black,
And she ran right out of the monster's lair.

She slows to a trot as she finds a shack,
Because she needs to hide, that is a fact.
As the monster finds her, the girl starts to screech,
And she feels herself start to fall back.

She sits up with a scream, clutching her sheets.
She throws the blanket off of her sweat-soaked feet.
She looks outside, and sees the ground covered in sleet,
Then with a relieved sigh, she falls back to sleep.

*Brianna Daly, Grade 8*
*Penn-Kidder Campus*

## The Ocean

The ocean is like one big mystery
A wonderful sight to embrace and see
The way the pleasant waves crash and roll
No one will be able to disagree

When you are there, it makes you feel whole
It's like it has its own deep soul
Though no one can understand its astounding characteristics
It feels like it takes over control

The ocean is like a painting, beautiful and coloristic
Just like a forest, so naturalistic
Its amazing the way the blue water flows
Its array of colors, greatly artistic

During the night, the water glistens and glows
Even better than a cold winter's snow
You can feel the misty breeze as it blows
It's always the place to be, you just know

*Julia Tonelis, Grade 8*
*Penn-Kidder Campus*

## The Unbearable Battle

Gooey giants gored from a bite,
raging red ones run from a fight,
clinging clear ones climb to the top,
are pushed to the bottom but they don't stop.
Yielding yellow ones await their doom,
I sweep them up my hand is the broom.
These bumbling bears were so tasty and sweet,
when I opened the bag they met their defeat.

*Emily Dorshaw, Grade 7*
*Pennbrook Middle School*

## The Pottery Factory

Can they?
Yes.
And they will.
Just let them strike you still.
We are wet clay.
The method is systematic.
Forget the converging static.
And slowly the stream will erode away
To a smooth and perfect form.
Until you forget
It was any different.
We are wet clay.
Broken porcelain wouldn't care otherwise.
Our purpose is merely that of worker bees and flies.
If you could chip away the rosy paint and gloss
Strength would vaporize into loss.
Designs.
Not our own
But engraved.
It's no bitter pill.
If you let them strike you still.

*Macie McKitrick, Grade 8*
*Independence Middle School*

## Oblivion

Breeze violently ripping through my hair,
Kneeling, praying for any kind of miracle,
But, no the Gods only mock me, they only stare,
Yelling, crazily laughing at myself, I'm so satirical.
Screaming at the wind,
My hope pinned,
To the dying sound of the 'copter.
The sound does fade,
And so do my hopes,
So I drown into the dark, evil shade,
And something reaches out, gropes.
I curl into a ball,
Rocking, trying to remember what was once given,
Then I fall, fall, fall,
Into the lonely deep oblivion.

*Abigail Zenone, Grade 7*
*Cambria Heights Middle School*

## Just One Kiss

A kiss is all it takes
B ecause it shows the love between two people
C ares and worries vanish
D evotion to one person
E very time you kiss you get butterflies
F alling head over heels in love
G etting closer with the one you love
H aving trust in your love
I love you; just those three words make your heart melt
J ust one kiss can make you fall in love

*Katherine Fegley, Grade 8*
*Ephrata Middle School*

## Hope Prevails

A child who was born into a loving, healthy family.
A mother who works hard to keep up with an active family.
A father, who climbs trees, day after day to support his loving family.
She was the first born child.
Her first brother was born five years later, uneventful.
Three years willow by.
As she looks upon a little brother of the third month.
Alas, everything was not right.
The men with the healing magic reluctantly brought the loving family to terms with the situation.
Her brother of the third month had a problem as grave as midnight,
He was to be sucked into the dark, black shadows of no return due to his critical state.
She was sucked into an abyss of shock, sadness, and depression.
Her two life forces had a choice to make,
He could live all his life in the dark,
always bound by the wire chains that held him down.
Or they could take a chance and disconnect. Hope a miracle happens.
They chose the latter.
Alas, that day he was hit by a ray of light from above,
Ever since that day,
He just got farther away from those dark shadows of no return, and closer to his loving family.
Some say it was luck. But anyone who saw him at his worst, and sees him now,
Knows that he is a miracle child.

*Ruth Stabosz-Danyo, Grade 8*
*FSEMS - Avon Grove Middle School*

## Our Love Connection

We were friends but you wanted more, I told you no so you left
but now that we're older and I've seen who you are
and my heart starts to break as I watch you kiss her, I'm jealous
I need your love to get me through the day, so I won't be neglected
wandering around like a stray dog, I'm foaming from the mouth
ready to rip your love away from her and steal it back for me

You don't know where your love belongs or are you giving false signs?
Just let me have my chance to press your lips against mine
but you don't lock your eyes into mine, is it because you lost the key?
Or did you throw it out to sea so you couldn't see the real connection between you and me?
I wish I hadn't blown my chance with my ignorant gasoline, will you please try to fix my heart?

I wish we could be together forever like two birds of a feather
or two peas in a pod or two halves of a heart
and not this facade, how I wish it was me you would give your loving kiss
I started falling into a scary, dark abyss
and hoped you would be at the bottom to catch me but without realizing it, you let me fall
because you had no intention of catching me
but the hardest part isn't hitting the ground when no one stops you from falling
it's watching the one you love fall more in love with someone else

*Aurora Ryan, Grade 8*
*First Philadelphia Charter School for Literacy*

## A View from My Window

My woods and the backyard, the shop is to the left next to the shed. I see snow falling rapidly everywhere. I remember me and my friends would ride four wheelers in the snow. I see the old fort we built, torn down, left to be covered in the snow. I see far in the distance a deer wandering peacefully, looking for food next to a creek with no water.

*Timothy Pullman, Grade 7*
*Garnet Valley Middle School*

### Nature Path

Looking up at a disruptive car bridge that hangs over a dirt path.
I see a bright blue fluorescent sky that illuminates everything except the shady nature paths below.

I hear boat motors humming, chipmunks chirping,
and the sound of water that sounds like a lion's roar as it flows over the waterfall.

What are the other people's purpose for being here? What was my purpose for being here, on this nature path?

I'm impressed by the amazing scenery. The beautiful green scenery, scenery filled with wondrous noises of nature.

Peaceful.
Peaceful.
Peaceful.

*Cole Bower, Grade 7*
*Saucon Valley Middle School*

### The Student I Should Have Been

The student I should have been looks like a miniature adult.
She wears sophisticated clothes and carries around a briefcase with her books and papers.
The student I should have been has a brilliant mind and amazing concentration.
She can stay focused for hours and always completes work efficiently.
The student I should have been says, "Oh, no! My essay is due in only three months! I'm behind schedule! Sorry, but I can't go to the movies next weekend."
The student I should have been skipped five grades and was valedictorian of her class.
After graduating from Princeton in three years, she will have a spectacular career and become famous for many important accomplishments.
The student I should have been never took a break from all her studying.
Many years from now, she will look back on her childhood and wish that she'd had some time to have fun and be a kid.

*Katie Wenger, Grade 7*
*Strath Haven Middle School*

### I Come From...

I come from a family of six who love me and teach me to stand up for what's right, and who took the time to wait years to complete our family by adopting two children from China.
I come from a school where I have friends who care for me, who won't turn their backs on me, and who are always waiting to give me a comforting hug.
I come from a church family who I get to know more and more, a youth pastor who teaches me to grow in Jesus, and who teaches the young to serve others and become more like Christ.
I come from Lancaster County, an area that values farming and hard work, that has taught me to love the outdoors and hands-on-activities like swimming, walking in the woods, and smelling farm fresh country air.
I come from a country that allows me to be free in worship, so I can praise and glorify my heavenly father.
I come from a world that hates Jesus, but I have the hope that when I die, I will go from this world to be with Him forever more.

*Mariah Mast, Grade 7*
*Conestoga Christian School*

### These Longing Winter Days

I came across a frozen lake one early morning.
The water was glass.
The sun was only just rising like the people in the town.
The air was brisk and dry but I didn't mind, because not long from now it would be summer time.
That thought is what keeps my mind sane.
These longing winter days cold, cold and dreary.
In June this lake will be full of life with children splashing and adults dipping their toes.
But for now it is cold and dark but soon enough it will be bright and warm.

*Molly Danemark, Grade 8*
*Centerville Middle School*

## Bullied

You cry watery tears of pain
The slap! of their words hits you in the heart
Like their punches
Your soul is stabbed, shattered and smashed
Into billions of pieces
Your personality that was rock strong
Now crumples into weakness and sorrow
The hurt you feel is like no other
You always ask yourself
Why me, what did I do wrong?
Yet it is a question that was never answered
You hope there's light at the end of the tunnel
But all you hear is the cackling of their laughter
It will all go away, it will all disappear
The bullying and punching will all fade away
I will be strong; I will have a better life
For it is too late
Because of these cold-blooded people
Your life has come to end

*Aida Mujkovic, Grade 7*
*William Penn Middle School*

## Their Love for Each Other

A spark of emotion and a delicate kiss
The love in his eyes, you could not miss
She was beautiful, as pretty as a rose
This time for them was bliss

Their love for each other really showed
It was as if the time had froze
He was handsome, as hot as can be
This romance was like a symphony being composed

He adored her so, that was something anyone could see
He pulled her from that dark place and set her free
They were far from sorrow and woe
The lovers were perfectly happy, though surrounded by calamity

There time was up, but he didn't want to go
He said he really loved her so
The girl was confused, little did he know
Their time was up, they both had to go

*Erica Bicchetti, Grade 8*
*Penn-Kidder Campus*

## Summer Snow

Sweet summer weather
is warm every day.
Happy fruit grows
like the fire
and the light sun
between falling snow.
You like to dream by night.
You feel good.

*Jared Shaffer and Dustin Vanderhoof, Grade 8*
*Saegertown Jr/Sr High School*

## The Broken One

You're the reason why I've built up walls
you lied,
wooden walls went up around my heart.
You were a jerk
those wooden walls were torn down
new brick walls replaced them.
You forgot about me and moved on to her,
those brick walls were plowed over
brand new cement walls went up
permanently.
But there's a door with a special handle
you had the key, but I changed the lock.
Those walls have been broken down, built up.
Whether it was attempted, or not.
They've been through a lot
just from you.
You've hurt me the most,
the worst.
All this building up, breaking down.
They'll never be fixed, ever again.
Just call me the broken one.

*Leanna Miller, Grade 8*
*Spring Grove Middle School*

## The Boardwalk

When you go to this place
There are many seagulls that you chase
All the rides, all the fun
So many choices, can't pick one
Cakes, pizzas, funnel fries
Looking up seeing bright skies
So many places where you shop
So much fun just can't stop
At this place you're always walking
On the phone, always talking
Going on the rides is the best
Seeing who can stand it is the test
On the boards, to the end
Walking home with your friend
Still have the smell and sound of the boardwalk on your mind
Cannot wait until next time

*Adriana Camiola, Grade 7*
*Pennbrook Middle School*

## In Your Memory

The hallways rang with silence I never wished to hear.
The eyes of all the school filled and flowed with tears.
Your locker is a memorial to memories of the past.
A life so young lost in a moment, lost in a tragic crash.
Your laughter echoes through the halls you'll never tread again.
Our team will make it to the game you always dreamed we'd win.
We know that you are with us; still the pain is hard to bear.
I wish that you had never gone.
I wish you were still here.

*Mackenzie Rodgers, Grade 9*
*Knoch High School*

### Buzzer Beater

Clock ticking down
Running down the court
All I could hear was
Squeaky sneakers and the crowd cheering
My heart was pounding out of my jersey
Sweat was falling down my neck like a waterfall
When I got
At the end of the court
All I could hear was the
Ball crashing into
The net
The swish echoed
The crowd went wild
The ref blew his
Whistle RANG!
We won the game
The other coach murmured
My buzzer beater

*Matthew Weatherington, Grade 7*
*William Penn Middle School*

### The Buzzer Beater

The clock ticks away
Just like my energy.
Fourth quarter,
Tied score,
Fifteen seconds left.
The point guard pounds the ball up court.
I could taste the victory,
And feel the intensity at my fingertips.
We fired the ball around the arc.
The crowd was silent,
And my heart was beating nervously.
The ball came to me faster than a rocket.
We had to beat the clock.
My shot went up.
It seemed like the ball was airborne for an hour.
And…swish!
Our side of the crowd went wild.
We won the game with my shot.

*Jake Northrup, Grade 7*
*William Penn Middle School*

### Dance

When competition comes
I know it's game time.
The music playing louder and louder
As my adrenaline gets higher and higher.
My heart thumps like taps in rhythm.
Hearing the announcer announce my name
Makes me want to throw up all the tickling nerves
That build up inside of me.
*Turning* like an open music box figurine.
Trying to make my mom proud.
Jumping gracefully but with attack
As my legs *fly* through the air.
Kicking higher than ever.
Then all of a sudden it's over.
The crowd cheering and chanting
As I walk off the stage.
Then receiving my award
For giving it everything I had.

*Kaitlyn Jones, Grade 7*
*William Penn Middle School*

### Hunter's Dream

One sunny spring morn
While I was looking for a bird,
A strange thing occurred.
Suddenly my eyes caught a flash of red —
Furry and red, sitting in a green bed.

"What's that?" I said. Let me look once more.
It has a sharp nose and black pointed ears,
A fat, bushy tail — it's a fox! That's clear.
We set up our telescope and saw three brown bundles
Playing around and taking some tumbles.

I called my buddies to come in a blitz.
"You've got to come see this fox and her kits!"
So together we decided to creep near its lair,
Then we parted our ways and came quite near;
And we saw rabbits and feathers scattered around.
So this is the story of what we found.

*Sheldon Peachey, Grade 7*
*Rockhaven Christian School*

### The Jet

It is like a speeding bullet
Whizzing past the cows like a pesky fly.
It is as loud as the atomic bomb
But it is far more dangerous
For the nose is as sharp as a spire.
If it crashes the explosion will be as loud as a shotgun.
But if the controller is put in the right hands
It is as graceful as an ice-skater
For I am that person.
It is a jet.

*Drew King, Grade 8*
*Ephrata Middle School*

### Stop the "Snakes"

I hate it when people bully a person,
Then that person goes a cursin',
They get tired of all this stuff,
And they can't keep being tough,
It's really hard to see them struggle,
When they need a friend to cuddle,
I would really like to help them through this,
When all those "snakes" hiss,
Don't worry this will soon all be done,
And a new friendship will have begun!

*Lydia Drass, Grade 7*
*Cambria Heights Middle School*

**Up to the Clouds**
Every day I dream of the misty, gorgeous mountains,
Cool, crisp towers that keep watch over the miniscule world below.

Along the rough terrain, and atop the breathtaking peaks I've traveled,
For every mountain that shows its face with a warm, welcoming smile.

Yet one single mountain, whose large, navy figure
Lies shadowed against the sky, is simply an everlasting nightmare.

It mocks me as I cringe at the sight of its frightening shape.
Yet I live on ignoring it, and watch the climbless days endlessly pass by,
and watch the climbless day endlessly pass by.

I am summoned one gray morning, as the despondent clouds part and reveal my fear.
But I gather my equipment, and let out a sigh with heavy breath, soon arriving at the mountain with the guidance of the clouds
above me.

I stare up as an unruly storm draws near, yet my foot somehow finds its place upon the beast before me.
And I begin to make my way up to the mysterious, glowing peak in the midst of turbulence.

I smile nervously as I approach the top
And complete the final step, standing like the captain of a ship.

The conclusion of my trek ends with a smile of triumph,
As I close my eyes and feel the mountain below
Smile back at me, both of us acknowledging the journey I had made up to the clouds.

*Kylie Manuppelli, Grade 8*
*Pine-Richland Middle School*

**Cancer Took You**
Cancer took you
Cancer took you, and I don't know why?
When you left this Earth I cried.

Cancer took you, and when it took you it took me too.
When you left me, my heart couldn't take it,
I could've sworn I never would've made it.

Cancer took you, I wanted it to take me too.
Now and again, I dwell on the past and try to look to the future,
But the memories I've had from the past pull me back in just like you did as I was leaving your house.

Cancer took you, why the heck would it do that?
You were my father figure and my best friend
You were the mend — to my sad sad heart,
and now you're gone without a goodbye or a kiss goodnight.
Cancer took you, after it did,
It was like a slap in the face and a whisper in my ear "FORGET YOU" in the soft devil's voice.
I feel so alone your home isn't a place I can call my own — any more.
Cancer took you, and I can't wrap my head around why?
You were my cousin and I cry every night, hoping your death was a dream.
I wish cancer would've taken me too, my tears fall like a heavy flowing stream,
I wish your death was nothing more than a messed up dream.
Cancer took you, and I wish it would've taken me too or even instead.

*Leayana Brinkley, Grade 8*
*First Philadelphia Charter School for Literacy*

### The Seasons Around Us

When willowing winter changes to colorful spring
The blazing sun does this shining thing
When the snow starts to wither away
Then, I know the brightness the sun will bring

When summer starts to come my way
Then every day is a sunny day
A burst of sunlight rains down like a beam
I know it is here to stay

The autumn months feel like a dream
When the sun from summer runs out of gleam
Leaves start to fall, one after another
And one falls gently on a stream

Winter swings back bringing everyone together
When there is below-freezing weather
There is no trace of birds, not even a feather
And the cycle goes on forever

*Malorie Gorman, Grade 8*
*Penn-Kidder Campus*

### Basketball

Everyone knows I get the inbound pass
Got to take this possession like it is the last
Coach tells me to take the shot
So I take it rather than not

My team loves that I pass a lot
After the shot I start to trot
Then the coach wants to sub me out
So I take a sip of my drink I brought

The coach will put me in without a doubt
And the other team starts to pout
I know we are going to win this game
And the fans are starting to shout

The team is starting to foul, it is kind of lame
The other team's coach wants to blame
But my team is always playing the same
And I end the game with a fade

*Rocco Twardzik, Grade 8*
*Jim Thorpe Penn-Kidder Campus*

### Summer Dream

During a summer dream
her beautiful imaginative mind
brought gentle happiness
to the wonderful season.
As squirrels scamper across the ground
under the warm sun and the bright sky
The children run and play until the dark hours of the night
During a summer dream.

*Hayley Acker, Grade 8*
*Saegertown Jr/Sr High School*

### What Could We Have Done?

What could we have done?
There in that place, we would have all been
Killed.
We did not know, but how could we, for they hid their
intentions well.
What we did know was the pain of starvation,
the desperation to find a scrap of food.
We saw the dead that were thrown in the trenches
Left to rot, naked and without dignity.
We were not allowed to close our eyes, to say the prayers of passing.
What could we have done?
Poisonous.
The smell wafted around us.
An ever-present sickly sweet smell. It pervaded our pores,
Always with us.
There was nothing we could have done,
but be the sub-servant delinquents they believed us to be.
We were merely Jews that got in the way of everything they did.
And so they disposed of us when we were no longer of
use to them.
What could we have done?

*Rachel Serfilippi, Grade 8*
*Susquehanna Community Jr/Sr High School*

### Cloud Nine

You don't have to stand in line,
You can lie under the great pine,
You can pick grapes from the grape vine,
Everyone will laugh when you finish the punch line,
You will always cross that finish line,
Your name will be a big dollar sign,
You can smell the sweet white wine,
You'll always look fine,
You can talk to your friends for hours on the phone line,
Everyone will enjoy your design,
You won't ever have to cross the picket line,
You will hit that gold mine,
You will catch many fish with your fishing line,
You will never have to resign,
And ocean side you will dine.
This is what it is like on Cloud Nine.

*Emily Burkland, Grade 8*
*Danville Area Middle School*

### Dance

Twirling, and swirling around in circles.
Though you might not think it's a sport, really, it is.
I dance.
Lyrical is my favorite thing to do.
Leaps and turns make you dizzy sometimes.
I love to dance.
It makes me happy when I'm sad.
Dance is all about emotion, happiness, sadness and attitude.
I love to dance.

*Sarah Shaw, Grade 8*
*Saegertown Jr/Sr High School*

**As He Went**

Sitting on hard cement,
Harsh hissing met his ears.
As lines of bright red bent,
To show what he did hear.
Laughing as it went.

Relatives and friends came round,
As the anxious firemen passed.
The children tried to block the sounds,
Of screaming, pleading people rasp.
Crying as they came.

He pulled on the iron bars,
As if maybe, they might move.
Forced to watch the fire char,
Burn a world he hardly knew,
Laughing as it went.

And sadly dying for a sin,
He wasn't guilty of,
His now orphaned children,
Became what he thought of,
As he went.
*Jessalin Urbano, Grade 8*
*Conestoga Christian School*

**Glad to Have Seen**

Sitting down at the edge of the shore
I didn't know what I was looking for
Expectant to see something marvelous
Right before my desperate eyes

I lounged a while longer
My eagerness getting stronger
Then "Ahh" what a sight!
Seagulls taking flight
Across the sunset sky
Just minutes before night

After contentedly sitting alone,
I figured I'd go home
On the walk there I smiled
Pleased with the scene I saw

When I arrived, I tried to boast,
But it was helpless — my sister,
With no life outside the screen,
Such a scene so serene
Would mock her
Only a pixelated dream
*Shelby Nigon, Grade 7*
*Elizabeth Forward Middle School*

**I Have No Finish Line**

The cool wind whistling on my face
As I run
But in no race
My legs moving 1000 miles beneath me
And I'm going to run as far as I can see

All the sudden I don't know if I breathe
And I don't know if I sprint
Or if I wreathe
And I'm trapped in a world inside of me

There is no place I have to go
Where am I going
I don't even know
When I stop
I don't care
Where I stop
Anywhere that's fair
When I run there is no time
When I run I have no finish line
*Jake Lambert, Grade 7*
*Pennbrook Middle School*

**I Come From**

I come from a family where the women
are independent and strong.

I come from a school where friends
are loyal and education is important.

I come from a household where God
is with me always.

I come from friends who treat me
fairly and care for me.

I come from a country where there's
love and war.

I come from siblings who argue a lot,
and yet, they still care.

I come from a God with unfailing love,
and a Lord who saved me.
*Emily Bernard, Grade 8*
*Conestoga Christian School*

**The Monster of Frankenstein**

Without beauty
Above monstrosity
Under sorrow
Between good and evil
To hatred at his creator
Over his warm heart
*Kyler Chance, Grade 8*
*Wattsburg Area Middle School*

**Dandelion Yellow**

The soft
Fuzzy yellow
Of a peach
The bright sun shining on me
And sparkles on the lake.
The sound of kids
Laughing loud on the playground
The taste of a sweet and sticky lollipop
In my mouth.
Feeling *smooth*
Touching the fluffy
Soft blanket.
The smell of
Yankee Candle Vanilla Cupcake
Floats in the air
Dandelion yellow
*Julia Price, Grade 7*
*William Penn Middle School*

**What a Lacrosse Player Knows**

The whistle blows
Everyone knows
It's time to go to
Work
Win the face off
Score
Work the ball
Get the call
Score a little more
Behind the back
Pick up the slack
What?
You hit the post
No need to boast
Get back to work and
Win!
*Connor Fahie, Grade 7*
*Easton Area Middle School 7-8*

**Mom**

Why can't you let me?
You say I'm not old enough.
I am certain that I can be,
Responsible enough so let me!
It isn't a crime,
So just say yes!
I get angry when you don't say,
The answers so I can get away.
If you understood me,
You could see the way I am.
It would mean the world to me,
If you would just let me be.
Mom,
If only you would let me.
*Becka Davitt, Grade 8*
*Wattsburg Area Middle School*

### The Uncast Outcast

That poor kid in the corner
Aching to be set free,
Is his own mourner.
Trying so hard just to flee.

As they bully and tease him,
They don't understand how he feels.
As the time passes, the light in his eyes grow dim.
He is standing on the edge of his heels.

The son of a single father,
That paints a smile on his face,
Has no way to turn back,
The memories remaining unerased.

As Kurt lies in his mind all alone,
He prays that God shall take him home.

*Francesca A. Petrella, Grade 8*
*Ephrata Middle School*

### I Am

I am kind and lovable.
I wonder what it would be like to not wear hearing aids.
I hear the waves in the ocean.
I see the sunrise on the beach.
I want a puppy.
I am kind and lovable.
I pretend to be a famous singer.
I feel happy when I am around my family.
I worry when my family is sick.
I cry when I think of my loved ones in heaven.
I am kind and lovable.
I understand what it is like to be hearing impaired.
I say practice makes perfect.
I dream of getting a puppy.
I try my best in school.
I wish my pop gets well soon.
I am kind and lovable

*Danielle Guth, Grade 7*
*Strath Haven Middle School*

### Pearl Harbor

Gunshots ringing through the valley
Fire burning everywhere
Screams unforgettable
Children running anywhere they want
Cars beeping uncontrollably
Suddenly I look up
Bombs flying towards me
You wince, close your eyes, and brace for impact
BOOM!
The lights go out
You wake and see the destruction that has been done
Hawaii is ruined and Pearl Harbor is gone
You can feel the damage
Smell the carnage
Taste the sand in your mouth
Hear the massacre that once was Pearl Harbor

*Zachary Ayers, Grade 7*
*Towanda Jr/Sr High School*

### Summer Field

There is no air, there is haze
It surrounds everything, scorching the newly planted corn
There is no water, just sun
The morning rays suffocate everything left
The stench of smoke started to fill the air

Charred bricks lay still on the scorching ground
Barren land shows the remnants of his old life
All hope is gone
The sound of sirens start to fill the air
But they are too late

He closes his eyes to relive the memories
The red waves engulfed me, leaving me helpless
You can open your eyes to stop the memories,
But they never really go away
Summer field

*Kristen Spencer, Grade 7*
*South Side Middle School*

### Game Time Noise

CLAP! CLAP! CLAP!
The crowd claps for me
I played a great game
Everybody could see
There were four seconds left
The ball came to me
We were down by two and I shot a three
Everything was silent
The net went SWISH
Then the crowd erupted
Everyone was screaming
And everyone cheered for me, the game's MVP.

*John Orlando, Grade 8*
*St Luke School*

### I've Finally Won

In this industry we're just a big family.
And this is all just some sibling rivalry.
But it sucks being the youngest out of the bunch.
Always being last to get breakfast, dinner, and lunch.
But right now I'm rising to the top of the can.
So bro, you're no longer the man.
That must be a bitter pill to swallow
That it's filled with sorrow, like it's hollow.
I'm sorry but now I'm the man, you're the son.
In this battle, I've finally won.
And now I'm the one who's victorious.
And the taste of victory, it tastes so glorious.

*Jordan Aposhian, Grade 7*
*Bellwood Antis Middle School*

## Dad

You were the one, who was always there for me,
You were able to make me smile and laugh when I would be upset.
You get anyone to laugh when they would be upset.
Some days I just wish that I could hear your laugh again,
And feel your hugs.
There's so much I wish I could tell you, but it'd take too much time.
I know that there are times when it's like so much has been happening and you aren't here to see me grow up anymore.
You will always be in my heart.
No one could ever take your place in my heart.
If our family was a solar system, you'd be the sun that would heat up our solar system.
You could make anyone happy if they were sad, and you just stayed positive and helped people when they most needed it.
I don't understand why you passed, neither does Grandma or Grandpa.
What I would do just to see you and have you here on Earth with me.
People judge others for what they look like on the outside, and it's not right.
Don't judge others until you take a step into their shoes and what they have been through.
You always told me since I was a little girl.
I dream about being your little princess again and going back to all our memories.
On Father's Day it's hard because a lot of kids get to have their dad and you are in Heaven.
Forever in my heart, and never forgotten.

*Deanna Gockley, Grade 8*
*Ephrata Middle School*

## Letter to Dad

Hey Dad,
Just know that I didn't have a choice in this.
My homosexuality is my mentality and I didn't have a voice in it.
But what you did was wrong. You left me all alone in the dark with the shades drawn. Did I embarrass you? Is that what it was?
Am I the son you never wanted? The one you left with no hugs and unloved?
Or was it me that drove you away? I can't apologize for what I've done
Because this is me in every way. But I wasn't the only one confused
When you learned what was so-called "wrong."
You kind of got caught up and froze. But that's when I needed you the most.
You by my side. Your support could have gotten me through the darkest of times. While you were being selfish, who was I to run to?
All I had was my confused conscience and the little memory that I had of you. Why were you afraid of me? Was "unconditional love" not fond enough for you to save me?
I'm not coming to you out of anger or a way to get you back.
But to let you know that nothing that you do will seal up my cracks. But don't worry, because the truth has set me free. I fly high above the people that look at me as though they hate me.
This woman I call mother is here caressing my hand, wiping away these tears, and telling me her love is indefinite.
Your absence is infinite and your heart isn't listening. Never forget, Kyle

*Markeeta Davis, Grade 9*
*Motivation High School*

## The Winning Score

BOOM, POW, SLAM
The pain that rushes through your body when you get hit really hard
You are so nervous that that might happen again
The ball is thrown, the air is screaming, your stomach feels like a million raging bulls running
The ball gets closer and closer and closer
BOOM, SMACK, YAY
You catch the ball and the millions of people watching scream
The referee yells TOUCHDOWN and the scoreboard reads 27 to 26
Your team runs over, puts you on their shoulders, and runs what seems like a mile to the sideline
Every football player's dream

*Quentin Potts, Grade 8*
*Centerville Middle School*

## Philippines

Palm trees surrounding me
The bright sun beats down
Against my skin
Smiling faces of people
Feel at home
Island to island
Feeling the soft white sand
Between your fingers
Like a pillow: soft, puffy, and smooth
Looking over
The blue ocean, fresh
As dawn brews in,
Delicious ethnic foods
Is what I enjoy.
I am a Filipina at heart,
These are a part of me.
*Amor Amante, Grade 7*
*William Penn Middle School*

## My Miracle

I asked God for a miracle,
One especially fine,
And in a way so pleasantly,
He gave me friends divine,
Whether blonde, brunette, or ginger,
I know they're always there,
To help me through my troubles,
Because they really care,
They aren't dressed in robes of silky white,
They don't have the soft, white wings,
They don't have the sparkling halos,
None of those fancy things,
But God did send me angels,
Only in human form,
To brush away my darkness,
And help me to reform.
*Alyssa Voland, Grade 7*
*Slippery Rock Area Middle School*

## Fall

Leaves fly and dance
Through the space
Like an airplane dives
When flown by an ace

They fall to the ground
And sit for a while
Waiting to be
Raked into a pile

And one day
They will be gathered
But for now
They are still scattered
*Justin Orefice, Grade 7*
*Pennbrook Middle School*

## Canoe Creek

Riding my bike
Down a long winding path
Wind in my hair
Trees swaying
And sunset downing

Swerving around turns
I look at the sky
Sporting a beautiful bird
As I speed past
Seems like the world isn't so fast

The sounds are amazing
Birds chirping like a chorus
The water's waves
My wheel going round and round
And the slow breathing of the air

The dirt on my feet
From my tires spinning
I thought that the trail would never end
But now it was
So it's time to reunite with my family again
*Cheyanne Sisto, Grade 8*
*Bellwood Antis Middle School*

## Just Say a Silent Prayer

When your burden is heavy,
Too hard for you to bear;
Just bow your head and close your eyes,
And say a silent prayer.

When everything seems to be going wrong,
And life seems so unfair;
Just bow your head and close your eyes,
And say a silent prayer.

When your world is turned upside-down,
And no one seems to care;
Just bow your head and close your eyes,
And say a silent prayer.

When the sun is blocked out by clouds,
And gloom hangs in the air;
Just bow your head and close your eyes,
And say a silent prayer.

I know that you've had many troubles,
Maybe more than your fair share;
But doubts can rise and fly away,
When you say a silent prayer.
*Lydia Beiler, Grade 7*
*Shade Mountain Christian School*

## The Ocean

The sun gets angry
and attempts to burn my skin.

Mysteries hidden
underneath…
wanting to be discovered.

The sun looks down at the water,
spreading its bright
bold
and beautiful
reflection.

Waves gently carry the broken seashells
onto the shore and set them down
on the wet slimy sand until
the liquid mountains come back
to claim the shells as their own.

As they are being carried back
underneath the ocean,
they get closer and closer
to their resting place
for the next few days.
*Makena Szejko, Grade 7*
*Schuylkill Valley Middle School*

## Africa

Depression lingers in the air
No food, no fresh water to share
Filthy clothes on their backs
Cold, sad, scared
Looking for a home to stay
Urging for an education
Selfless
No one to love
Dying of starvation

We can…
We can sponsor
We can share
We can be selfless
We can be caring

There can be…
More going to school
More with clothes
More with food and fresh water
No more depressing times
No more cold or scared
No more gloomy days
*Rebecca Westrom, Grade 7*
*Indian Valley Middle School*

### Forever

I was on a never-ending road
stretching out in front of me
like a long ribbon going on into eternity.

To my right was pure sand, untouched,
just daring me to take a step into the unknown
to disturb the peace of the blinding calmness.

To my left was an ocean of souls
lost in its depths, crying for help
they called me forward
but my feet were glued
to that never-ending road.

I was an obstacle on my own path
where it led, I don't know.
I just hope that someday I will get there.

For now, I am leaning on sorrow;
I am standing on hope.

To my left is an ocean of souls
to my right is an undiscovered desert

I want to make a choice,
but my feet are forever glued on that
never-ending road.

*Rachel Boward, Grade 8*
*Moon Middle School*

### Why?

Why do fields of wheat and rye
Filled with the rewards of bountiful life
Have to be tarnished with wear and tear
To be bludgeoned aside without a care

Why does doubt enfold our minds
Covered in webs of wicked disguise
An arrow that seeks to destroy
Any noticeable peasant boy
Or any man or woman that wants the freedom to think

Why do we think as we do
In a place where our selfish thoughts yearn to be true
When we will do as we must to get what we desire
And cause the world's problems to swell higher

Why do we lie
Why do we fight
Why do we hate
Why do we try
To thwart each other's actions
When all we need to do
Is agree

*John Morris, Grade 9*
*Holicong Middle School*

### Who Are You?

You were my best friend.
We were close like two peas in a pod.
You had my back, I had yours.
Then someone came along…everything changed.
Words,
Actions,
Friendship,
Now I don't know who you are.
Whatever happened to the times we used to have?
All the laughter,
Memories,
Smiles
Now all there is between us is
Fighting,
Lies,
And secrets
Whatever happened to the person I used to know?

*Jessica Weber, Grade 8*
*Donegal Middle School*

### My Teacher

I once had a teacher,
Her name we will not speak.
When I first met her,
I didn't care much for her,
But in time,
And by time I mean hours after school,
She grew on me,
She grew on me to the point
That I don't know what I'd do without her.
Through literary magazines and drama club.
I know the day must now come soon
That I will say goodbye,
Not goodbye forever but for awhile
I will not forget how much she means to me,
A second mother if you will,
And I hope she will not forget me either.
Always my second mother.

*Joe Carter, Grade 8*
*Bellmar Middle School*

### The Race

The engine revs, saying "Ready to go."
Bang! The starter gun yells "Go!"
The wheels turn and run, panting as they go.
The wheels yell and scream as they lose rubber on a drift.
The whole car yells, pushing itself.
The engine groans to keep going.
A pit stop keeps the tires running.
The tank sighs after its drink of fuel.
Final lap, second place right behind —
the tires scream, the engine roars, the axle squeals in pain.
The tires can't hold on, but they push
and the car passes in a photo finish.

*Derek Yenser, Grade 7*
*Tulpehocken Jr/Sr High School*

## Best Friends

**B** est Friends are Forever!
**E** xchange funny and weird stories
**S** omeone you can trust
**T** ell you the truth

**F** inds ways to make you smile
**R** andomly laughing over all the memories
**I** always want to hang out with them
**E** ncourage you through everything
**N** ever will let you down
**D** orky and dangerous but I love them!
**S** omeone you cannot live without

*Kathleen King, Grade 7*
*Northgate Middle/High School*

## I Don't Know Why

I don't know why she won't talk to me
I really want to know
We have been friends since preschool
And then in 5th grade it all started
She didn't talk to me at all
I tried asking her why
But she doesn't seem to respond
And we still don't talk today at all
Maybe it was meant to be
Maybe she found new friends
So I guess we have gone
Our own separate ways

*Sabrina Bojarski, Grade 8*
*Wattsburg Area Middle School*

## Sunset

Sun, that was once so high
Sliding down the horizon
Inch by inch,
You fall with a sigh.
Your blood-red streaks at twilight go
Remaining is your glow.

There you go, out of sight,
There is now no light.
You'll be back tomorrow bright.
I'll say goodbye again at night.

*Christina Kowalski, Grade 8*
*Bellwood Antis Middle School*

## Fire and Water

Fire
Dangerous, bright
Burning, heating, flickering
Inferno, blaze, deluge, monsoon, dripping
Falling, plopping, essential
Relentless
Water

*Ari Feldman, Grade 7*
*Strath Haven Middle School*

## The Whisper Shadow

My eyes come and go but they're always open.
Millions reaching to pierce your soul.
Black as a sinner's heart, my teeth could cut you just from smirking.
My mouth never closes.
It's always wide in a sickening grin.
You shudder as you feel it in the inner depths of your soul.
White as chalk, but just as grotesque.
My rancid body can take on many form.
Never knowing which one I'll show up as.
I whisper in your ear, telling everything you don't want to hear, the truth.
You may try to run from me, changing the subject, but I never entirely leave.
Light is my enemy, and I despise the feeling.
Oh, I may retreat and plan for the right time.
That is the only time I scowl.
But when your heart is vulnerable and ready to be stolen.
When I frown and you think you've gotten rid of me.
I'll still crack a smile, to think of ways to ruin your day.

*Candace Price, Grade 9*
*State College High School South*

## 4 Seasons

While it snows all day in winter
I'm inside being a baker
Kristen's outside making snowballs
The water is frozen on a small pond

In spring it all thaws
Flowers bloom…
Roses are red
Violets are blue

When summer comes around
We run out of school
Jump in the pool or
Take a nice stroll

As fall comes,
Colors are a radiant sight
When it comes to an end
Leaves die
Winter begins our cycle again

*Sarah Heffler, Grade 7*
*North Pocono Middle School*

## Important Me

The important thing about me is
That I am me
I don't try to be someone else
And I am quite ordinary
Sure, I am good at football and wrestling,
And I am smart,
And my favorite color is green,
But the important thing about me is
That I am me

*Matt Shirey, Grade 8*
*Penn Middle School*

## Weeping Willow

As the willows weep at night,
I hear the cry of the wind,
They tell the willows to speak,
As if they were humans

As the willows weep at night,
I see the moon that peeks,
Through the cotton candy clouds,
And the bats reaching for the sweet treat

As the willows weep at night,
I hear the branches screech for help,
Weeping from loneliness,
And no sun to give them hope

As the willows weep at night,
I walk out the door,
I see the moon, the trees, the bats,
And the clouds,
I lay down as they rock me to sleep

*Desirae Butler, Grade 8*
*Ephrata Middle School*

## Fear of the Unseen

The future is a ghost,
Who can decide its path?
When you try to run,
Why is it always one step ahead?

It is the unseen, the invisible,
The distant, the unreachable
When will the moment arrive?
That it becomes real?

*Sonnet Woodrow, Grade 8*
*Penn Middle School*

## Goal

5 seconds,
Left on the clock
Puck is passed,
My heart
R-a-c-e-s,
As I drive the puck,
To the net,
I take the slap shot…
!!!Score!!!
0-1 is the final score,
As we win the cup,
The team cheers,
They skate onto the ice,
As the stands cheer,
The team hugs the goalie,
They bring the cup out,
We hold it up in the air,
Then the astonishment,
Kicked in and I was,
Happy.

*Kyle Santos, Grade 7*
*William Penn Middle School*

## Better Yet

Bombs blazing,
Bullets flying,
Men on the ground,
Motionless,
Homes worried,
Are the safe?
Are they hurt?
People dying,
No one to help.
There is a better way,
We just have to,
Drop our weapons,
Fight no more,
Come home from war,
*Better yet*,
War is over,
*Better yet*,
*All* people stop fighting,
*Better yet*,
World peace.
*Timothy Hanlon, Grade 7*
*Indian Valley Middle School*

## The Future Grows Green

Imagine a beautiful breeze
   little, gentle, and warm.
It makes your heart blossom,
it continues through the night,
      past the moon,
where the future grows green.
*Kaylee Luchansky, Grade 8*
*Saegertown Jr/Sr High School*

## The Ocean

It's a place that will calm your senses,
   And carry your worries away.
      Waves are pulling at you,
         Begging one to stay.
      Hungry seagulls fly above,
         Ready to attack.
   For if you drop a piece of food,
   It will become their tasty snack.
      Stop for just a moment,
         To slowly smell the air.
      Do you sense that saltiness,
         Drifting everywhere?
   Children are laughing loudly,
      Their imaginations free.
      The ocean is our home,
         A place for you and me.
*Olivia Miller, Grade 7*
*St Luke School*

## The World We Live In

The world we live in.
Full of pain, full of sadness,
Full of heartbreaks, full of madness.
The world we live in.
Full of love, full of smiles,
Full of laughter, full of style.
The world we live in.
Full of confusion, full of hate,
Full of unknowns, full of fate.
The world we live in.
Full of people, full of sweets,
Full of music, full of beats.
The world we live in.
We might not always get our way,
But we were born for a reason,
So let's live another day.
*David Rosen, Grade 9*
*Susquehanna Township High School*

## World Peace

The world is a beautiful place
filled with many religions,
which includes the entire human race.
It's like a stone unwritten.

God is the key to the lock
like the unwritten rock
feel the need to have peace again
yet the world is in so much pain.

Every religion has its own ways.
Just count all the days.
It's just like lilies on the moon,
also like the summer sun in June.
*Cassidy Blankenbiller, Grade 7*
*Tulpehocken Jr/Sr High School*

## Modesty

when i think of
simplicity
i dream of
whiteness
found in the
oddest of places.

most will think of
naïveté
country cottages
flowers blooming
paint drying.

but i believe it's
more than that
like hidden forests
small towns
light rain.

how about little lies
told out of friendship
or family gatherings.

life is full of
simple pleasures.
*Joseph Montesrin Jr., Grade 8*
*L B Morris Elementary School*

## Poverty

Poverty isn't my cousin
Poverty isn't my lover
Poverty isn't my preacher
And poverty isn't my teacher

Poverty is not my wish
It isn't the song I sing
It isn't my answer
And poverty isn't my dream

Poverty isn't my brother
It isn't the hand I hold
Poverty can't be my anger
Poverty isn't my spirit or soul

But poverty is real
It's stuck in our minds
It slashes through our hearts
And leaves us all deaf and blind

Poverty stays with us
It's our haunting companion
It's the aching cold we feel inside
Because poverty
Is what we become.
*Saige Kling, Grade 7*
*Indian Valley Middle School*

### For the Future

I am from the Chesapeake Bay at Charter Hall,
And fishing with family all around.
From washing dishes in a steamy vacation-house kitchen,
And slurping root-beer floats around a big table.

I am from reading a good book in front of the fireplace,
And riding bike on a hot summer day.
From playing flute in Ephrata marching band,
And singing crazy songs in chorus.

I am from sledding down a super-steep hill,
And hot chocolate waiting inside the frosty windows.
From elementary coloring with worn out crayons,
And pastel painting with rainbow-colored hands.

I am from encouraging family and friends,
And many moments I never want to leave.
From past and present,
And hopes for the future.

*Karly Potts, Grade 8*
*Ephrata Middle School*

### When I Thought That I Had It

When I thought that I had it in class that one day
It turned out I didn't. There's not much to say.
I knew it was perfect, yet the goals were not met.
There was still technique he said I can't get.

My yell was not strong enough. He said it was weak.
My eyes were not fierce enough. They hadn't reached the peak.
Yet I know it meant well; that's what I'll always think.
He will always know what's wrong before I can blink.

It truly is great having a Grandmaster like mine.
He will always be there to show me the line.
Not only does he teach me more Taekwondo skill
But also more character, such as spirit and will.

Like an eagle he hovers over me in the class
And picks off the rats that scuttle in my grass.
If not for him in my life in this way,
I wouldn't be the person that I am today.

*Stefan Jablokow, Grade 7*
*Pennbrook Middle School*

### March Harmony

March creeps through the grass
like a leprechaun moving unperceived toward a pile
of gold that seems to gleam.
He searches for shamrocks and anything green.
And when he sees the month is no more,
he scurries back to Ireland
where there's always an open door.

*Alex Opdenaker, Grade 7*
*Garnet Valley Middle School*

### Rainbows

Black is the pitch dark filling the sky
White is the fluffy snowflakes that fly

Red are blossoming roses glistening to me
Orange is a big juicy orange on the tree

Yellow is bitter sour lemons you can't beat
Green is crunching leaves that the caterpillars eat

Blue is the warm beach ocean water
Violet is the fire when it gets hotter

These colors make a big lollipop

*Andrea Zook, Grade 7*
*Pequea Valley Intermediate School*

### The Beach

The tide comes rushing in
To the shore
I walk along the coast
My friend Bailey is at my side
We surf, build sand castles
And laugh at the way we wrote our name in the sand
She doesn't look
A wave throws her into the sand
The water topples me then, too
As we look at our strange appearances,
We laugh until a wave hits us again
And once more
We are covered in sand and seaweed

*Hannah DeBone, Grade 8*
*Bellmar Middle School*

### Wishes

I wish I could fly to the moon,
I wish I could swim to the bottom of the sea,
I wish I could be as tall as a tree.

I wish I could breathe fire like a dragon,
I wish I could do everything there is to do,
I wish that all my wishes would come true.

*Vanessa Charles, Grade 8*
*Lancaster Mennonite School - Locust Grove*

### Veteran

V ery strong passion to fight for our country.
E verlasting strength.
T rusting to protect us.
E veryone giving up family for others.
R egiments that stuck together no matter what.
A ir force.
N avy.

*Scott McGarvey, Grade 7*
*Cambria Heights Middle School*

**Stay Awhile**

I wrote our names
Side by side
Come with me
Along for the ride

Trust yourself
I know you'll get by
Just one chance
To make me cry

It doesn't work
It never could
Why don't we just stop
We knew we would

But then I found
The words to my favorite song
Written on your hands,
And on all of the stalls

So we relax and forget
Try not to smile
But we laugh too much
As you say "Stay awhile."
*Stefanie Gorson-Marrow, Grade 8*
*Paxon Hollow Middle School*

**All I Wanted Was You**

Almost seven years ago
but it seems like yesterday
that you left me
on a cold October day.

I never saw it coming
it made my family fuss
never thought it would be me
not my family, not us.

You told me you loved us
but it didn't seem that way
you left in a hurry
as I watched you drive away.

All I wanted was you
to watch, to care
but it never occurred to me
that you wouldn't even dare.

All you cared about was her
while I was home very sad
barely seeing you at all
and all I wanted was you Dad.
*Ashley Hildebrand, Grade 8*
*Spring Grove Middle School*

**Tiger Cat**

I run around the room
Jumping on everything.

My owner laughs and giggles
When I pounce on my
Gray, little, rubber mouse.

And the little girl
That loves me so
Watches me with large blue eyes.

She pets my fur which makes me purr
Slowly I drift off to sleep and dream.

I dream of a fierce tiger running.
A fiery color as it bolts past,
Its green eyes glowing in the dark.

Slowly sneaking behind
Plants of all kinds
Stalking its prey
In the dead of night.

Suddenly I wake up,
And imagine me being that
Fierce cat.

A tiger cat.
*Andrea Seitz, Grade 9*
*Bishop McCort High School*

**Poverty**

Deserted roads sad souls
Poor families no food to share
Worse thing is
Not many people care

No chances for kids
That are very smart
They are too poor
To afford a chance
In this cruel world

We can give we can share
Reach out a hand
Just show you care
I can see hope on the horizon
Join together make a difference

It's getting better
People are donating more and more
This money makes a big difference
Of the lives of these poor people
Maybe for once everyone can be EQUAL
*Vito Davi, Grade 7*
*Indian Valley Middle School*

**This Is Home**

The place we always want to see,
The place we always want to be,
How do we forget,
This is home.

Where so many memories are made,
Where we all laughed and played,
The place we all belong,
This is home.

The place we all love,
The place that is high above,
The place where everyone is free,
This is home.

The place we know is right,
The place we think of every night,
The place that is long-awaited,
This is home.

Where people hope to go,
One place all Christians know.
The place that God has shown.
Oh, this is home.
*Nick Chroscinski, Grade 8*
*Coventry Christian Schools*

**Memory**

These tears will subside.
This pain will ease.
I only want you here with me.

This time will pass.
These days will leave.
I only want to stop this dream.

These eyes will see.
This voice be heard.
I only want to spread my word.

This pen will fall.
This page will turn.
My name forgotten.

These eyes will close.
This body will numb.
I will go to my grave with words unsung.

But all the while your thoughts will stray…
Thinking of some distant day…
A brown-eyed girl with golden hair…
Is hiding in your dream somewhere…
*Cristin Sweeten, Grade 9*
*Hughesville Jr/Sr High School*

## What Does a Softball Player Know?

Strikes and balls
dives and falls
slap the ball off the wall
coaches yelling
fans booing
now I know what I should be doing
bats swinging
children singing
and we're only just beginning
*Hannah Wieller, Grade 7*
*Easton Area Middle School 7-8*

## A Journey to Success

The wind fills my sails
There is no turning back
Leaving the darkness behind me
There is nothing I might lack

The journey ends at the horizon
I have hopes and dreams
The path is straight in front of me
Living life to the extremes
*Brendan Bogolin, Grade 8*
*Pine-Richland Middle School*

## Not a Dream

Boom! The door slammed shut
Nobody heard it, not even my mutt
I went over to check it out,
Then suddenly, I heard a loud shout
I felt a chill run up my spine,
As the wind blew through the blind
I woke up relieved, it was only a dream,
Until I heard that same shrill scream.
*Alex Fisher, Grade 7*
*Garnet Valley Middle School*

## Hot Wing

**H** ot out of the fryer.
**O** h how I love you.
**T** antalizing my taste buds.

**W** ish I could eat you every day.
**I** just love the taste.
**N** ot nice if you don't share.
**G** ood thing there's one more left.
*Collin Dian, Grade 7*
*Pequea Valley Intermediate School*

## Hawaii

The sun is bright in the sky.
The birds overhead fly.
The ocean is steps away,
And beautiful palm trees sway.
*Anna Woznicki, Grade 7*
*St Luke School*

## Jolly Rancher

I watch. The basket of fruity colorful ranchers,
Goes around the room.
Rows of classmates eagerly choosing flavors.

They're just about ready to eat when — No! Not yet.
Learning to describe nouns and actions of you and the Rancher.
Waiting and waiting until, finally, the sound of unwrapping,

Fills the room like air in a balloon.

Pink, purple, blue, and red
In the mouths of those savoring them.
The taste of grand grape grows great in my mouth.
Slowly, I savor it all the best I can.

As it disappears, I taste the last of my purple Rancher,
Until it dissolves to nothing.

What was once a bouncing burst of flavor was now still.

Now with my purple tongue,
All that is left of that once juicing Rancher.
Knowing it's over,
I look back to see tables of kids with no Ranchers.

Here I am, unwrapping another one, starting over that sweetening experience.
*Antonia Sarria, Grade 8*
*Danville Area Middle School*

## Till' Death Do Us Part

One day while I was walking
I saw a light on the top of a hill.
When I saw this light I decided to follow it.
The light continued to move and sway with the wind.

The darker it got outside
The brighter the light got.
It shined and shined until the world was bright as day.
It shined and rose up into the sky and reached for the stars.

When the light finally reached the midnight sky
It looked almost as if it replaced the sun,
The way it brightened up the world
Like the smile of the woman you love, it brought joy to the world.

All of the lights in the cities went out for everyone to focus on the activity
Going on below, another light, just the same, rose up next to it.
These two lights were very similar
And you knew that they were meant to be with each other.

These two lights never went out
And they stayed by each other's side every moment.
They shined and continued to brighten the earth together,
Until the day when they went out, happily, together.
*Joey Rump, Grade 7*
*Redeemer Lutheran School*

## The Past

Can't you realize
The past is the past?
You ain't ever going back.
It's over now, honey.
Just start new,
You'll be better off.
Don't be scared
I'll always be
In your heart.
When it feels
Just right and
There's nowhere
Else to turn,
You'll have me.
But, just remember
The past is the past,
We ain't ever going back
*Audrey Tyler, Grade 8*
*Blue Ridge Middle School*

## Spring Flowers

The vibrant colors of the flowers
That spread across the field,
Are a result of the spring showers
That rarely ever yield

In the midst of July
This is what I favor most,
For when they disappear I sigh
These flowers only come to boast

They are dying now,
Many of them already are
Their little tiny heads they bow,
The days of fall are not that far

Their life will resume next year,
Bringing me yet more cheer
*Lindsay Pembleton, Grade 8*
*Lake-Lehman Jr High School*

## Relationship

I was relaxing one summer day
remembering our date
I miss his gentle embrace
Walking together giggling
as we talk about our future
We stopped to talk about our future
We stopped and stared at the clouds
trying to guess what they looked like
we gazed into each other's eyes
as he told me he loved me
that's when I realized
that I love him too
*Emily Morris, Grade 8*
*Saegertown Jr/Sr High School*

## Kayaking

Kayaking is lots of fun;
Downstream we will float.
We'll paddle through the rapids,
Through rocks we'll guide our boat.

Silver ripples lining
The path that we have took,
Rainbow trout are leaping
From the sunlit brook.

'Round a bend we're gliding,
There, upon a rock,
A snapping turtle splashes
Back into the brook.

Now the sun is sinking,
The western sky turns red.
We'll beach on yonder island,
Eat, and make our bed.
*Walter Unruh, Grade 7*
*Rockhaven Christian School*

## The Meaning of Life

The meaning of life to me,
Means most certainly a lot.
I tell myself to live life to the fullest,
Because life is all I got.

I have not yet made a bucket list,
Yet I have been told I should.
I'd rather allow my future to happen,
And live all the experiences that are good.

Dr. Seuss once said,
That life's a big balancing act,
To always step with great care,
As well as to step with great tact.

Now remember all these things,
That I have shared with you.
For if you are asked the meaning of life,
All answers may as well appear true.
*Ally Bish, Grade 7*
*Landisville Middle School*

## Markkuss

**M** inecrafts
**A** wesome
**R** adically
**K** illing
**K** iller Creepers
**U** sing
**S** ilver
**S** words
*Nicholas Cosentino, Grade 7*
*Northgate Middle/High School*

## Path of Life

When in church we bow our heads
A blessing for the food he gives
I walk with Jesus as he guides me
With the love from him, I always feel safe
I talk to Him, it holds my faith
As I travel down this path called life
I run into situations that cut like a knife
He pulls me back and holds my hand
And I know, things will be okay
My days get better as I pray
Day becomes night and night becomes day
I keep him close all the way
He is my best friend I can always trust
He takes his time, never in a rush
Just walk with the Lord
Always keep your faith
The angels watch from the sky
A bright blue place
Empty is a wish upon stardust
Send one upon Christ's light of love
Send a prayer of Jesus dove
*Oasiz Whiting, Grade 8*
*Penn Middle School*

## Free

This wooden board
Keeping my back straight,
Will eventually break my bones
This familiar world the sun hasn't shone
This is my last reflection
When the moon has shined its last light
Into the dark waters
And the stars take place
Change me to see the colors of this world
Before it disappears to white
I move to the sunrise
Where I belong
Gone to the sky,
Off the sand,
My footprints are washed
My path is cleaned
And time takes me further
To the start of the game
I think of my farewells
And feel the light glaze me
I am free
*Mariann Do, Grade 9*
*North Hills High School*

## Spring

A gentle breeze blows through the air.
The leaves rustle ever so lightly.
The songs of nature fill the air.
Spring has approached us.
*Kassandra Whiteford, Grade 7*
*Cambria Heights Middle School*

## Shattered Soul

As the sweetest moments
Turn into the deepest despair
All that is left is a shattered soul
Striving to become whole again
It's a shade with no corporal form
It starts, but never ends
Deceived by her black heart
Destroyed by her chaotic beauty
It wanders unknowingly
Without her touch
That's so potent it kills
But so addictive
That once felt, you can't get enough
Otherworldly with its presence, it takes life
Like a lion does a lamb
Held between life and death
As the lion dances and the lamb goes motionless
One is sated, the other obliterated
Life goes on in this despair
While this soul is still shattered
Beyond repair

*De'sia Blackwell, Grade 9*
*Multi-Cultural Academy*

## Back Then Today

'Twas not far in the greatest past,
lived two families, three civil brawls last.
While thither, it was fate that thou met.
It was the greatest story two loves hath made,
for it was in Verona where both have stayed.
At the ball, under the masks, incognito they are.
Thus foe families their love was forbidden.
Behind beauty and charm their feelings were hidden.
Both figures are star-crossed and young.
On the balustrade the mood was set,
but yet one knew of his untimely death.
It was love that brought them to rest.
For on the day they lived and passed,
they knew their love would never last.
They were taken into a piece by Will.

*Elizabeth Ruth, Grade 9*
*Southern Lehigh High School*

## In My Own Little World

In my own little world I see her.
Or maybe not.
I can see him.
Or maybe not.
In the real world I can touch their graves.
This is about it.
In my world I can feel how sad they are.
My world may not be normal or what you want.
But I am not normal either.
Or am I?

*Tyara Snyder, Grade 7*
*Schuylkill Valley Middle School*

## 00:54 Seconds Left

I was breathing hard as I brought the ball up the court.
*Dribble Dribble*
I glanced at the clock
00:54 seconds left in the game.
We were down by two and everyone was shouting
"C'mon! Concentrate!"
I felt like the world was on my shoulders.
I made a mistake
And the defense quickly became offense.
*Dribble Dribble*
I was sprinting as I took back the ball.
I crossed back over half-court like a jaguar.
The buzzer sounded...*beeeeeep*
I didn't think,
I just let my instincts take over and I shot the ball.
*Swish*
I didn't comprehend that I won the game
Until my teammates lifted me up onto their shoulders
And cheered and cheered.
Wow!
I won the game for my team, we are undefeated.

*Sierra Stevens, Grade 8*
*Bellwood Antis Middle School*

## Valentine's Day Sorrow

Valentine's Day was to be full of joy
But all I got was the loss of my sweet boy
He was hit hard by a careless driver
Crawling back came my little survivor
I waited for the call shocked and scattered
Only to find out, his spine had shattered
The only option was for him to die
All I wanted was to lay there and cry
I've seen my dad cry for the first time ever
Who would've known we would see so much terror
I miss him smiling and wagging his tail
Every day after seems like an epic fail
I never knew losing you could be so hard
Thinking about you catches me off guard
You were always so cheerful and lively
All I say now is, "I love you, Riley"

*Lauren Hite, Grade 7*
*Cambria Heights Middle School*

## July

Blazing hot days
Beautiful night gaze
From swimming to tanning
Fireworks to tasty popsicles
To staying up late, watching the sun set
To grass tickling the soles of your feet
To butterflies kissing flowers, bee stings and beaches

Oh, summer! Oh, summer! Please come to me.

*Marisa Hornberger, Grade 8*
*Ephrata Middle School*

## Dreamed Love

The day I met you was the best day of my life.
Our eyes met,
Time stopped,
Everyone seemed to freeze.
True love at first sight!
We met in front of the café
On the corner of my street.
Between the coffee and the laughter,
I knew we were something to be.
By the time a year came around,
You approached me with a ring.
My eyes teared up and my legs started to shake.
I nodded my head as the words yes broke through my sealed lips.
As we stand at the altar of our church,
I recite my poem to you as my vow.
From this moment to the day I die,
But even then,
My heart will still grow
Because your love keeps me alive.

*Amanda Conway, Grade 8*
*St Luke the Evangelist School*

## Time for Peace

You see it every day,
Everywhere
Hate, bullying, crime, drugs…
Why can't we just have peace?
Peace and love is all we need.
It was once said by a wise man,
"Give peace a chance…
Imagine all the people, living life in peace…"
If we'd all imagine it, then it could be!
There would be no vandalism
No murders
No drugs
No suicides
No bullying
No hate
Only love
And that's the way it should be!
Ignore the haters,
Live, breath, sleep, peace.

*Teresa Bridge, Grade 8*
*Danville Area Middle School*

## Just Me

I wish I knew how to become invisible
then I could just disappear
but I do know that I would be better right here

I wish I could fly like a bird
then I could be free to explore and soar
but I know I can explore on my own by traveling the world

I wish I was a dog
then I wouldn't have any responsibilities at all
but I know I have a good life as I am

I wish I would freeze time
then I could have more time for fun
but I know I will have time after my work is over and done

I wish to be a movie director
then I could work with what I love
but I'm happy just being me.

*Andrea Kleckner, Grade 8*
*Pine-Richland Middle School*

## Baseball

Bottom of the ninth
Two outs bases loaded
I'm stranded out on this island
All alone on the pitchers mound
No one in front
No one behind
Neither the sides
The wind up
The pitch
Crack!!!
The bat screamed!
The ball whistled past my face like a steam engine
I look back to the short stop
The captain who is supposed to make plays
At a time like this
A dive...
Smack!
The ball hit his glove,
Game over we had won

*Dante Sienko, Grade 8*
*Pine-Richland Middle School*

## Strong

When people accuse you of something you did not do,
Everyone knows that's it is up to you,
To stand up for yourself and stay strong,
Even when you know they are wrong.
Don't sink to their level, just let it go by,
Don't give them the satisfaction of seeing you cry.
Stand with your head up high.

*Christie Guthridge, Grade 7*
*Pennbrook Middle School*

## See Me

One window is all I need to show you the real me
To prove the real me is here
To show you what I can be
For people to appreciate me when I am near
To do my best in everything I do
And to show you I am someone too
One window is all I need

*Nicolas Karg, Grade 7*
*Pequea Valley Intermediate School*

## People

People
Going places
And running everywhere.
Time is escaping them
Fast.

*Tyler Varvel, Grade 8*
*Northern Lebanon Middle School*

## Weather

Some sunny,
Other days cloudy,
Many are very rainy,
Few days are extremely hot,
But the weather is very unpredictable.

*Paul Maust, Grade 7*
*Holy Sepulcher School*

## Easter

White lilies,
Painting Easter eggs,
Sights and sounds galore,
New life in the church,
Easter candy and chocolate in baskets.

*Ashley Blazczak, Grade 7*
*Holy Sepulcher School*

## Best Friends

Best friends stick together
No matter what the weather
Having fun
In the sun
Best friends forever

*Erin Ball, Grade 7*
*Easton Area Middle School 7-8*

## The Sleepy Reader

Olivia was reading a book,
Standing upright in her nook.
But, she fell asleep,
Dead on her feet.
And the book didn't get a second look.

*Olivia Stouffer, Grade 7*
*Big Spring Middle School*

## Swimming

There once was a girl named Jule,
She loved to swim in a pool
The fly and the free were her best,
She swam without even a vest
And all her friends thought that was cool.

*Julia Baur, Grade 8*
*Lake-Lehman Jr High School*

## A.D.D. (Attention Deficit Disorder)

A.D.D. is a gift from God
A gift that comes with a lot of responsibility
A gift that can focus your mind on things more important
But you can make you think about the wrong thing
You see from a whole new perspective
You work in different ways

People think that it is something bad
But it's not so bad at all
You can do things that others can't
You can learn in better ways
And of course it has its defects
But so does everything else

People wish they did not have this gift that God gave them, well don't
When people say you are special, it's in a good way
You are different from anyone else
But no one is the same
So take this advice I am offering to you
And make sure your choice is wise
Use your gift not as an excuse…

…Use it so you can be a success

*Luc Waugaman, Grade 8*
*Penn Middle School*

## Goodbye Winter

Spring comes to shake away our winter blues.
Flowers begin to peek out from the earth.
Little buds start to appear on tree branches.
Sunrises greet me in the mornings,
And sunsets shine through my window at night.
The smell of freshly cut grass and dew fills my nose,
While I'm on my way to school.
More and more children can be seen playing outside on the weekends.
Winter clothes get replaced by swimsuits, skirts, and t-shirts.
Jackets become thinner, pants become shorter.
Toes begin to peek out of sandals and flip flops.
The end of school seems so close yet so far away.
Classes are occasionally held outside under the rays of sunshine.
Summer vacations begin to be planned out,
Beach trips and parties get closer and closer.
Thank God for spring!

*Angela Charis Wise, Grade 9*
*Coventry Christian Schools*

## This Piece of Paper

This piece of paper, dull with nothing on it, lifeless,
Waits and waits to become something better than it actually is.
It is a seed, the first step of something magnificent.
And now it becomes a caterpillar waiting to become itself.
Now it is a cocoon developing changing.
Now it has become a butterfly, what it always wanted to be but could not achieve.
As I see this, I am amazed at what this paper has become.

*Harrison Leonard, Grade 7*
*Garnet Valley Middle School*

### Rainbow

The sun is shining bright as day,
No rain or sadness could take it away.
Yet, in a split second a thunderstorm can hit,
And all hope is lost and I'll have to quit.

Harder, harder the thunderstorm gets,
Never knowing when it might end.
Scared like a child,
But I will live.

Sing a happy song like the Frey,
And everything will be clear as day
The sun is back again,
And I'll finally win.

After all the sun and rain;
The happiness and sadness,
A perfect rainbow has formed.
A rainbow that will last a lifetime.

*Destiny Troutman, Grade 8*
*Pine-Richland Middle School*

### Summer in July

Staying outside in the bright warm sun
Placing the hot dogs in their crispy buns
Watching the fireworks burst in the sky
Flying my kite in the park so high

The sound of all the people lawn-mowing
As the grass is constantly growing
The motor running at the fastest pace
Leaving that fresh grass scent in its place

We celebrate our independence on the fourth day
Children love to go outside and play
Water slides and pools fill the backyards
Trying to cool down can be a little hard

The smell of juicy and greasy burgers on the grill
And the sound of kids rolling down the hills
Laughing and feeling on top of the world
Summer is definitely in full twirl

*Larry Rupp, Grade 8*
*Ephrata Middle School*

### Teachers

**T** each students important stuff.
**E** arn money when they work.
**A** ctions help students learn.
**C** omes on time everyday to teach.
**H** elps every student reach the fullest potential.
**E** very student counts.
**R** eally helps kids that want to learn.
**S** ticks up for every kid.

*Tyler Scott, Grade 7*
*Cambria Heights Middle School*

### Ocean Waves

Walking through the sand, sun beating on my face
Like a flame set fire to my nose, mouth, and eyes
I listen to the ocean, splash, crash!
On the sand
Oh dear, how wonderful it sounds
Sweet sea salt, fresh fish, and food are filling my nostrils
Crash, bang!
The ocean is colder than ice
I look down the beach one way,
No end
I look the other way,
No end
I look out to the ocean,
No end until the ocean meets the sky
The perfect blue forms
As I walk to the big blue water,
I feel the sand squish between my toes,
Shhhh…quiet now,
As I hear the ocean
Wash away my
Soul…

*Lindsey Southworth, Grade 7*
*Bellwood Antis Middle School*

### Abstract Art

Swirls, splatter, streaks
Dots, lines, designs
Splatter and globs of paint of a canvas
What do you recall abstract art is
A puzzle that needs to be pieced together
A puzzle that has multiple colors
A puzzle that just comes to mind
A design that comes straight from imagination
Shapes, spirals, people
Objects of your imagination
Dark dreary sketches
Ravens, dead trees and leaves, and red moons
Or cheery sketches
Those are full of color and design
Or just circles and squares that make up a picture
What do you think of abstract art

*Samantha Murphy, Grade 8*
*Ephrata Middle School*

### Gone

When I saw you I became sad.
All I wanted to know was why.
Why are you laying there skinny and pale?
Why are you sitting there silent and speaking no more?
Why can't you get up and cook our dinner?
How did you sit there and let yourself go?
Now you're not here…
You're gone.

*Casi Wolf, Grade 8*
*Wattsburg Area Middle School*

### April

April darts to us
Right after March
Rainy and wet, a bucket of water
It soaks the ground
With its determined tears
Tears drying, hands waving
It says goodbye as it solemnly leaves
*Martina Zuppo, Grade 7*
*Garnet Valley Middle School*

### June

June skips
Out the school doors
With children playing and laughing,
Jumping in the pool,
Making a big splash,
It swims away,
Leaving the pool for July to dive in
*Angela Burke, Grade 7*
*Garnet Valley Middle School*

### July

July darts
up high in the sky
with a field of fire.
It cooks the world
with its red-hot eyes.
It silently creeps away after all of its heat,
cooling down for August.
*Savannah Hake, Grade 7*
*Garnet Valley Middle School*

### Potter vs Dark Lord

Harry Potter
Benevolent, mortal
Running, saving, seeking
Only one can live
Chasing, killing, hiding
Sinister, immortal
Voldemort
*Brianne Balmer, Grade 8*
*Ephrata Middle School*

### Baseball Is Life

Baseball is home runs
Baseball is wins
Baseball is team
Baseball is second base
Baseball is double-plays
Baseball is everything
Baseball is life
*Ward Taraba, Grade 8*
*Fred S Engle Middle School*

### The Game of Hockey

I tie the helmet, slip on the gloves,
Slide on the jersey, and lace up the skates.
The ice is calling my name, and I sprint to the spotlight for the game.

The face-off begins, and I win the battle with pride.
Launching the puck to the other side, launching the puck to the other side.

A cross-check to the board leaves me dazed, but the whistle hasn't put a stop to the play.
My head might hurt, and I might feel the pain.
It might be hard to stand up, and I might feel ashamed.
That's the game of hockey.

My recovery is short, and the puck comes my way.
With the night burning away, I decide to take the final shot.
The adrenaline pumping through me is like a battle well fought.
I'll never know the result until the time runs out, but that's the game of hockey.

The lights dance around me, and time has stopped.
The swoosh of a goal puts me on top.
A new me is released, through the game of hockey.
*Carly Duncan, Grade 8*
*Pine-Richland Middle School*

### The Pool Over the Summer

Over the summer, the pool can be
As refreshing as an icy glass of lemonade.
When the hot sun is beating down,
Just jump into the water, like a pig jumps into mud.
It will cool you off in an instant, like a fire is put out with water.
It will be a huge relief, like that great feeling when
You finally complete a project.
When the sweat starts pouring down your forehead,
Like water runs out of a spigot, dive into that coolness,
Like a bird dives down to catch its prey.
You can relax in the pool, like a hippo wallows in the muck.
I promise you all of this when you jump into a pool over the summer,
Like your mom promises you that you will always be safe with her.
Unless, the pool you jump into is heated…
*Erica Sensenig, Grade 8*
*Ephrata Middle School*

### Jealousy Is Not Worth It

I have it
You have it
We all have it
Most of the time we don't want it
But have to live with it
Jealousy is in everyone
Even if you have everything
You always want more
Love can turn jealousy over the top
In time, love, live, and learn
Don't be jealous, be happy for what you have and don't want to loose
Dream if you can and live like you're dying, and have a life of love
*Abigail Ferraioli, Grade 7*
*Villa Maria Academy Lower School*

**The Snow Fall**
I sit and stare out the window
And watch the flakes fall
I wonder why they fall like confetti
As if we're happy it's here

Through the woods I walk and watch the world around me
Not looking for there is nothing to see
For it's all the same everywhere I go
Same shovel same snow

I strive to shovel the ever coming snow and
Shovel the super sliding slush and snow
As much as I can bear
For I keep putting it way as it keeps appearing

But as it drags me down, I can't help but smile
Winter is over the war is won
Spring is a coming
Spring is a coming
*Joey Weaver, Grade 8*
*Pine-Richland Middle School*

**I Am**
I am curious and caring
I wonder what animals are really thinking
I hear bells ringing
I see birds singing
I want life to be stress-free

I pretend that I don't care what people think
I feel my body ready to crash down
I touch the line of accomplishment
I worry that someday I will lose my real friends
I cry over things most people don't care about
I am curious and caring

I understand that people don't always get along
I say let's all be friends
I dream that one day life with be drama-free
I try to be the best person possible
I hope that one day everything will be okay
I am curious and caring
*Regan Donecker, Grade 7*
*Pequea Valley Intermediate School*

**Thanks**
I hear the loving, loud laughter of my family
As they arrive happily through the door.
Spending time with each other
A special day to be together.

Round the table we all come
To enjoy the meal that took all day.
The table is a mountain of colors
We give special thanks today.

The scent of the roasting turkey
Floats in the air like a cloud.
In a flash the food is gone
And all the hard work is done.

As we slice the pumpkin pie
The dishes cleared and washed,
We think of all the fun we had
And say goodbye until next year.
*Brittany Berg, Grade 8*
*Pine-Richland Middle School*

**Broken Heart**
The wind in my hair
the darkness in my eyes
each day comes more despair
you've been telling me nothing but lies

As I look up at the sky
I don't know what to do
but then I wonder why
I always think about you

But I'm trying not to care
or think about you
or wishing you were there
I'm trying to find someone new other than you

No matter what I do I can't have you
but I'm still outside as cold as ice
the wind is ice and I am frozen
sitting here with my heart broken
*Jeffrey Reaver, Grade 8*
*Spring Grove Middle School*

**Springtime**
Winter's time is up soon.
No longer will the freezing bite of winter
Linger anymore.

All of a sudden, spring barges in the front door
With vibrant bouquets of flowers
And plants of all sorts.
*Zack Swetz, Grade 9*
*Bishop McCort High School*

**Rapture**
Would you kindly? Rapture is
A capture. A place art and minds
Come together. A city where others
Are great and the ocean is like a mystery
Waiting to be discovered. Rapture is just like a city
that has been left from a vacation place but dangerous.
Would you kindly? Join the city of Rapture.
*Kylie Hoffman, Grade 8*
*Donegal Middle School*

### My Friend
My friends make me laugh a lot
They are fun to be around
My friends are trustworthy

My friends and I
Like to go to the mall together
We like to get ice cream
We love to go roller skating
We like to ride horses together

My friends are always nice
They believe in me even
When I do not believe in myself

My friends are always there for me
When I am down
They are always there for me
In good times and bad
*Kaitlin Fuller, Grade 7*
*Pequea Valley Intermediate School*

### The Dragonfly
Flashing by,
Is it a butterfly?
A zip of green,
Too fast to be seen,
A swirl of blue
Barely seen by you
A flash of red
A creature of dread?
Zig-zagging
Never lagging
Up, down, left and right
Is the pattern of its flight
It buzzes past
Going so fast
It doesn't land
It's hardly bland
It touches the sky
For it is a dragonfly
*Cory Kendall, Grade 8*
*Punxsutawney Christian School*

### Across from Me
On the train, there I see
A brown-eyed boy, across from me.
His name I will never know,
A stranger going to and fro.
I saw he was a Phillies fan,
I saw a Rubik cube in hand.
I know he had a smiling side,
I saw his braces flashing wide.
I know that again I never will see
That boy on the train across from me.
*Jona Lieberman, Grade 8*
*Paxon Hollow Middle School*

### Patacon
My baby scurries around,
He wants to see all of town.
With his strong smelling nose,
His curiosity grows.
But he is small
and can easily fall.
Off of edges and curbs,
His wandering wretches my nerves.
So he lives in his habitat,
He's nocturnal like a bat.
His hair is the color of snow
Every day my love for him grows.
Just a hamster he is not,
He is more like home,
And my heart he has got.
*Johanna Vallejo, Grade 8*
*Barack Obama Academy*

### The Guesser
I guess
I thought
You guessed it.

I guess
I thought
You knew.

Maybe I'm
Too fixed
On guessing

And not on
Finding out
The truth.
*Emmalyn Erisman, Grade 7*
*Shippensburg Area Middle School*

### Seagulls
Gracefully and vigilantly flying
It glides down at the sight of food
While watching the beach

Quickly, loudly, and violently
Fighting against an army of seagulls
Annoying the tourist on the boardwalk

Carefully and cautiously
Remaining still instead of searching
On the nest of its eggs

Sadly and unfortunately
The ocean seagull starves
And is brought back to the ocean
*Matt Choi, Grade 8*
*Penn Middle School*

### If I Was in the Air Force
If I was in the Air Force
I'd do some fun things fast
I'd make the best out of every day
Considering it my last.

If I was in the Air Force
I'd be cautious on patrol
Not knowing what I'm up against,
I could easily lose control.

If I was in the Air Force
I'd be always on my guard
Waiting, watching, every day
Timid where I play my cards.

If I was in the Air Force
I'd watch my every step
Venturing where they tell me to
Making sure to prep.
*Casey Campbell, Grade 8*
*Penn Middle School*

### Pollution
The sky is a murky gray cloud of darkness
There is an acid sour smell in the air
The ground is covered in filth
Waste is hiding the beautiful world
Filled with flowers
Gleaming sunlight
And warmth
It's your world and mine
Let's make it shine

Make a change for the better
we can do it together
Make a pretty world
Fill our world with happiness
Once again
People don't know
How much they can do
Make these gray skies
A beautiful blue
*Hannah Knol, Grade 7*
*Indian Valley Middle School*

### What a Cat Knows
The luscious smell of fish
The sound of food in a dish
Silent footsteps
The deepest of depths
How to chase mice
How to "play nice"
Playing with string
And springy toys: PING!
*Anna DeVault, Grade 7*
*Easton Area Middle School 7-8*

## Regala

Because when I was three,
I rode a horse,
Before then I never knew,
The joy of riding a horse,
Since that first ride, I always knew.
As if I was born to ride a horse,
The meeting of my own,
Led me to know,
She was the one,
That told me I knew.
That I was her rider,
That she was my steed,
While good days,
And bad days were in our way,
That nothing could take us apart.
Her name was Regala,
Who is now my soul mate,
We could never part,
Because we will love till the end,
When we ride the feeling will never be like any other,
Because together, we will always be champions.

*Isabella Schmidt, Grade 9*
*Holicong Middle School*

## Keep Up With the Beat

The trumpet screams a high C,
Sending chills through the crowd.
A bari sax belts out a soulful low A,
A soothing, warm feeling spreads.
Two slides and a half step later,
The trombone glistens in the glowing, glorious spotlight.
A twangy C chord escapes from the strings,
The guitar is ready to solo.
The bass walks up the fret board,
Deep and smooth, playing the blues.
A striking piano riff startles the audience,
Flying over the glossy, slick keys.
Paradiddle, double stroke, rim shot —
The drums cry out, like a sonic boom.

Jazz: the rhythm of my life.

*Natalie Kulak, Grade 7*
*Pennbrook Middle School*

## Spring Day

Buds pop up here and there,
While big bumble bees fly through the air.

You awake in the morning with the sight of dew,
While flowers pop up to see the view.

Spring is here,
So don't be late...
Jump up and celebrate!

*Kate Matyas, Grade 7*
*Landisville Middle School*

## Small Piece of Serenity

When you close your eyes
And think of the most pleasant place to be
You may picture something I call
A small piece of serenity
Where you may be at peace

The grass is green, very green
High waterfalls create a mist screen
Big tall trees of maple and pine
With rivers as long as the Rhine
With mountains that stretch across the horizon
And rocks and hills with running bison
Where you may be at peace

Colorful birds chirp like flutes
Trees catch your eye with tasty fruits
The sun shines the light of day
With the seasons of warm May
And you see a lake like the Victoria
That fills your little mind with wonder
And shows you a beautiful small piece of serenity

*Jonathan Bucci, Grade 8*
*Daniel Boone Middle School*

## A Journey

Wonderful, weird, wayward words,
Scattering themselves along a track,
Grouping with other words to make,
Cliques and sentences.

Simple, satisfactory, searching sentences,
Lined up like ants.
They move together to create,
Companies and paragraphs.

Pyknic, pyrrhic, penitent paragraphs,
Are gargantuan giants waiting to be
Beaten by a hero too shiftless to.
They cry together and form
Planets and stories.

Salient, soporific, sardonic stories
Simply sit there and
Are read and analyzed until not
One soul knows what they are rambling about.
They are compiled into series unread.

*Linda Yang, Grade 8*
*Danville Area Middle School*

## The Tear from the Sky

The light blue tear drop falls from the dark sky
Crying with sadness from leaving the $H_2O$ cloud
To begin a new life again
And again.

*Deven Corona, Grade 7*
*Fort Couch Middle School*

## Heat

Sweat trickling down my face,
Temperature skyrockets into oblivion,
Mercury in a thermometer explodes!
My body is melting butter on a sizzling skillet,
No food, no water, no creatures
Lifeless.

A tiny scorpion comes pinching my way,
I see illusions of water in a haze,
I run to it.
Nothing, Empty,
Lifeless.

My body heat goes up like instant wild fire.
My time has come,
My dreams are done,
I'm ready.
I'm ready.

I close my eyes and get into full poise,
But I snap them open as fast as lightning when I hear a noise.
Wind spinning 'round and 'round,
A helicopter above,
My flat hair fluttering in the breeze.
I'm saved, I'm rescued,
I am free.

*Shalaya Minor, Grade 7*
*C.C.A Baldi Middle School*

## April 15, 1912

The ground has slanted more now, nowhere to escape this hard,
long death. I can see the panic on the passengers'
faces as they run frantically through the crowd,
to escape the water rushing up the halls.

The lights glisten in the water at night.
Illuminating the pitch black sky are the distressed fireworks
rocketing through the night, to alarm others around us.

The panic muffles the usually loud crashing waves
as some women and children surface the ocean,
cries from the wives of the men still onboard,
grow softer as the women are lowered to survival.

So many questions race through my mind,
they said she would never go under.
Surprisingly the lights are still on.
How many people survive this death trap at sea?

Sadness rises in me as the reality of the situation hits me
the tragedy that people won't survive one more night.
I soon became frantic, thinking of my family,
and my life back home, that I should have never left.

Will I ever see that life again? Will I ever see that life again?
Will I ever see that life again?

*Shannon Boyle, Grade 7*
*Saucon Valley Middle School*

## Pictures Worth a Thousand Words

In a jewelry box I would keep
Pictures of my favorite memories
Photographs of places I saw before
And friends and family
Those pictures are worth a thousand words

There's a picture of the beach
Where I built my first sand castle
And also my first pinch from a crab
My little finger is red and numb
But the memories of that day was great

There's a picture of my first day of school
In my little uniform
I have my backpack on one shoulder
And a big grin on my face
Even though I was nervous that day

What picture is next for my jewelry box?
What adventures will I seek?
How much will I achieve?
Every step I take will be photographed
And they will be worth more than a thousand words

*Jenny Zheng, Grade 8*
*Sacred Heart Elementary School*

## A Cupcake:  Beginning to End

My life would being
As the offspring of flour and milk
Mixed together in a bowl

Then I would be tucked into bed
And set to keep in an oven
Where the sizzles would send me asleep

Later in my life
I would meet my perfect match
A fluffy, blue dollop of icing

We would get married
And set on a shelf
Where we would live happily together

The together we would experience
That sequence of moments, both magical and mundane
Before being snatched from our corner of paradise

We would fulfill our destiny
By together being devoured
By a smiling boy with greedy fingers

*Lydia Forsythe, Grade 7*
*Schuylkill Valley Middle School*

## The Future of My Life

I woke up this morning feeling mighty fine
Why, because I knew the world is all mine
To conquer all things that school has for me.
Yes, I want to make all A's and B's
Sometimes it seems hard, but that's okay
I got to keep pushing it day by day.
Pushing to become the lawyer I want to be.
That's not all, to sing and let the world hear me.
I know I have a lot of odds, a lot of odd I have to beat,
So I am determined I won't take defeat.
I encourage all children like me
To keep your head up and get all those A's and B's.
Not for other people, do it for yourself
Surely you will be happy seeing that diploma hanging on the shelf.

*Treshaunna Moore, Grade 7*
*Northgate Middle/High School*

## A Day at the Beach

On my favorite beach,
I was looking out for seagulls.
In the distance the vendors are adorned
with my favorite smell.
The sand is laid out and soft,
with the young and the old.
The air steaming hot,
and the sea's surface cold.
The waves hitting the ground got my ears ringing,
along with the seagulls going around singing.
The air being natural and smelling fresh,
with hot dog and popcorn stains in my breath.
What a delightful sight,
seeing the sun so big and bright.

*Taea Burks, Grade 7*
*Northgate Middle/High School*

## A Winter Snow

A winter night
Darkness falls
The clouds will burst
With a new snowfall
Powdery white dust
Glittering as it falls
Blanketing all
Untouched by all
Pure it is
This beautiful snowfall
Pure not for long
Slushy it will be
I love when it snows
But that's just me

*Joshua Liddy, Grade 8*
*First Philadelphia Charter School for Literacy*

## Prey Race

The legs of the beast ran at a rapid pace,
As he was in front on the prey race.
Paws throwing dust behind
Left all the other opponents blind.

The prize was inches ahead
When all of a sudden another predator jumped above his head.
The others behind lost interest instead,
But two were still after the prey ahead.

The predator right behind got caught on a root,
So the other one raced ahead a foot.
The last one left the other behind,
As the last got his dinner tonight.

*Devin Sneed, Grade 7*
*Northgate Middle/High School*

## Forever Friends

Friends will be there till the end
Sticking by your side day after day
Texting on the couch, I keep clicking send
I love them in each and every way
Some people come in your life and leave you
But true friends would not hurt you like that
They will always have a little clue
Without them I would be as blind as a bat
Friends building castles in the sand
Surfing, swimming in the sea
Without them my life would be bland
My friends are always there for me
To their every wish I will comply
Our friendship will never die

*Aislinn Galvin, Grade 8*
*Penn-Kidder Campus*

## Friends

I love all my friends,
They are all special to me,
When I'm sick, get well cards they'll send,
And I know when I need them, by my side they'll always be.

I know if I tell them a secret,
Not a soul they will tell,
They won't ever leak it,
Even if they had it to sell.

My friends and I,
We never aren't having fun,
And when we say good-bye,
I know the next time will be just as fun.

*Lauren Wanat, Grade 7*
*Northgate Middle/High School*

### Love Is Like…

Love is like broken glass…
it can shatter before your eyes

Love is like mud…
sometimes you can get stuck

Love is like a candy cane…
long and sweet, but can be gone before you realize it

Love is like a book…
you have to read the other person to understand them

Love is like a mountain…
it can be rocky and dangerous

Love is like a boat…
always swaying back and forth

*Breana Friday, Grade 8*
*Ephrata Middle School*

### To My Parents

Love is not simply a word, but a proof
Through a long time, to a family;
True lovers are neither clingy, nor aloof
But respect each other and trust firmly.

While both were young, love was novel and sweet
Like the stars shining, fair and appealing;
Years passed, with the pressure of life, love was beat
The heavy clouds kept the stars from brightening.

But the love turned warm when a baby arrived
Like a thread of sunshine cut through the night;
From the smile of the angel, joy was derived
Made love a treasure as precious as the twilight.

Love could be challenged as problems appeared
But the true love would never disappear.

*Simeng Wu, Grade 9*
*Linden Hall School*

### Dancing

Dancing helps me free my mind
  Where all my worries go out the door
    Where the only thing that needs to catch me
    Is a cold hard floor
Dancing is my escape
  It's the closest thing to flying
    It's another way to express yourself
      Where you always have to keep trying
Dancing becomes another part of you
  With every step you progress
    Where you have to dare to be the best
    And nothing less

*Stefanee Sybo, Grade 7*
*Northgate Middle/High School*

### Her Greatest Trait

As Lady Liberty holds her torch up high
People of all nations: Irish, German, French come by
They come to our golden kingdom
To end their search for freedom
With their old life they could not cope
But in America they will find hope
They come from everywhere, all over, far and wide
The poor and homeless will have pride
She might be mute but she is not deaf
She hears your cries for "F…R E E D O M"
Because to the sick, tired, and homeless, America is a gem
Her torch lights up a pathway
To all looking for success, that won't ever decay
The joy and delight on all of their faces
Stays true through all the country's great places
America the beautiful, the strong, the great
Liberty is, by far, her greatest trait.

*Sean Diehl, Grade 7*
*Grey Nun Academy*

### The One Hit

When they called my name
There was one out and the score was one to zero
At the plate I was getting ready to smack a baseball
Through a cloud-filled sky
A pitch came rushing towards me and it was a strike
Afterward I was prepared for the next pitch
Another pitch came in and
Bang!
I started sprinting to first and I looked up
And saw the ball flying far
I heard the siren
For the homerun only to slow my pace
Only because I wanted to live that moment forever
When I reached home
I was as happy as a kid on the first day of summer
I still look back just to think
It was my first homerun.

*Adam Bowers, Grade 7*
*Bellwood Antis Middle School*

### Emptiness

That emptiness you feel inside
That has no hope to be filled
A cold, empty chamber
Void of free will
It whispers a painfully silent sound
It's great at hiding when it does not want to be seen
It feels like all hopes have been flushed away
It's where dreams turn to nothing, where hopes vanish
It's where you feel like a vacant house on a lifeless street
Like a deflated basketball gasping for air
Where all hopes and dreams are exhausted from waiting
That emptiness you feel inside is detaining you from achieving.

*Durrell McClendon, Grade 8*
*First Philadelphia Charter School for Literacy*

## Slow Down

A little girl in her mother's shoes,
Tries to tiptoe daintily around.
She wears bright red upon her lips,
Smearing it just a tad.
The dark green dust above her eyes,
Is sure to make her mother mad.

Crash! The makeup falls to the ground.

The little girl is surrounded by glass,
As swirls of colorful dust fly and dance.
She wants to grow up, far too fast,
And catch a boy's admiring glance.

Slow down little girl, take some time to breathe.
Hold on to your innocence,
For life won't stay like this.
All too easily is glass shattered,
All too easily does life make you tattered.
Soon your pretending will become reality.
Soon your hopes will run towards you rapidly.

*Jessie Wollum, Grade 9*
*West Chester East High School*

## Found

I was lost now I'm found
I found hope shinning brightly in my path

I turned my back numerous times,
My mind always battled the brightness

Every day I turned my back,
And fell deeper, sinking in the darkness.

Strode along like nothing was wrong
Knowing very well

But I have grown and come to know,
The light which laid brightly shinning.

*Larice Mejia, Grade 7*
*Lancaster Mennonite School - Locust Grove*

## The Way Things Were

The colors slowly dimmed into bland shades of gray.
Past has become an unimportant mystery.
Love has been shattered piece by piece
Person by person
Heart by heart.
The glorious calls of birds were muffled into
Distraught
Silence.
Hills faded into lines
Choice faded into order
Life faded into nothing.

*Anna Morreale, Grade 7*
*Strath Haven Middle School*

## Where Is the Love?

Every day
They cower in fear of what might happen

Their life is like a black hole in space
Dark and cold, never ending
But never beginning

They need hope
They need you
They need LOVE

Why can't we respect the races of our people?

People sheltering, wishing, helping
Where is the love?

But there is hope, you just have to look a little harder

A world filled with judgment, and fear
Praying for a better place
Filled with happiness and full stomachs

Their hearts walk along a dark lonely path
We must reach out and WANT to help
Soon happiness joins them
They no longer fear or worry
A little hope
A little love <3

*Phoebe Rogers, Grade 7*
*Indian Valley Middle School*

## Battling Seasons

Screams and cries cannot be heard
Over the deafening sound of water
Submerging friends and family
Belongings swept away
None can be saved
Is it our fault? This may be

Global warming may wash away your family
We will build the World back up
And emerge from the rubble
Then we would have no more trouble
But the floods will not recede
Until we change, our polluting ways
Recycle, save a life
Don't fight against the earth defend it

The winters will get colder
While we're just getting older
But, together we can
Change the world, global warming
Can, and will be put to an end!
The battle of the seasons is over.

*Cara Plummer, Grade 7*
*Indian Valley Middle School*

## Walking the Line

Once again
The battle ensues
Between life and death
The dark jaws of death
Close around the soft, fragile thing called life
A struggle begins
To escape the grasp
Of pain
Darkness
Death
Nothing is working
Until...
A flicker of light
A flicker of hope
Pierces through the darkness
But to no avail
The darkness fights back
And wins
Death's jaws close
Around that soft, fragile thing
Called life

*Rachel Dodaro, Grade 9*
*Holicong Middle School*

## Happiness

From every corner of the world happiness runs
Like wood feeds the fire happiness feeds the heart
Before the day begins and after it ends the joy pulls us through like
A dog on a leash
Aboard a bus, above a bird, even below a wet cardboard box in a
Dirty alley in Detroit — You can find happiness
Anywhere the gentle wind sings through the smiling mountains joy
Can be found
As it goes faster and faster sweeping up the glob the place we call
Home becomes easier to live it
Into our hearts — Out of the trenches
Around and around us engulfing our minds
Until nothing is left but fuzzy feelings
Instead of feeling sad and gloomy we pick ourselves up
Near the edge of sadness happiness pulls us back
During our darkest hour joy is there to comfort
Instead of hating us it's there when no one else is
Throughout the ages it's always been there
Until the sun's last breath it will stay
Without happiness we are nothing
In us joy will always shine — And like us it will never end

*Abby Doohan, Grade 7*
*Fort Couch Middle School*

## Life Is a Show

The lights sine as bright as the stars
Way above, blinding you
Line after line coming closer and closer
To your shining moment
Butterflies in your stomach
Released into the crowd through the shiny star you are
Notes as beautiful as the sunsets
The crowd erupts into a fury of screams and shouts
Of one thing only, your *name*
The lights now blinded by you and your excellence
That shy but talented girl now shines
More brightly than the sun
But stronger than an ox
Your life, now a show with you as the star
Look at how far it took you

*Victoria Cantini, Grade 8*
*Penn Middle School*

## The Rocking Chair

I wait in the parlor
for you to come;
when the moon is out
and sometimes the sun —
my arms are strong
to hold you tight;
with your children
it's such a delight!
My movements are slow and comforting, too;
not just for children,
but also for you.
So come on down,
rock for a spell;
I have many great stories
that I may tell.

*Sarah Williamson, Grade 8*
*Conestoga Christian School*

## Nature

Trees are green, brown, and leafy.
Branches are blowing like sand in a sandstorm.
Wind is howling, blowing everything away.
Grass is green with rain coming down.
Everyone is taking cover in their houses.
Branches are swaying with their leaves in the air.
Leaves are blowing everywhere.
Not a person in sight anywhere.
Soon the wind dies down, putting the leaves to rest.
Trees are brown, green, and leafy.

*Jordan Zonin, Grade 8*
*Donegal Middle School*

## Alicia

Her smile puts the city lights to shame.
The happiness in her heart was a burning flame.
Everyone listened when she would sing.
She was a goofball, it's sort of a funny thing.
She had the loudest feet ever!
Our friendship was one you couldn't sever.
She took advantage of everything in life,
and never showed a moment of strife.
She was as delicate as a rose,
and I know love will follow wherever she goes.

*Rachel Koehler, Grade 8*
*Centerville Middle School*

## World Hunger

We lay our heads down at night
Hoping we will wake up to everything all right
We don't realize the kids around us
Searching everywhere for just little food
Their stomach rumble
As they face those dreadful days of hunger
A tiny slice of bread is such a big feast
With the looks of starvation
All they want to do is eat
We don't have to live like this
The world can make a change
Kids scramble for food
Like an abandoned hamster just left in the cage
While dying from hunger
Not playing games
Their rib cages popping out of their skin
we can all join together
Let us gather as one
Let us end world hunger
Our new lives have just begun

*Kristen Gibbs, Grade 7*
*Indian Valley Middle School*

## Living on the Ranch

I am a rancher in case you don't know me
I have a lot of animals, and horses you see
I love to hunt and to be outside looking at the trees
I am the cowgirl running my steeds with the breeze.

The goats majestically graze
As they gently play
They eat a lot of hay
When they neigh

The chickens lay lots of eggs
Counting them by the kegs
They Free range and still lay
Allowing them to still play in the hay

The rabbits don't do much
Just eat in their hutch
I show them in the Fair
The ones that have perfect hair
Living the life on my ranch

*Breona Hollen, Grade 7*
*Cambria Heights Middle School*

## Real

Walking through the hall, you see everyone smiling kindly.
Putting on fake faces, not letting the real show,
It's all for entertainment, all this innocence I see.
When we all know we're guilty, for sins we can't foresee.
We always say I'm sorry, and I take it back, please.
But, all of us know, it's not the real we see.

*Makenzie Wright, Grade 7*
*Elizabeth Forward Middle School*

## Close But Not

I didn't know you very much,
I even try to think of such,
I envision you when you were young,
Before you died from the failure of your lungs,
You were a retired vet,
Yet someone who I barely met,
I hear good stories of you and my dad,
In the 60's he was born, then 70's were rad,
Then 80's he got married and you let him go,
But then a surprise you didn't know,
Four beautiful children were now born,
But as they grew older the family was torn,
We grew further and further apart,
And it broke my sweet innocent heart,
As your dreadful time grew close,
Those are the memories I'll treasure the most,
I love you,
And I always will,
I just know there's no need to be sad,
Because I'll see you again someday and that's why I'm glad.

*Rachel Shreve, Grade 8*
*Wattsburg Area Middle School*

## I Love How You Love Me But I Hate How You Need Me

I know I'm lucky to have you
But I didn't want you
Although you don't speak like me; your eyes comfort me
I love you
But I don't want to take care of you
I didn't want to take care of you
I was told that I'd grow to love you
And I did
But I won't grow to love your needs
Although you are easier to take care of
Compared to most of your type
You are more responsibility than I want
Than I need
I love watching you sitting in the grass
Looking into the horizon just sitting so calmly
I love when you greet me at the door
I love when we run together the way you smile
The little tricks you do, since you will only do them for us
I love how you love me
But I hate how you need me

*Sylvia Garner, Grade 8*
*Donegal Middle School*

## March's Gifts

Like an officer, you save me from winter's crime
She has stolen away all the warmth
Paint the earth with your tenderness and beauty
Deliver spring; she has gifts to bring as delicate as lace
Clear the sky so the sun can shine like a spotlight and
Display your alluring masterpiece

*SunHi Moore, Grade 7*
*Garnet Valley Middle School*

### The Leaf

The leaves dance in the soft breeze,
A leaf falls then two more follow.
The leaves chase each other like children playing tag,
When on their journey they pass the Great Blue Swallow.

Then fly over the grassy moor,
As if they grew legs and ran.
They then pass the old red barn and rest,
Their journey ends as fast as it began.

But, no, one leaf still drifts lazily in the wind,
The bright colored leaf paints the moor.
Like the stroke of a paint brush across the green and gold field,
Earth's entire problems end now, for this little green leaf is the *cure*.

*Kaitlyn Musante, Grade 7*
*Landisville Middle School*

### Cycle of Life

There are deep woods that you have to travel through
There is wind blowing through the branches
There is a summer and winter in life
And most importantly you are the one to experience it

Life can bring new dreams to the table
Or life can bring darkness upon you
You may be able to hear the bells ring
Or hear the bells shatter to pieces

Autumn could suddenly hit you with great force
And overwhelm you with the darkness of night
Or summer could come dancing in
And make all your dreams come alive

*Zane Unitas, Grade 8*
*Pine-Richland Middle School*

### Colors, Colors, Colors

Green is the color of nice cut grass
Yellow colors zoom by when the cheetah runs fast

Blue jeans ruffling in the dryer
Brown mountains go by when the hiker climbs higher

Red blood dripping from a cut
Gold retriever running around, "oh that mutt!"

Purple grapes shinning in the bowl
Orange jumpsuits for those on parole

Dark blue is the color of the night sky
Pink is the color of a tulip growing high

*Lauren Kaeser, Grade 7*
*Pequea Valley Intermediate School*

### Slow and Steady

**S** lowly slithering
**N** ot too slow though,
**A** lways keeping a steady pace.
**I** n the end they will reach their destination and
**L** ove every minute of the journey.

*Keegan Peterson, Grade 8*
*Ephrata Middle School*

### Spring

Life everywhere,
Animals exploring naively,
Warm breezes gently whistle,
Lush grass spreads like wildflower,
Flowers blossom in beautifully picturesque clusters.

*Alex Stoeckle, Grade 8*
*Holy Sepulcher School*

### My Rainbow

Rainbow
colorful stripes
gliding down in the sky
feel happy and free to be me
Colors

*Rebekah Umble, Grade 7*
*Lancaster Mennonite School - Locust Grove*

### Transformation

Morning turns to afternoon
Day turns to night
Sinners turn to Christians

Fall turns to winter
Spring turns to summer
Sinners turn to Christians

Mess turns to organized
Bent turns to straight
Sinners turn to Christians

Dirty turns to clean
Diseased turns to healed
Sinners turn to Christians

Gray turns to black and white
Black and white turns to color
Sinners turn to Christians

Ugly turns to beauty
Lame turns to able
Sinners turn to Christians

Broken turns to fixed
Dead turns to alive
Sinners turn to Christians

*Emily Struhala, Grade 8*
*Armbrust Wesleyan Christian Academy*

## Childhood Memories

The living, laughing, and loving are all in your heart,
It's like you're shopping, memories overflowing your cart.

Crafts, toys, and blankets that are warm,
You do not know yet of any harm.

Childhood memories will always be with you,
Wherever you go, whatever you do.

And then you get older, day by day,
Bedtime stories are packed away.

And whatever happened to your fun-loving smile?
I have not seen it there for a long, long while.

You lost the dolls, no kissing goodnight,
No more stories about how bugs bite.

Your mom is sick, and won't live to see much more,
And this is when you open your childhood doors.

The memories come pouring out,
You miss these times, there is no doubt.

Playing with all those dirty things like mud pies and slime,
Now you wish you were there for more time.

These memories are pictures, in your mind being drawn,
Because you just realized, one day, everything will be gone.
*Natalie Ciepiela, Grade 7*
*Landisville Middle School*

## Me

I'm a rock,
Skipping across the water's surface,
Soaring through the air,
Just to slam into the water,
And then soar again.
Each time in the air getting shorter
And less meaningful…
Hurting more each time I fall.
But I can't show pain…
I'm a rock.

I'm running out of skips.
This thrill will soon be over.
All I will have to do is lie here,
And wait…
Wait for someone to pick me up again.
Me,
Out of this seemingly infinite span of rocks
At the bottom of this dark pond.

I fear that I may turn to sand long before then.
*Jasmine Miles, Grade 7*
*Northgate Middle/High School*

## New Challenges

The world is full of many things
No matter what season, summer, fall, winter, or spring

There are always new challenges that lie ahead
All you have to do is get out of bed

The early bird will catch the worm
In the face of a challenge, never squirm

Whether it be a new challenge or old
Put your chin up and never fold

An old dog can learn new tricks
Even if it's like pushing through a wall of bricks

There's no mountain that's too high
There's no plane that you can't learn how to fly

Some people can go back to school and graduate
Even if the challenge is so big they feel like they will suffocate

All you have to do is push through
And good things will be on the other side for you

You can try a new sport
Or take on a whole team down the court

Just take life head on —
Because sooner or later it will be gone
*Aidan Towsley, Grade 8*
*Sacred Heart Elementary School*

## Bells

In the night
The bell rings
Someone is calling
Something is calling
As the bell tolls you wonder
If you should answer it, it could be fate
If you don't, it could be a problem avoided
The ringing keeps coming and you wonder what to do
As you open the door and answer the calling
The world opens up, you are enlightened
You have discovered your road
And as you drive you try to avoid obstacles
But they keep coming
And the old man above gives you tests
And he tells you
"Once you learn to drive the road,
You will truly see how the bell tolls"
And now you hear a different bell
And this time you don't wonder
You are sure
This is how the bell tolls
*Francisco Carattino, Grade 8*
*Sacred Heart Elementary School*

### Softball

On a warm summer day, softball is the best sport to play
Love to run through the breeze
Hear the ball hit off of the metal bat
The game begins
One nervous hitter, one nervous pitcher
The batter is up to hit
She has three chances to hit
She misses and misses
She has no hope, but suddenly she has faith
They all stare at the ball
When they turn around, she's at home plate
They scream and cheer
Her teammates give her a pat on the back
Good job, girl
We're going to All Stars for the first time
Thanks to you
We won!

*Alyssa Hayes, Grade 8*
*Wattsburg Area Middle School*

### Summer

What a wonderful time of year.
Hot days; warm nights,
Sleeping in the moonlight.
Toes sinking into soft warm sand;
Laying in the sunlight with lotion at hand.
Diving into light blue water,
As the days get hotter and hotter.
Some days it gets as hot as an oven,
But others are perfect.
The sunsets look so beautiful,
As all the colors combine and make the sky look far from usual.
All the memories that are made,
The memories to come,
And the memories that have always stayed.
I can't wait for it all to start again,
But until then,
I can only fantasize about the fantastic days that lay ahead.

*Samantha Matthews, Grade 8*
*Centerville Middle School*

### Winter

Snowflakes fall to the ground,
as quiet as a mouse, they make no sound.

The snowflakes are dancing as they are falling from the sky,
dropping from the clouds way up high.

The wind whirls wildly from the west,
so I grab and put on my hat, gloves, and vest.

I walk through the snow that's up to my knees,
then ride on my sled and feel the cool breeze.

I see an icicle and I break it off with a snap,
I know when I'm done, I'll need a long nap.

As the snow piles up higher and higher,
I go inside and drink a cup of hot chocolate near the fire.

*Stacy Hartz, Grade 7*
*Frazier Middle School*

### Happy Birthday

Don't worry about it now.
Today we all bow,

Down to you, because today's your day,
The day where everything goes your way.

Wipe away your sorrows.
Leave them for tomorrow.

Breathe a steady beat,
Because your life is one of your biggest feats.

As I said before,
I'll say this once more,

Today is your day, your birthday.
Keep living your life to the fullest, all the way.

*Anastasia McClendon, Grade 8*
*Abington Heights Middle School*

### Autumn

Autumn.
Where everything is changing.
Where life is rearranging.
Last chance to renew,
For winter is coming soon.
When winter comes those chances die
And that's when you start to realize,
That autumn only brings truth and sorrow.
So you bid autumn and gentle good marrow.
Nothing more. Nothing to say.
Your chances have all faded away.

*Isabella Salpietro, Grade 8*
*Pine-Richland Middle School*

### Me

Just because I am autistic

Doesn't mean I am boring,
Doesn't mean I am stupid,
Doesn't mean I am untalented.

What's wrong with being autistic?
What's wrong with being shy?
Do you have to judge me?

I think everyone should like me for who I am.

*Emma Billingsley, Grade 7*
*Prospect Park School*

## I Dance…

I dance because I need to
I dance all that I can
I twirl, spin, leap, and soar
Until my feet can hold me no more
The blisters on my feet
Stay for seven days a week
The pain can't hold me back
That is a fact
While I'm dancing on the floor
Blood, sweat, and tears is what I endure
*Regan Fleming, Grade 7*
*Cambria Heights Middle School*

## Spring Is Near

Hop, hop
The Easter bunny drops
Chocolate and jelly beans
Means Easter's here
A mere sign that spring is near
Grass grows
The sun shows
As temperatures rise
And the cold wind dies
I know spring is here
*Mary Thomas, Grade 7*
*Landisville Middle School*

## New Eyes

With my new eyes,
there are many things that I now realize.
I have learned not to judge,
or to hold a grudge.
I have learned to see
that you must respect everybody.
I have learned to not be a cynic
and to instead be optimistic.
With my new eyes,
there are many things that I now realize.
*Erica Hodgson, Grade 7*
*Strath Haven Middle School*

## Never the Same

A stray flower sitting on the open land,
Mr. Sun stretching out his warming hand.
A fresh gentle breeze flows up high,
Trees with beautiful leaves lie nearby.
The sky is bright, crisp and blue,
Everything reminds me entirely of you.
The clouds are a perfect white,
Baby birds chirp with such strong might.
The tiptoe sounds of a babbling stream,
Can only now be the place where I dream.
*Tara Korch, Grade 7*
*Our Lady of Mount Carmel School*

## What Life Is

Life is something special

Life is laughing and having fun
Running through the rain and having no care in the world

Life is not worrying about the time and living in the moment
Trying something new and not letting anyone control you

Life is never giving up and trying as much as you can
Dancing like no one is watching and singing like no one can hear you

Life is knowing everything happens for a reason
Crying at something sad and laughing at something funny

Life is knowing someone will always be there for you
Making mistakes and learning from them

Life is living every day like it's your last
*Madison Kladnik, Grade 8*
*Penn Middle School*

## Color Guard

We prepare ourselves in shimmering uniforms,
And board the bus to the game
When we arrive at the stadium
We all get off with pride and no shame
We march to our seats,
And put the equipment in its place
When the football team comes out in their cleats
We each go on the field and stand on our space
Then the music starts,
And flags go flying, dancing in the light
As we execute every part
Then when it's all over I try to hold in my excitement with all my might
When the audience starts to applaud we all know
We were the stars of the show.
*Sophie Monboussin, Grade 8*
*Penn-Kidder Campus*

## Love Is…

Love is like the moon
That shines brightly in the night.
If plagued, it can become a typhoon,
For it is forged with as much darkness as light.
Love is lovers lying beneath the night skies.
Looking at stars twinkling in darkness
While gazing into each other's eyes,
Mesmerized by the spark of fondness.
Love is like a song sung in the rain.
To the one true love, the lyrics are sent.
But only if lovers are sincere will they survive the pain,
For their love is pure to the greatest extent.
Love comes in various shapes and sizes,
So cherish the love you are given for it's the most valuable of all prizes.
*Sydney Xinyi Wang, Grade 9*
*Linden Hall School*

## Prevent Poverty

Dirty, gray and dark
Noisy, weak and bound
Reach inside your heart
And feel that pounding
Driving your destiny
See the people
In the mist of poverty

We hate
They ache
They break
We take
Take things for granted

Give them hope
Give them a smile
Give them a chance
To break the chains of poverty

Reach inside and look
Look for the person you should be
Lend a helping hand
Help to end poverty
*Briana Reuss, Grade 8*
*Indian Valley Middle School*

## Soccer

I love soccer
That isn't a shocker
Let's play the game
I'll put you to shame
It's just something I do
The crowd will boo you
I'm obviously winning
So please, no crying

The score's not tied
But isn't the field wide?
But you still won't pass me
'Cause this is victory

Isn't this fun?
I'd say so, Hun
Let's be real here
'Cause your eyes show fear

Soccer's MY game
And I'm putting you to shame
Victory is my name
I can't and won't be tamed
*Monica Beshay, Grade 9*
*Tamaqua Area Sr High School*

## Championship Game

It was a never-fading memory
The whole park was cheering
They were undefeated
Only one more out

The whole park was cheering
We were winning by one
Only one more out
I've never been so nervous

We were winning by one
"Strike"
I've never been so nervous
Until now

"Strike"
They were undefeated
Until now
It was a never-fading memory
*Mary Kate Kavanagh, Grade 7*
*Garnet Valley Middle School*

## Lost

"Shh" said the ocean
"Hush hush" said the door
She lays with her memories
Scattered on the floor

"Shh" said the rocking chair
"Hush hush" said the halls
She watches deep orchid paint
Peel from the walls

"Quiet" said the curtains
"Be still" said the lamp
Her flushed cheeks are still
Tearstained and damp

"Quiet" said the mirror
"Be still" said the fan
She can hear the sad cry
Of unborn Lucy Anne
*Kendall Master, Grade 8*
*Centerville Middle School*

## Ninjas

Ninjas are like a stalker
Watching you without your knowing
Ninjas are like the BOSS of night
This makes every night a fight night
They almost never die
And I don't know why
But ninjas are really cool
Like an ocean BREEZE
*Zachery Pepe, Grade 7*
*Schuylkill Valley Middle School*

## The Flag

Red, White, and Blue
Waving high
The struggles behind it

Red, White, and Blue
The wars fought
Freedom won

Red, White, and Blue
The American Dream
Being fulfilled every day

Red, White, and Blue
Not just a flag
But American liberty high in the sky
*Christopher Rust, Grade 8*
*Pine-Richland Middle School*

## What I Found in My Purse

a pair of sunglasses
chewed-up gum masses

quarters and dimes
a watch with no time

eyeliner and blush
a pretty pink brush

a random pen
a picture of some hen

water bottle caps
Exton mall's map
*Kelly Saalbach, Grade 7*
*Pequea Valley Intermediate School*

## Spring's Serenity

Flowers have finally gotten here
After those cold winter months.
The flowers bloom then glow
At the bottom of tree trunks.

The months with all the snow have gone
As if they never came.
A mother deer protects her fawn
wild and untamed.

A beautiful breeze blows all day
Making everyone lighthearted and happy.
It shoves the flowers
And blows the trees making them all noisy.
*Rebekah Zimmerman, Grade 8*
*Ephrata Middle School*

## My Night of Paradise

What do you think of
when you see me?
Do you think of Shawn Johnson
doing giants on bars?
That's what I think of.
I walk in.
I see the empty vault tracks waiting to be raced on
like the Daytona 500.
I hear the coaches
instructing the students;
getting them ready for competition.
I smell the sprinkle of chalk in the air
and taste the cool, refreshing cold of water
after an excruciating workout.
Touching the bar;
feeling the rip on your hand
while you fiercely swing.
I am Tarzan, swinging on my vine.
All of this is mine
every Thursday night.

*Tori VanDerMark, Grade 7*
*Towanda Jr/Sr High School*

## The Sea

How I'd love to live in the sea.
It's the perfect place for a girl like me.
I'd swim with the dolphins, but not the sharks.
They creep me out with their spots and marks.
I would look for Atlantis, the sea's lost city.
Not being able to find it would be a pity.
Eventually, I'd grow gills.
I'd never miss the ocean thrills.
I'd watch the vivid colors of the reef,
To keep me calm and give me relief.
Floating on the surface of the sea all night long,
Watching the stars glow bright and strong.
Living as a mermaid,
Land memories will fade.
As reality becomes my grave,
Once again, I become its slave.
To live amongst those who judge,
Living in a land of trash and sludge.
I wish I was in my fantasy land,
Instead of staring at it from the sand.

*Ashley Warner, Grade 7*
*Landisville Middle School*

## Someday

Someday I wish to meet my goals
Someday I wish to be called nothing but beautiful
Someday I want to be successful
Someday I wish people would stop fighting
Someday I wish drug use would stop
Someday I want to be treated with respect

*Dana Brill, Grade 7*
*Pequea Valley Intermediate School*

## Fathers

A father is someone who will always be there
Someone who will help you when things are tough
Someone who will never let you down

A father is someone who will help when you get stuck
When you fall he'll be there to get you back up
When you are sad he'll cheer you up

A father is someone who will share your joy
When you get a good grade he'll be happy
When you win a prize he'll cheer and smile

A father is someone who cares about you
As you grow he'll grow too
When you're in trouble he'll help you out

A father is someone who is honest and true
Someone who is not perfect but is trying everyday
Someone who loves you no matter what

*Julie Weeks, Grade 9*
*Holicong Middle School*

## The Beach

I can feel the sun's warmth on my face,
On a summer's day, it never feels out of place.
The ocean's waves roll in and out,
As squawking seagulls swerve about.

The sand is an endless road,
Made of rocks, shells, a constant load.
People pray that there won't be a day
Where the blue sky will turn gray.

The crabs that are there are like ticking time bombs
Just waiting to burst.
If someone dares me to touch it,
I am NOT going first.

As the day comes to a close
When we go back to learn,
Realizing my feelings go high from low
Knowing I will return.

*Jessica Corace, Grade 7*
*William Penn Middle School*

## Beautacious Life

My beautacious life
The sun brightens my heart,
With a cool breeze on a fall day.
Warm weather and clouds in the sky,
Wildlife and sparks of green.
The dancing leaves, and flowers that blossom,
It makes me happy,
In this beautacious life I have.

*Becca Siple, Grade 8*
*Saegertown Jr/Sr High School*

### Lies

I should have seen right through your lies.
All your words meant nothing.
I hid behind a wall of emotions,
Shielding me from the truth.

What I found deep inside,
Was a knife cutting deeper.
The lies need to stop.

From now on, life's only a dream.
I've reached past the lies.
The wall of emotions came crashing down,
Never to be seen again.

I never suspected from the start
That all these lies would tear me apart,
Although they never had the best of me.

I'm better now that the world's brighter.
The dark clouds have since gone.
No need for shielding anymore,
And free will to begin once more.
*Kaitlyn Garris, Grade 8*
*Penn Middle School*

### Cotton Candy Pink

Sleeping on a warm, fluffy cloud,
Smelling the soft, sweet air,
Trailing off into the sun —

Laughing and singing
Tasting heaven on a magical evening —
Bringing joyous smiles to my face

Like a wonderland —
Having various dreams
One after another,
Carefully prancing cloud to cloud —
Carelessly leaping,
Light as a feather

Twirling and whirling,
Dancing in the sunlight
Quickly becoming evening,
Dusk is brewing —
Starry night is falling —
Sweet night has come.
*Abby Johnson, Grade 7*
*William Penn Middle School*

### Cherry Blossoms

Cherry blossoms bloom
In the midmorning sunlight
Covering the ground
*Kayla Culhane, Grade 7*
*Easton Area Middle School 7-8*

### My Friends

My friends are
Helpful, supporting
Funny, truthful, and caring

My friend is
Helpful when she helps
me with my homework

My friends are
Supporting with my problems
They are support with
My health problems

My friends are
Funny when they
Make me laugh

My friends are
Truthful when they tell
Someone something they were
Not supposed to tell them

My friends are
Caring when I am sad
They are caring when one
Of my friends or family member died
*Nashalie Cruz, Grade 7*
*Pequea Valley Intermediate School*

### If I Had a Million Dollars

If I had a million dollars,
I'd spend it all on me.
I would buy a bunch of candy,
As far as the eye could see.

If I had a million dollars,
I'd buy a huge TV.
I'd go to the station demanding,
"I want a channel dedicated to me!"

If I had a million dollars,
I'd buy a brand new car.
I'd keep it locked up in my garage,
And not drive it very far.

If I had a million dollars,
I'd buy a private jet.
Not worrying about how much it costs,
I still won't be in debt.

If I had a million dollars,
I would look back and think,
That my old life with nothing
Really did stink!
*Zach Meyer, Grade 8*
*Penn Middle School*

### Enjoying Life

Life is like a rollercoaster.
It has its ups and downs.
So, take some chances,
No matter how scary it sounds.
Don't worry about other people,
Just do your own thing.
Randomly break out in song,
Even if you can't sing.
You can't just sit back and watch.
Live your life every day,
Go outside and enjoy the weather,
Even if the skies are gray.
Dance in the rain
And fall in love
I hope you can do
All of the above.
*Aubrey Cintron, Grade 8*
*Bellmar Middle School*

### Up in the Starry Sky

Morn in the starry sky
How the moon is way up high
Purple-orange light starting to rise
Up in the starry sky
Morn is coming, hills are showing
Moon starting to dim
As sun starts to brighten
Up in the starry sky
Morn is ready to start
Moon winding down
Birds waking from their midnight slumber
Up in the starry sky
Sun breaches through the surface
Moon disappears
Sun ready to start its shift
Up in the big blue sky
*Conner King, Grade 7*
*Garnet Valley Middle School*

### The Forgotten

We are the last of our kind,
The rest gone with the wind
All that's left but we don't mind,
Those who destroyed us grinned.

The lost are here,
Unstable and queer,
Watch the world quake,
Enveloping the innocent in their wake.

They take our world for a glance,
As the towns lay rotten,
They take an offensive stance,
We are the last, The Forgotten
*Ben Hoover, Grade 8*
*Wattsburg Area Middle School*

## Easter

Really peaceful,
Full of joy,
Jesus Christ has risen,
One of my favorite holidays,
A happy day celebrated by Christians.
*Jacob Rechenberg, Grade 7*
*Holy Sepulcher School*

## Ghost

ghost
haunting, scary
frightening, green, creepy,
scares people at night
spooky
*Ally Tanase, Grade 7*
*Easton Area Middle School 7-8*

## Miss Ruth

There once was a girl named Ruth.
She sat at a restaurant booth.
She loved to bake,
Her favorite was cake.
She had a very sweet tooth!
*Megan Dugan, Grade 7*
*St Luke School*

## Thunderstorms

Thunderstorms while you're sleeping
Crackle Flash!
As lighting collides with thunder
Drip drop like water dripping from a sink
Pit pat as Mary Poppins dances in the rain
*Nick Patrone, Grade 7*
*Pequea Valley Intermediate School*

## Return

Spring's back,
Flowers are blooming,
Birds are all singing,
The snow is all melting,
Now the rivers are filled up.
*Caelan Hinterlang, Grade 7*
*Holy Sepulcher School*

## Spring

New life,
Animals are born,
Flowers start to bloom,
Leaves start growing on trees,
Spring brings new scenery and life.
*Lauren Gibbs, Grade 8*
*Holy Sepulcher School*

## I'm All Alone

I'm all alone…
No one to help me,
No not even…someone to save from the darkness.
Can someone help me?
Can someone save me?
Or will I stay alone and be in the darkness…forever?
I'm all alone.
I am like an outcast.
I bet some people think of me as a question mark.
They don't even know me.
They don't want to know me.
And so now I'm still all alone.
I'm all alone.
I am like the wind; when I blow past, you feel me, but you don't react.
Was I born to be alone, or is it because of my personality?
My mom loves me, my dad loves me, so why can't anybody else like me?
Either way I look at it…I'm all alone.

But I will promise you this…I will have someone to accept me.
I will have a friend to have and play, I will escape the darkness.
I promise that one day…I will not be alone.
*Cristian Diaz, Grade 8*
*First Philadelphia Charter School for Literacy*

## Time

**E** veryone has to go sometime.
**F** or everyone has their own way to go.
**G** oing into the light, as some say, isn't so bad.
**H** aving someone to meet sometimes and others have no one at all.
**I** have always wondered what could be waiting for me,
**J** ust because I don't know what may happen over time.
**K** illing is never the way we want to go,
**L** iving is always what people want.
**M** any don't know what it is like to actually be hurt to the point
**N** o one is wanted near you.
**O** n and on, it just keeps going on and you want it to stop.
**P** eople think that you are going crazy, but no one actually understands.
**Q** uiet is always nice to be around but there is always someone there,
**R** eal friends stay by your side and fake don't.
**S** ometimes you think about the impossible but,
**T** imes can be hard and you just can't think at all.
*Taylor Reider, Grade 8*
*Ephrata Middle School*

## The Blue Dragon

The dragon's fire is as hot as any sun and as bright as a supernova
The dragon's wings are not as smooth as leather but as hard as scales
The dragon's claws are as flawless as ebony
The dragon's teeth are a million times worse than any sword
The dragon's eyes are like flawless sapphires with no smudges
The dragon's ears are as keen as any owl's
The dragon's scales are bluer than any ocean
The dragon's beauty is like no other
The dragon is like no other.
*Justin James, Grade 8*
*Donegal Middle School*

## Our Health, Our Future

**O** ur
**U** niverse
**R** uns in our

**H** ands
**E** arth
**A** nd all
**L** iving
**T** hings
**H** ere

**O** n it
**U** nderstand that we
**R** un the

**F** uture
**U** ntil
**T** he
**U** niverse is in
**R** uins
**E** ternally

*Autumn Byes, Grade 7*
*St Peter Cathedral School*

## Music

Music is harmony,
Music is smooth,
Music is my remedy,
Music is my muse,
When I'm listening,
I don't have a clue,
The music just takes me,
To another place,
Somewhere far away,
Maybe outer space,
I love the beats,
And the rhyme,
I listen to it all the time,
When I'm down,
I feel like it's the only thing,
There for me,
Music tells a story,
Maybe the story of my life,
The best feeling is when you can relate,
To the great lyrics,
That music creates.

*Dominique Manning, Grade 7*
*Pennbrook Middle School*

## Rain

Mourning fields of golden grain
Waiting for the evening rain
Whirling clouds, a violet haze
Pouring down to renew and raise

*Gabrielle Sergi, Grade 7*
*St. Luke School*

## The Girl in the Mirror

When I look in the mirror,
I don't like what I see.
I see me, well, part of me.

My voice is silent,
sound, estranged.
Far away, I hear my name.

The girl in the mirror is blowing away.
The girl in the mirror isn't here to stay.

I hated that girl.
She hated me, but in that girl,
Lay my destiny.

Other girls take the stage,
Sometimes pounding
On the mirror in rage.

I need that girl.
At last, the first girl is back again,
and she dons an evil grin.

I stare back and meet my fate,
To fight yourself,
It is too late.

I wait.

*Kathryn Scott, Grade 7*
*Beaver Area Middle School*

## The Ride

Walking into the park,
With the smells of wonderful things.
Then the sound of scream comes along,
But they are drowned out by the fun.

Go to the first ride,
The roller coaster.
As a boat on roaring water.
The rider gets on and the ride begins.

Tik, tik, tak, tak,
The sound of anticipation
And it stops, just before the edge,
Then it is as if someone had dropped him.

But the rider ends up on top,
Through the zigs and zags,
The ups and downs.
It's over a sudden darkness and a stop.

The journey is over,
Until next time.

*Rusty Batykefer, Grade 8*
*Pine-Richland Middle School*

## Things a Bully Knows

What does a bully know?
The difference
Of others,
Making them cry to
Their mothers.
People at their
Weakest,
Thinking they are
The sleekest.
People shy or
Bold,
Bullies can be
Very cold.
Bullies know what's
Not right,
Keep them out of
Your sight
Strange tall or
Small
Bullies make fun
Of them all.

*Alexis Gasparetti, Grade 7*
*Easton Area Middle School 7-8*

## Kill It All Before It Kills Me

Drops of sorrow drip down my face
No way out of the tunnel of death
I look around at the dirt
There is no one there I'm all alone
What happened to my life?
I envy the day
I have freedom
I dream of the day I feel full
Full of life, hope and happiness
Yet it is all so far away
I try to get up but
I fall back down
I am overwhelmed by
The big thing inside of me
The pain, the sadness, the death
Why do I even bother to try
Big flying birds drop
Crates from the sky
We open it up and look inside
It is just like paradise but
Paradise doesn't last forever

*Catherine Pileggi, Grade 8*
*Indian Valley Middle School*

## Ninja

Amazing skill
Fast, decisive, smart
Makes you feel safe
Shadow

*Josueph Salas, Grade 7*
*Easton Area Middle School 7-8*

### Polluted

Ice melting crumbling into the ocean
Polar bears their fluffy white fur
Matted with brown.

Trash covered sidewalks brown grass
Smoke and car exhaust billowing into the air
The air is so polluted it hurts to breathe.

Beaches their sandy shores littered with trash
Water black and oily seaweed replaced by food wrappers
The stench of garbage fills your nostrils and burns your nose.

Is this really how we want our earth to be?
A prisoner held captive in the palm of global warming's hand?

Grass will be greener the air much cleaner
If only we just care
We can stop global warming in its tracks.
Nurture our earth.

After all, it's the only home we've got.
*Cate Hayes, Grade 7*
*Indian Valley Middle School*

### All We Need Is Food

Most basic need of life,
We all dread the man with a scythe,
So why let them all die,
Without even saying goodbye,
All they need is food,
There is no reason to exclude,
A bowl of rice is all they get,
But even this is not surely set,
Contribute to the execution,
And help be part of the solution,
Any amount will do,
This revolution isn't new,
It's just finally come to a head,
It's in many books to be read,
It's on the news to be seen,
Time to activate the dream,
Could you really turn your back?
They hack away the pain,
Day or night sun or rain,
Help make it go away,
Let's make it happen not tomorrow but today.
*Sterling Fitser, Grade 7*
*Indian Valley Middle School*

### Stars

Stars
stars shine from above
gleaming, beautiful and bright
the moon says hello
*Veronica Lopez, Grade 7*
*Lancaster Mennonite School - Locust Grove*

### Deceiving Utopia

The mellifluous echo permeated my skull.
Swaying to the melody,
My thoughts drift to the glorious Heavens.
What is this alluring music?
Is it the downy, snow white feathers singing to me?
A blissful gleam emits from far ahead,
Twinkling upon my eyes like a personal star.
Smiling, arms extended to snatch,
Flying afar, a firefly evading me.
I giggle, carol, skip, chase.
Buzzing away, it halts, beckoning me forwards.
Engulfed in a white sea of foam,
A halo of pure light, expanding ever so greatly,
Until nothing created of darkness is present.
All of a sudden, darkness swallows all.
A damp wind whispers my name,
As ghost hands clutch my shoulders.
Spine shivering, goose-bumps rise,
Peace has turned into nightmare.
Like the flip of a switch,
The aroma of hope shifts to the stench of decay.
*Kimberly Hess, Grade 9*
*Holicong Middle School*

### Nightmare

Running and panting, survival at stake,
I try to determine the next move he'll make.
The rain poured down hiding the tears in my eyes,
The wind whispered loudly, it muffled my cries.
I look back and notice the rage in his face,
He knows that I'm frightened, I quicken my pace.
I trip and I slip, a result of the mud,
I finally fall with a deafening THUD.
I get myself up and I gain my composure,
I hold back my screams to prevent my exposure.
I turned my head 'round and I noticed in fear,
A dark silhouette, my pursuer is near.
Then I realized I needn't be scared anymore,
This is all too familiar, this has happened before.
A recurring nightmare, I conclude that this is,
I have to wake up; I'm no victim of his.
I wake with a jerk and I let out a sigh,
I laugh with relief, though I feel I could cry.
Though bad situations may drive us to tears,
Some aren't what they seem; we can face all our fears.
*Gina Ghamo, Grade 8*
*Wattsburg Area Middle School*

### Sincerely, a Future Leader

To you, I am just a child, young and free,
But to the ones that know me, they most definitely see.
I can be whatever I want, big or tall,
Because to you, I may be small,
But to the world, I can be it all.
*Ashley Passamonte, Grade 8*
*Wattsburg Area Middle School*

### Spring Dreams

The essential wet rain,
The present breeze,
The little birds,
The lively flowers,
The blue sky,
And the beautiful green ground.

It almost smells like spring,
But all this is just a dream.

*Emily Johnson, Grade 8*
*Saegertown Jr/Sr High School*

### Backpack

A big bulky backpack,
Draped across my shoulder,
Weighing me down
Like a ten ton boulder.

Full of binders, notebooks, and folders,
With assignments to submit.
So much to go in
I hope everything will fit.

*John Vanderwolf, Grade 7*
*Strath Haven Middle School*

### Serenity

I love the forest rich and rare,
It has no worries, but can share
The birds, the bees, the mink and bear;
And we thank God for all His care.

And farther on there is a brook
For catching fish upon my hook
Or lazing by it with my book,
And all my worries I forsook.

*Trevor Koehn, Grade 7*
*Rockhaven Christian School*

### Feelings

**L** ove
**A** rgue
**U** gly
**G** rin
**H** appy

*Kayla Napoli, Grade 7*
*Easton Area Middle School 7-8*

### Arctic Air

Out in the white cold
the snow drips from the trees
the wind also told us
that it's coming from the sea,
the ground, hard like a rock,
is covered with the soft, silly, white stuff.

*Lauren Lucas, Grade 7*
*Garnet Valley Middle School*

### The Sea at Sunrise

Where am I?
It is dark, but not frightening.
I lean down to a small puddle and drink.
I spit out the salty water too salty to drink.
I hear birds crying out as if they were searching for a friend.
I walked on something cool and gritty.
I hear it crunch.
Soon I find my feet wet.
I hear the crashing of waves.
I feel them pull and push.
I look out onto the blackened water.
Soon I see a light of red and pink, orange and purple.
The sky is set aflame
Lighting the Earth with hope of a new day.
I stand ankle deep in water feeling the small fish swim against my legs.
I stand silhouetted against the painted scene.
Bathed in the light of the glorious dawn
I watched the sun rise over the ocean.

*Brande Robison, Grade 8*
*Bellwood Antis Middle School*

### Paradise in the Simple

A splash of bitter sweetness,
Tingling on my tongue.
A rush of luscious magic,
Carrying me away,
To a world of dreams,
Where big black elephants run towards the glowing white crystal ball,
And tall, thin, brown grass shoots from the shield,
Than it hit me.
Icy cold waves,
Refreshing Like a newly made Earth,
In this glorious paradise I see
Them surrounding me.
Watching me passionately, high in the trees.
But eventually the time runs out,
And the paradise disappears
But it's okay
Because they'll be back for me Someday.

*Angeline Gabel, Grade 8*
*Nazareth Area Middle School*

### You've Imprinted on Me

You could have had the best of me.
You could have grabbed the love I had for you from me,
But the only thing you got from me was tears, pain, and an empty dream.
If you love someone, you'll let them go but, I can't with you.
I just want you to know my love for you burns icy cold.
That's why I could never let you go.
You've imprinted on me…as I did to you.
Now I'm seeing you in a different way…a way I never thought would come out of you.
You kissed me once and I pushed you back.
Now I'm regretting ever doing you like that.
When I cried; you held me tight, but now I'm crying and you're not here with me tonight.

*Eliree Yakpasuo, Grade 8*
*Cornerstone Christian Academy*

### Goal

Last summer a game of a lifetime was upon me
The second of the whistle so loud like a boy screaming
The start of the game
The touch of the ball
I spring past the other team
A break of wind across my face
A click and clack of my cleats hitting the ball
A break of speed so fast, faster than light
An excitement that I'm so close to the goal
A break of adrenaline rushing through me
As I pull back my foot
Ankle stiff as a board and toes straight down
As I hit the ball
So quiet
Quieter than space
My eyes watching the ball
The goalie's eyes watching the ball starting to move
I looked around, everybody's eyes on the ball and goalie
I looked at the ball slowly making its way towards the goal
The goalie slowly jumping towards the ball
The ball was as fast as light, then I knew it was a GOAL!

*Nic Mallory, Grade 8*
*Bellwood Antis Middle School*

### Heroes

Heroes lay their lives down so that strangers can live.
They can't save everyone but, that's just how life is.
They live every day without glory and fame.
Heroes hold their heads high when no one knows their name.
They believe that fear is strong,
But, will never do what's wrong.
Their voices ever confident, firm and yet fair,
Always speaking with patience, tenderness and care.
Heroes protect both those unknown and those that they hold dear,
Through times of laughter and through times of tears.
We live in a kind of world which can be hard to bear.
Thank God for these people and how greatly they care.
Do ponder new heroes and what they will face.
And pray for their safety no matter their place.

*Christina Shragher, Grade 7*
*Our Lady of Mount Carmel School*

### Won't Stand for Change

Won't stand for change…
Because of the lies I have received
Because of the hate I have experienced
Because of the life that has been taken away from me
Now as I vent the ugliness within, I feel free!

I will stand for change…
Because of the truth I was given
Because of the love that took the hate away
Because the life that was returned to me
Now, as I'm complete on my quest, I don't just feel free, I am free!

*Mark Philhower, Grade 8*

### Change

Change is something we can see
And something we strive to be
It doesn't have to be big
But if we really want it we have to dig

People will look near and far
And wish upon a shooting star
We have to realize it comes from the heart
Almost like working on beautiful art

All we have to do is believe
And change, we will achieve
Let's extend our arms out wide
Coming together and never divide

Friends, family, and people are alike
Including the ones who act childlike
Change can start with us
Let's be peaceful and discuss

We may have to sit
To grasp the intriguing concept of it
Good or bad change is coming
It can be as loud as drumming or soft like humming

Change!

*Madalena Psillidis, Grade 8*
*Sacred Heart Elementary School*

### In the Dark

Bit by bit, piece by piece
We are descending into darkness
Where hate thrives and evil silently lurks

Crack by crack, inch by inch
Love is crumbling at our mercy
Honesty and trust are disintegrating before our eyes

Ignorance is ruling the world
On her mighty throne of twisted black
Strangling empathy, extinguishing hope

Who's caring?
Who's noticing?
Who's helping?

If one person starts caring
If two people start noticing
If three people try to help

Light can be found
The dark can be chased away
Humanity saved from itself
A perfect world full of love in our grasp

*Jocelyn Edwards, Grade 7*
*Indian Valley Middle School*

### Love

Love springs from the heart joyfully and free.
Lasting forever and always within.
In my mind I truly thought it would be.
This elegant story will now begin.

Walking down the long path, love to wander,
To the warmth and thoughtfulness of the top.
Idea of love comes to mind to ponder.
A puzzle needs its piece don't want to stop?

All of this a game, it becomes crafty
You find yourself in curiosity
Flowing like water as if it's drafty
Finding joy not harsh animosity

Your love will now blossom, all pieces fit
When it comes to love you know it's legit.

*Katie Myron, Grade 8*
*Pocono Mountain East Jr High School*

### This Must Be

I close my eyes and I can see
Your sparkling smile aimed right at me.
I feel the rush when I'm around you;
My head starts to spin from the adrenaline

Butterflies in my stomach, I'm weak at the knees.
I'm not sure I can breathe with you this close to me.
This must be how it feels to be in love.

I look up and my eyes meet yours;
You smile and then you look away.
Thoughts of you race through my mind,
Can you tell I am dreaming about you and I?

Butterflies in my stomach, I'm weak at the knees.
I'm not sure I can breathe with you this close to me.
This must be how it feels, how it feels to be in love.

*Tiffany Power, Grade 9*
*21st Century Cyber Charter School*

### Anything Will Happen

Anything will happen,
You can't control your life,
It is what it is,
You can't take it back,
But you can take your mistakes and learn from them,
You'll trust your heart with the wrong people,
And it will hurt,
It will be broken,
Then it will feel shattered,
You can bandage the damage,
But you can't ever really
Fix a heart.

*Carli Hoffman, Grade 8*
*Wattsburg Area Middle School*

### Life

Life is like a pretty flower
One day you sprout and are happy
The next you are sad and withered
Stuck in the same place every day

It doesn't matter where you are
Life is like a pretty flower
You always want to go places
Not everything goes your own way

No one cares about your color
I wish life was like that today
Life is like a pretty flower
Nobody cares what you look like

Dream your best dreams and make them real
Don't let someone stand in the way
Always make the best of your days
Life is like a pretty flower

*Rebecca Crouse, Grade 8*
*Beaty-Warren Middle School*

### Hope

Hope is the shoulders on which dreams lie,
The feet which carry you home,
The wind beneath a bird's wings,

The food in a famine,
The rain in a drought,
The foundation of the future,

The light at the end of a long, dark tunnel,
The enlivening of the gray lackluster world,
The rainbow after the storm,

When I fall, hope's helpful hand is never far,
When the world eschews me, hope never leaves my side,

Hope is something I've never seen,
But hope has never deserted me,
And with all the help hope's given to me,
It has never asked a thing in return.

*Brianna McGovern, Grade 9*
*Holicong Middle School*

### True Friends

Friends will let you cry on their shoulder
True friends will cry with you
Friends will encourage you to try
True friends will try with you
Friends will tell your secrets to their best friends
True friends will ask why anybody asks
Friends will leave you stranded in the middle of the desert to starve
True friends will starve with you

*Kaylie Wilson, Grade 7*
*Park Forest Middle School*

## Each Animal's Role

On the farm, each animal plays its role
Pigs fatten up to become bacon and pork
Swans in the pond bring grace to the soul
Horses eat nonstop, like a bottle without a cork

Pigs fatten up to become bacon and pork
Hens lay fresh eggs as they call and they cluck
Horses eat nonstop, like a bottle without a cork
Cows moo from the barn where they are stuck

Hens lay fresh eggs as they call and they cluck
A kitten searches for a playmate without much luck
Cows moo from the barn where they are stuck
Dogs loyally follow farmers in both tractor and truck

On the farm, each animal plays their role
A kitten searches for a playmate without much luck
Dogs loyally follow farmers in both tractor and truck
Swans in the pond bring grace to the soul

*Alexa Potts, Grade 8*
*Ephrata Middle School*

## The Diamond

This diamond is made of dirt and grass,
It is not made of glass.
You can play on it night and day,
On this diamond, you want to stay.

The crowd claps and cheers,
For the batter named Piers.
The crowd makes an impact,
As the fielder does a juggling act.

Many of the players wear stirrups,
They all play for the Champion's Cup.
All of the players wear cleats,
They are wondering who they might beat.

This diamond is like a field of dreams,
The dark green grass shimmers and gleams.
This beautiful diamond is a playground to all,
The game starts when the umpire says, "Play Ball!"

*Nick Romano, Grade 7*
*Pennbrook Middle School*

## All About Life

you start dying the second you are born,
so don't make your life an 80 year scorn.
don't be a slave to every rule in the book,
because back on your life you will look.
don't regret chances you have never taken,
and all the things you have mistaken.
yet on the contrary, I want you to see,
don't rob yourself of whatever you want your life to be.

*Glade Sparks, Grade 8*
*Spring Grove Middle School*

## Soccer

A lot of people love to play soccer
You're really excited for the coin toss
And when you block a shot, you're a blocker
But when you can score, you feel like a boss

You might get a foul for troublesome tricks
And be suspended with a yellow card
But work hard and carry a lot of bricks
And you can even play in your backyard

When you're in the field, try to be the best
Don't become nervous when you run downfield
And feel proud when you differ from the rest
Block the other team's goals like a strong shield

When you're about to win, people will scream
Then you will go out to eat some ice cream.

*Marvin Roca, Grade 8*
*Pocono Mountain East Jr High School*

## Soldiers

Soldiers will give up their lives every day
And it's amazing how they have no fright
On the battlefield some dead soldiers lay
Even though they may be scared they still fight

Some soldiers stand in awe at what they saw
He throws a grenade then runs away
The sergeant tells the men when to withdraw
After some just go home but some just stay

The sound of the land machine guns at war
The tanks rolling by let their guns go off
Some soldiers get shot and fall to the floor
Lots of soldiers who get sick start to cough

Even though soldiers don't want us to fuss
Soldiers are really important to us

*Jillian Cubelo, Grade 8*
*Pocono Mountain East Jr High School*

## Guess Who?

She's as quiet as a mouse,
She's shy but she always says hi,
In the morning she can be hazy,
But I ensure you, she's not that crazy,
She's as nice as can be,
But once you get to know her you will see,
She's very talkative and lively,
If a rock could talk the rock would be louder then her,
She would rather be in the sun having fun,
Than be in a crazy cramped classroom all day,
She's a star student and a burst of energy,
Once you get to know her.

*Catherine Weaver, Grade 8*
*Spring Grove Middle School*

### Perfect Summer Day

It was a perfect summer day
Good weather
Green grass
All across the vast yard
Butterflies floating around
Aimlessly in the field
There is a slight breeze
Not too strong
Song birds
Belting out many different tunes
The blue pool
Offering cool refreshment
The bright yellow sun
Very warm
Nothing was wrong on this day

*Kevin Erb, Grade 8*
*Daniel Boone Middle School*

### Soldiers

There is a discipline in a soldier
You can see it when they walk
There is honor in a soldier
You can hear it when they talk
There is courage in a soldier
You can see it in their eyes
There is loyalty in a soldier
That they won't break your promises
There is strength in a soldier
That's beating from their heart
A soldier isn't a title any person
Can be hired to do,
A soldier is truly deep inside of them.
You have served our country first
And left your lives behind

*Jayla Coppetta, Grade 8*
*Sacred Heart Elementary School*

### My Friend

Tough as an ox,
yet soft as a fox.
Sometimes sweet,
sometimes sour,
sometimes a mix.

Pick on a friend,
he won't let.
Like a box of chocolate,
you never know what you get.
The rainbow brightened him.

He might fall, but he's friends with all.
No matter what hue, old or new,
He will be there for you.

*Brent Shue, Grade 8*
*Spring Grove Middle School*

### Music

Music is like the soundtrack to my life
Even though it doesn't tell a story
People dance to it, enjoy the nightlife
The lyrics can be explanatory
There are many different bands to choose
A Day to Remember and All Time Low
Jazz, pop, R&B, and even the blues
Oh how I wish I could go to a show
Up on the stage there is no place to move
Avenged Sevenfold is bloody awesome
I can't help but getting into the groove
Keys to my house after the show, lost 'em
Dude as they build up to a crescendo
Man, I wish the show would never end'o

*Kylie Meckes, Grade 8*
*Pocono Mountain East Jr High School*

### Music

I love listening to music each day
If the power's out, there is no sound
Music makes me feel like, I've run away
Without my music I'd feel like I drowned
Music is loved by all from coast-to-coast
It's like an x-ray going right through me
Without music I might just be a ghost
You can't just hear music; too you can see
Music can come in every shape and size
Everywhere you look you can make music
Listening to music, eating French-fries
No music at all would be no picnic
Listening to lyrics is such a blast
With no music, today would be my last

*Cassandra Swartz, Grade 8*
*Pocono Mountain East Jr High School*

### Blinding Darkness

A quivering girl cowered in the corner,
Of a dark and dusty room,
Feeling the loneliness of a foreigner,
Drowning in the vast gloom.

Darkness obscured her weeping jewels,
Teasing and tormenting her troubled being,
Clouding her view until she saw fools,
Of the precious ones who were now fleeing.

She could not understand why,
Not one person dared to intervene,
When her chaotic life had gone awry,
No one understood what this girl had seen.

*Kaitlyn Carr, Grade 8*
*Pine-Richland Middle School*

### The Great Race

You mount your horse.
You are waiting for the gate to open.
Suddenly, the gate opens and…
You go as fast as you can.
Around the first barrel,
Hoping you don't knock it over.
You're safe!
Now for the second barrel.
Safe again!
The last barrel.
You're safe yet again!
You made it to the end,
Now to see what place you got,
Maybe you won.
Your time comes up,
It's outstanding!
You beat them all,
You were the best.
you got the belt buckle!
The victory is yours!

*Sarah Miller, Grade 8*
*Danville Area Middle School*

### What a Cat Knows

What does a cat know?
Mice filled barns
Balls of yarn
Litter boxes,
Awful foxes
Barking dogs
Skinny logs
Hunting
And jumping
To purr
And to lick its fur
Trees and fleas
Ice cold water
And loudly crying daughters
To hunt at night,
In the moonlight
A loud noise
Playful toys
Purring
And other cats for reassuring

*Meghan McHenry, Grade 7*
*Easton Area Middle School 7-8*

### Flowers as a Symbol of Friendship

Friendship grows like a flower seed
There are so many things flowers need
As do friendships that have been for years
There is happiness and tears
When it eventually ends
Other people tend to fix things

*Hailey Reinbold, Grade 8*
*Northern Lebanon Middle School*

## Things a Janitor Does

They clean
and clean
all day
they don't
get a
good
pay
for all
they work
every day
*Blaze King, Grade 7*
*Easton Area Middle School 7-8*

## Childhood

**C** atch some baseball
**H** ide or maybe go seek
**I** see it everywhere
**L** ike riding a bike
**D** oing something every day
**H** ave a puppy
**O** utside
**O** rdinarily hyper
**D** oing it all over again
*Austin Via, Grade 8*
*Northern Lebanon Middle School*

## Grief

Grief is cold water
It pools at the bottom of your heart
And comes in waves of emotion
Stripping you of comfort with its current

It's suddenly upon you
Tugging and pulling
But the waves will always subside
And the flood will always pass
*Caitlin Bieganski, Grade 8*
*Saegertown Jr/Sr High School*

## Spring

Beautiful flowers,
Really warm weather,
School is almost out,
Rainy April sprouts May blooms,
Animals come out to play.
*Brett Jackson, Grade 7*
*Holy Sepulcher School*

## Man's Best Friend

Dog
Playful, excited
Run, jump, play
Happy, joyful, funny, thoughtful
Loyal
*Charley Darkes, Grade 8*
*Northern Lebanon Middle School*

## Rhetorical

An ocean full of questions overwhelms my mind.

Will I make it? Should I try to?
Am I running out of time?

My first and only sanctuary lays surrounded with doubt.

Is it worth it? Does it matter?
Can anyone here me shout?

And yet the world spins on and on like nothing is the matter.
But these questions we keep asking fuel or mind's endless chatter.

Why does he not love me? Why do I love him?
What else can I hold on to? Can I risk another sin?

Is this life worth living? Do others feel as I?
Why do I say nothing? Would they miss me if I died?

Why is the world so eager to point out others' flaws?
And yet somehow is not required to abide by it's own laws?

Am I alive? Or am I just living?
Is there a difference? What am I missing?

We'll keep asking and asking but never out loud.
And we'll find no reply only more and more doubt.

And I've heard all the roundabout answers, I've heard it's all metaphorical.
But I'm just wondering, could it be?
That life's greatest questions are rhetorical?
*Kirsten Crawford, Grade 8*
*Valley Middle School*

## I Am My Own Worst Enemy

There's a time in the day when I become bored
Then I hear the monster in my head telling me it's okay
So I begin to bite my nails
Without a care in the world

I mess up the pretty nail polish
Then the monster goes away
I regret what has been done
But I don't worry, they'll grow back

I go on about my life not noticing them
But there's always going to be a teacher or a friend telling a boring story
I wish I could control it
Although it's as if I black out and don't know what I'm doing

One day I'll overcome this bad habit
But until then I'll always be cautious about people looking at my nails
So don't be surprised if my hands are in my pockets
It just means the monster is taking a nap
*Olivia Young, Grade 8*
*Penn Middle School*

## Dance

She stands
Arms straight, extended
Her limber, long legs held up by her
Sharp pointed toes

Her white tutu wrapped up around her waist
Slippers tied up in a perfect bow
Beautiful long hair held up in a long ribbon
Not one piece falls

I sit there watching
Hearing the silence as she points
A tear falls down my cheek as I look down and see the
Wheels on either side of me

I wish I could just get up but I stop myself saying
"I will never get up"

She dances for me as she smiles from cheek to cheek
I watch her twirl, spinning
She takes me away to a beautiful place

I try to point my toes like she does
It's very hard but I manage to do it

I sit closing my eyes taking all this in
All this beauty and I…DANCE
*Hannah Huron, Grade 8*
*Danville Area Middle School*

## A Dream

Having your dream come true, is all that counts
No matter how big or small
If you have a goal,
Then strive for it
Don't let anyone bring you down

If you're as big as the president
Or as small as a student in school
Who says you can't live out your dreams
There is no one who can stop you
You're the only one bringing you down

If I had a dream to become the president
I would work at it with all my heart
And you should too
Because everyone deserves the best
No one can tell you differently

Sometimes it may seem impossible
Or you may feel like giving up
Just remember, whether it's big or small
Just strive for it
Because having a dream come true is all that counts
*Olivia O'Connor, Grade 8*
*Sacred Heart Elementary School*

## Her Love Is Forever

You were there for hello
I was there for goodbye
Now that you're gone I try not to cry

I saw you getting thinner
I saw you getting weak
I saw you get to the point where you could barely speak

Although I miss you dearly
I know you suffer no more
Because now you're in heaven and that's nothing to cry for

I love you, Great-Grandma
I always think about the memories we share
And about how losing you was more than I could bear

But what keeps me glued together
What keeps me from falling apart
Is this feeling I have deep in my heart

It tells me that I'll see you again someday
And I know exactly what you'll say
"Hello sweetheart, how are you today?"

So I say goodbye for now
With no tears in my eyes
Because I know that you, Great-Gram, wouldn't want me to cry
*Stacy Stotler, Grade 8*
*Penn Middle School*

## I Am From

I am from a rainbow trout in a deep creek.
Or a palomino that lurks underneath.
I am from an Ugly Stick fishing pole that bends when I got a bite.
I am from the bottom of the pond where the catfish rest at night.

I am from the deer head on the wall.
The chocolate white horns that stand real tall.
I am from the beard on a turkey that shakes when he gobbles.
The blast of a shotgun that makes his head wobble.
I am from the 20 foot tree stand where I get a good view.
I'll stay there as long as I can so I know I'm true.

I'm from the beagle bark when he's got a smell.
It's a big rabbit, that I can tell.
I'm from a long dusty dirt lane.
Where there's mud after a noon storm.
I'm from the crow flying overhead making sure he warns.

I'm from the depth and definition in the realtree camouflage.
The sound of the safety turning off when the deer is at a pause.
I'm from the family, friends and the outdoors.
I'm from the deer munching on the cut corn.
No matter what, I'm from the chocolate white horns.
*Quintin Miller, Grade 8*
*McConnellsburg High School*

## Horses

Horses
Majestic, swift
Muscles rippling
Soarin' like eagles
Never wanting to stop
Galloping
*Katelyn Hossler, Grade 8*
*Northern Lebanon Middle School*

## Flutes

**F** looding the room with sound
**L** ovingly creating the music
**U** sing smooth transitions
**T** urning notes into songs
**E** ach time making the music pretty
**S** inging beautiful notes
*Alyssa Clemmer, Grade 7*
*Pequea Valley Intermediate School*

## Perfection

Brown hair,
Hazel eyes,
Perfect teeth,
Half-smile,
Beautiful personality,
I love it.
*Alexandra Baez, Grade 8*
*Northern Lebanon Middle School*

## Elements of Summer

**S** is for swimming
**U** is for ukulele
**M** is for melon, water
**M** is for mountain pies
**E** is for entertainment
**R** is for reading
*Tyler Schenk, Grade 7*
*Cambria Heights Middle School*

## Puppies or Kittens

It's true that puppies may have fleas,
And true that kittens they will tease,
But kittens bite and scratch,
And kittens can't play catch,
So I'll stick with puppies, please.
*Brittany Keener, Grade 8*
*Ephrata Middle School*

## The Indescribable Temptress

Moon
Opalescent silver,
Glowing, flowing, pooling,
The indescribable temptress remains
Unchained
*Christine Croll, Grade 8*
*Northern Lebanon Middle School*

## My Special Symbol

It was a teeth-chattering night.
The air tasted like ice cubes, making my face smooth and tight.
Everyone was rushing and pushing around, all trying to beat the Black Friday crowd.
My family cried out, "It's right over there!"
We were racing so fast, that we ran over the stairs.
The coach store approached, pulling me near.
When I walked through the door, my face was covered in tears!
It was heaven to me.
Wallets and purses, that's all I could see!
It was so loud in the store, I could barely even think.
Everyone was clawing, trying to get the handbag in pink.
As soon as I saw it, I knew it belonged with me.
A mini plum wallet, decorated with "c"s!
I felt every stitch, imagining it mine.
Each "c" was unique, it was quite fine.
My sister offered to buy it, for Christmas later that year.
I felt so very lucky; it almost brought me a tear.
To this day, it reminds me of my sister.
How she bought me something special, it symbolizes her.
*Elizabeth Dougherty, Grade 7*
*J R Fugett Middle School*

## My Little Star

She looks upon me with curiosity in her big, brown, dancing eyes,
The way she moves so helplessly takes me by surprise.
As gentle as a butterfly, I try to pick her up,
She is so cute and tiny, like a newborn pup.

She is a petite angel, at least when she doesn't cry,
But when she does, I calm her down, by singing a lovely lullaby.
I will give her a kiss and hold her miniature hand,
As she slowly closes her round eyes and drifts off to her own little land,

When she smiles, I do too,
Then in a soft, soothing whisper I say "I love you."
She looks up at me; while I look down at her,
I am so very thankful that she is my little baby sister.
*Elizabeth Yi, Grade 7*
*Pennbrook Middle School*

## Tough Times Are No Match for Love

Life is not easy,
it's not like a walk through a wildflower field,
Tough times exist,
Pain,
Hurt,
Sorrow,
It's tough,
but what if something drowned out all that pain and hurt,
What if there was an overwhelmingly awesome feeling that makes you smile?
There is, Love
Love drowns it all,
it makes you forget that there is reality,
Like a crystal clear breath love is just as refreshing.
*Devin Landis, Grade 8*
*Park Forest Middle School*

## I Remember

I remember when I was really little and danced in my PJ's when I was getting ready for school,
I remember when I first got my brand-new puppy,
I remember when my dad picked me up, tickled me and my giggles filled the air,
And I miss those days so much.
I remember how it felt to not worry about anything,
I remember how I could fit in almost any space because I was so little,
I remember when my dad put my hair up to stick up out of my head,
Even when my parents used to take me to my favorite restaurant every Friday,
I remember being little and knowing so little about the world,
But my favorite memory's yet to come.

*Sabrina Ryan, Grade 7*
*Pequea Valley Intermediate School*

## Things That Remind Me of Home

Welcome Sign     inviting
Open space     plenty of elbow room
Quiet     no "New York City people laying on the horn"
Fields     a second backyard
Barns     place to hide in the hot summer days
Hot summer days     great time to be outside
Tractors     a ride to the fields in the summer
Tractor trailers     seeing them every day outside my window
Pasture fields     seeing cows graze happily
Fresh country air     wildflowers, fresh cut grass, freshly mowed fields, and freshly turned over dirt

*Cheyenne Dyarman, Grade 7*
*Big Spring Middle School*

## Beach

I know the beach…I hear the waves crashing on the seashore. I hear the seagulls chirping for food. I hear people yelling because they're having fun. I hear the lifeguards blowing their whistles at people telling them to stop doing wrong.
I know the beach…I see kids playing in the hot warm sand. I see people swimming in the ocean. I see the nice clear blue sky looking down at everyone. I also see the fish jumping out of the sea waving to the people on the beach.
I know the beach…I smell the wet sand on the ground. I smell the salt from the saltwatery ocean. I smell the good food from the boardwalk. I smell the grossness of the dead fish that washed up on the shore.
I know the beach…"Let's go surfing dude!" "Owww! A sand crab pinched me!" "Look at our amazing sandcastles!" "Hey look a jellyfish!"
I guess I really do know the beach after all…

*Lindsey Halerz, Grade 8*
*Ephrata Middle School*

## The Sister I Should Have Been

The sister I should have been has a slender body.
She has graceful arms and hands, so she can hug her brother.
The sister I should have been has the ability to understand her brother.
She is a good listener and listens to her brother's thoughts and feelings.
The sister I should have been says, "Oh, I can lend you money! You need it more than I do."
The sister I should have been is rich and her life is always pleasant.
Long ago, she lost record of how many days had passed since she said a mean word to her brother.
Now, she wishes she had loosened up and had what I had: a childhood!
With arguing, laughing, misunderstanding, and having fun.

*Rachel Kroch, Grade 7*
*Strath Haven Middle School*

### What Do Trees Know?
They are big.
They are small.
They're tall.
They're made into walls.
They see you from above.
They're great for turtle doves.
They're oaks.
They're smokes.
They are made into paper.
They're skinny as vapor.
What they see is you and me
They are home to bee's
They love us all
And some will never fall.
*Reanna Marie Worman, Grade 7*
*Easton Area Middle School 7-8*

### Gone Away
The leaves are gone
my heart is broke
he is gone left alone.
Why did he leave I don't know.
I miss him, I wonder if he thinks of me
I wonder if he knows I still
love him, so oh why oh why
did he go I am left
alone in this world
goodbye, adieu's
I guess I am better off without him
I will move on
And get him off
my mind.

*Amber Markley, Grade 8*
*Spring Grove Middle School*

### Swim Practice
Hot like the desert,
Wet like the beach,
And the smell of chlorine,
I have just arrived at swim practice.

I jump in.
The water as cold as ice,
Splash, splash, splash,
Racing through the water.

I can barely breathe,
My breath is taken from me.
Just one more thing to do,
Go run stairs.
*Abby Wentling, Grade 8*
*Pine-Richland Middle School*

### Clearly Written
My head hangs low
As I wonder,
Wonder if I
Want to be noticed.
Choose to be seen?
I try to hide it.
To shake it, and everybody off.
But it never works.
I just cannot wait to get
Home.
Home alone.
Just the music and I,
My mental healings and I.
Everything is in my way.
The crack in the road and the locked door.
I just want to stop.
Stop it all.
Stop the world.
*Paige Parshall, Grade 8*
*Bellmar Middle School*

### What a Catcher Knows
Strikes and balls
Dives and falls
Bases stolen
Runners coming
Coaches yelling
Give the signal
Here it comes
Bats swing
Now the cheers, ring
First, second, third
Now the runner comes home
The ball has no time to roam
It comes to me.
I catch and tag with glee.
The umpire yells she's out
The pitcher cheers,
Now I know what it's all about
We won
*Alison Nicolosi, Grade 7*
*Easton Area Middle School 7-8*

### The Path of a Thunderstorm
Clouds, darkness, chills,
Darkness, chills, rain,
Chills, rain, thunder,
Rain, thunder, lightning,
Thunder, lightning, pounding,
Lightning, pounding, cracking,
Pounding, cracking, flash,
Cracking, flash, darkness,
Flash, darkness, quiet,
Darkness, quiet, gone.
*Rebekah Pauley, Grade 8*
*Ephrata Middle School*

### Unique and Confident
I am unique and confident.
I wonder how I'm going to do this year.
I hear teachers.
I see classrooms.
I want good grades.
I am unique and confident.

I pretend to be an actress.
I feel my dog's bear-like fur.
I touch my hair.
I worry I won't do well this year.
I cry when I see sad movies.
I am unique and confident.

I understand I can't roll my tongue.
I say to be yourself.
I dream of having a lot of pets.
I try to work hard.
I hope to someday be successful.
I am unique and confident.
*Nicola Barrett, Grade 8*
*J R Fugett Middle School*

### Express
I dance even when in pain
Knowing there is something to gain

I dance to express

I dance for me
And for my loved ones to see

I dance to express

I dance all the time
Knowing that I shine

I dance to express

I dance with my best friend
Knowing that we blend

I dance to express…
Not to impress
*Lauren Kemler, Grade 8*
*Ephrata Middle School*

### Sadness Ends with a Broken Heart
Sadness is blue
It smells like rain
It looks like piles of tissues
It tastes like tubs of cookie-dough ice cream
It sounds like the cry of the winds
It feels like a broken heart
*Lauren Gerkovich, Grade 8*
*Northwestern Lehigh Middle School*

### Fading

Tell me why,
You leave me without goodbye.
Explain to me,
What we used to be.
They never last,
Fade into the past.
Forget your name,
Forget your smile.
That only lasts a while.
Let me go,
When I want to stay.
Tell me no,
I'll go away.
Why?
I'm fading away.
Into the past
Fading quick…
Fading fast…

*Emily Nichols, Grade 8*
*Wattsburg Area Middle School*

### Flyers

Flyers are the name,
Hockey is the game.
And the game is tonight,
It's going to be a fight.
They are playing their rivals,
The team from New York.
The hatred is going to be there
Like it is between a bully and dork.
As game time approaches,
The teams listen to their coaches,
And prepare themselves for battle.
It is game time now,
The Wells Fargo Center is loud,
And nothing else matters.
The puck is dropped
And the whistle is blown.
Who wins this game?
I guess you will never know.

*Joey Abel, Grade 8*
*Paxon Hollow Middle School*

### Lifeless

Why does it have to be this way?
The lies, the hatred, the anger.
We used to be closer than ever,
Thought we'd be friends until the end.
What happened to the joy?
The spark between us that used to
Shine to the world.
I wish it could be the same
Again my friend.
What happened?

*Rachael Kovach, Grade 8*
*Wattsburg Area Middle School*

### Mistakes

I'm not perfect.
No one is.
Yet I'm treated as if,
I can't make mistakes.
This makes my mind,
blow up into a million pieces.
I can only take so much,
until I become nothing.
My heart goes CRASH!
Right then and there,
I'm nothing but dust.
My inner strength can be,
as strong as a bull.
But if I'm pressured too much,
I'm as weak as a feather.
Mistakes are made,
just like babies crying.
It happens often,
but you have to stay calm.

*Marah Foltz, Grade 8*
*Centerville Middle School*

### Summer

Summer,
Summer,
Summer.

Warm summer,
Wonderful summer,
Sleep-like-a-rock summer,
Party-all-night summer,
Those are just a few.
Swim summer,
Sweet summer,
Dancing, swaying trees summer.
Sweet like chocolate summer,
Lazy summer, too!
On-the-run summer,
Traveling summer,
Don't forget sandy summer.
Last of all, best of all,
I like my family's summer.

*Nick Walter, Grade 8*
*Centerville Middle School*

### My Dad

He's not just my dad,
He is my hero.
He is one of a kind.
When he is around,
I feel safe.
Without him, my world isn't complete.
We're not just father and daughter.
But we're like brother and sister.

*Kendyle Bennett, Grade 7*
*Bellmar Middle School*

### Ballet Slippers

Small, delicate, pink
wrapped around my feet
helping me spin round and round
and never miss a beat

You're always there to help me
you never let me fall
keeping me on my tiptoes
towering above all

You compliment my skirts
leotards and costumes
watching as I turn
and leap around the room

Keeping my balance for my pose
making sure I look my best
taking careful care of my toes
first, fifth never rest

And at the end recital
when all is said and done
you're always there to see
the great dancer I've become.

*Megan Miller, Grade 8*
*Spring Grove Middle School*

### Disguised

She looks like she's happy
Without a care in the world
But if you look in her eyes
Her story starts to unfold

Her smile is forced
As she laughs with her friends
Her poise acts like a shield
Against the pain that never ends

Her perfection pretended
While she wanders the world
Her smile concocted
Her voice still unheard

Her makeup protects her,
A mask on her face
Her feelings are guarded
She feels out of place

Her struggles are great
Her dreams seem so far
But she must never forget
You should be who you are

*Raahema Durrani, Grade 7*
*Fort Couch Middle School*

### First of All, Stop Calling Yourselves Victims
to all of the people who cry on cameras when your "loved ones" are killed and then try to put away the innocent,
first of all,
stop calling yourself victims,
because you're not lying in a coffin

you're just distracting our justice system,
with your cries of "justice for all" that include hanging and filthy
prison cells,
because it's not the fault of police or prosecutors that the innocent
are put away as guilty,
it's you,
with your denial and need for a conviction at all costs

do whatever you want in your own home,
but I'm sick of you in a justice system
that should be focused on freedom and opportunity,
and I'm sick of you believing the world is so black and white
that revenge is unconditionally possible,
and I think you're sick for wanting revenge and painful justice even without proof,
and that you're animals,
hidden by bleach-blonde hair and boring tears
and precise suits

*Evan Boone, Grade 8*
*21st Century Cyber Charter School*

### Love
Love is a word that is overused, stereotyped, and often abused.
Those songs and movies about it have gone bad; it really is rather sad.
Some people pretend to love each other; I really wonder why they bother.
Don't just love someone 'cause you think they're hot; I'll tell you that is exactly what love is not!
Love shouldn't be in the same song as a curse; it also should not, at all, be forced.
People can choose how they want to portray it, but usually, when they do, they often betray it.
Love is beautiful, I have no doubt; love is something to talk about.
Don't save all of your love for Valentine's Day; spread your love every day and in every way.
Love is a song that holds the world in place; love is a feeling that cannot be replaced.
Love should be pure, happy, and never-ending; maybe you should think about that message you're sending.
You can have it your way, but just listen to what I say.
You only have one life, so you have to do it right; treat others with love, and your life will be bright.

*Rachel Whitten, Grade 7*
*Indian Valley Middle School*

### Haters
People look at me and laugh at me
People make fun of every move I make
I wonder why people always hate
Is it because of how I act?
Is it because of how I dress?
Is it because of who I am?
People don't just talk about me they do everything they can to humiliate me
I try not to care but it is too hard not to
Eventually I thought to myself why should I care about what people think?
While these people waste their time talking about me, I'm using my time to walk away and keep my head up.
People these days hate each other for no reason.
I learned not to give into haters.

*Pina Rocco, Grade 9*
*Pennbrook Middle School*

## Thinking of Summer

The cold bites through your coat,
As you recall the days when you could just float
All day in the pool,
Instead of going to school.
Now those days seem so far in the past,
Summer is just an old friend.
The long days spent at the park,
With the heat beating down on your back,
The times watching fireworks in the dark.
When you only went inside to grab a snack.
The cold has been here for so long,
Summer seems to have been just a dream.
The days that everyone hated then,
Are the days we hope for now.
the heat that came again and again,
Now makes us say "Wow."
Summer has been gone for so long,
We forgot that the weather could be hot.

*Kerri Little, Grade 8*
*Bellwood Antis Middle School*

## Clap of Thunder

Your eyes reflect the golden lightning
Upon dilated pupils, black as night.
First breathtakingly beautiful, then frightening;
Once open, they make the world ignite.
Thunder emits from your forceful yell,
But still it becomes even stronger;
Every one of your howls empowers the spell,
And allows your reign to last even longer.
You dodge trees as you run full speed ahead;
Contact is made between Earth and your paws,
Releasing more powerful thunder instead
Of coughing up dust; you have no flaws.
Pounce once, and everyone rushes to hide
From your furious, yet glorious, show.
You bring destruction, anyone can decide,
But still everyone loves the blinding glow.
A snap of your jaw is a clap of thunder;
A cliffhanger that leaves us all to wonder.

*Sarah Turturro, Grade 7*
*Pennwood Middle School*

## Kennywood

The Phantom flying down the hills
Hanging upside down on the Aero 360
Getting drenched on the Raging Rapids
Bouncing on the Kangaroo
Ducking where roller coaster tracks cross
Nervous people screaming on rides
The sun warming everyone
Cold water splashing up on the Log Jammer
Rushing wind while racing down the tracks
Stomachs flip-flopping before dropping down a hill
The excitement of winning a prize $20 later
Hot and cheesy French fries at Potato Patch
Ice-cold refreshing lemonade
Warm funnel cake with sweet powdered sugar
Fruity slushies from the Slush Factory
Eating ice cream while leaving the park
Falling asleep on the way home
Making memories with friends

*Autumn Alko, Grade 8*
*Penn Middle School*

## As You Grow Old

As you grow old your lights start to fade,
And you struggle with age,
As you grow old your limbs bend and break,
Just like a tree you grow and you die,
As the birds chirp and fly,
You wonder where your youth went,
As the young kids on their cell phones have 150 messages sent
You sit and wonder how your life went by so fast,
Your knowledge is like oceans vast

You start to complain about your son touching the heat
And young men and women help you cross the street
Your legs feel weak,
All your furniture is antique,
Your life is bleak
It gets harder to speak
You can't get the comfort you seek
"Ring ring," "Hello?" Your mother passed away last week

*Hunter Warnick, Grade 8*
*Donegal Middle School*

## I Remember

I remember my week at Alaska
I remember diving into the ice-cold water
I remember eating steaming Alaskan salmon
Ice plummeting from glaciers
I remember the warm beds
I remember playing chess in the lounge
I remember the giant boat we traveled in
Even all the beautiful cities we visited
I remember exploring the Alaskan wilderness
But my favorite memory's yet to come

*Connor Horst, Grade 7*
*Pequea Valley Intermediate School*

## Music Is

What a wondrous thing music is.
The reason to come to school in the morning.
The pathway beneath your feet, tread by so many.
The glimmer of light in the nighttime shadows.
The sight of truth when you are deafened by deception.
The promise of hope when you are discouraged by despair.
The invisible force that binds us together.
The wings that allow us to soar.
The spark in our souls that makes us…
Human.

*Hannah Rutt, Grade 7*
*Cocalico Middle School*

## Boarding

Swerving down the hill
carving out a path,
a signature
made in the hill's
white foam
that shines in the light.
More riders come
to tame
the white beast
with a toy
known as the board.
*Brandon Borel, Grade 7*
*Garnet Valley Middle School*

## Niagara Falls

The breeze in your face
The wind in your hair
The fresh water
The cool feeling
The crash, the beautiful sight
The calm, relaxing feeling in the air
The silence as everyone stands in awe
The majestic overlook
The shock when you first see it
Then, wow!
It's amazing
*JR Yenser, Grade 7*
*Tulpehocken Jr/Sr High School*

## Game Day

Shoes are laced,
Game faces are on,
And the crowd awaits.
Players take the field.
One, two, three!
The whistle sounds.
Dribble, dribble, and pass.
Kick!
Goal!
They've won!
And the crowd goes wild.
*Abby Selan, Grade 9*
*Bishop McCort High School*

## A Choice

A choice you have from good or bad
A choice you have from right or wrong
An important choice you have to make
Between happiness or sadness
To attend school and go to college
To be a good or bad person
A choice you have to make yourself
Be wise and choose wisely
It might change your life
*Nick Seidel, Grade 8*
*Northern Lebanon Middle School*

## The Day We Met

There I was, sitting like a mantis with bad posture, alone
Feeling like a rat at a mall
Wearing both my sorrows and regrets as a blanket

Why did he have to go?
He wouldn't say

That was before the day we met
When your sun reflected on my dark night and you held tightly as if
my hand was a pencil and we danced the night away

Our eyes and hearts connected like a puzzle when the music became slower than a snail
I could barely feel any part of my body because of the gentle force that hit me
when you held my hand on the day we met

We both share the same words except with your voice, it was an angel
We were two free birds just getting out of our cages both happy together

Then, my eyes awaken, still sitting here alone but almost sick
Until I see a wondrous creature coming up to me saying, "Let me hold your hand"
On that glorious day we met
*Erin Leso, Grade 8*
*First Philadelphia Preparatory Charter School for Literacy*

## Ocean

The waves crashing on the sand,
The smell of the salt water,
The sting in your eyes when the salt gets in your eyes,
The salty taste when you swallow some water,
You feel the plants and shells under your feet,
You watch as the dolphins jump in and out of the water in the distance,
The flow of the water as you float on your back,
Just thinking of the unexplored world below,
When you dive under and see all the amazing creatures,
To see all the happy friends and families together,
Everyone flying kites or tossing a Frisbee,
As you sit on the edge of the water you watch the sun turn into a full moon,
What is it you ask,
Think harder you can guess,
How about…the ocean.
*Caroline Choromanski, Grade 7*
*Our Lady of Mount Carmel School*

## Equestrianism

He paws the dirt ground of the racetrack with his strong hoof.
His tall, lean jockey grips the twists of light brown mane in his fists, tightly.
Screaming,
Yelling,
Tickets waving everywhere.
All the miraculous horse hears is silence.

This is Equestrianism,
This is MY obsession.
*Audra Morgan, Grade 7*
*Strath Haven Middle School*

**November**
November sweeps the fall season with tints of claret and orange
Says the burning winds that tamper with the greens and the soft leaves that fall from the trees
The tasteful colors burn to brown, like the petals of wilting flowers they hit the ground
Swift as the brisk last rains, as full as the celebrating feasts
November weaves its way for her brother, who is mothering the cold snowy beast

*Meghan Quinn, Grade 7*
*Garnet Valley Middle School*

**Hero**
There are many definitions of a hero
Like muscular and tall

But that's not necessarily true
They could be short and have no muscles at all

My definition of a hero is someone who has…

COURAGE, something
You need to be a hero

BRAVERY, a key ingredient
You need to be a hero

AFFECTION, you need a big heart is a thing
You need to be a hero

KINDNESS, is the most important thing
You need to be a hero

Someone who is fearless
And will do anything to help anyone

Someone who pursues good not evil

Someone who will help you up and dust you off when you fall
Everyone needs heroes

Without heroes the world would be terrible
We need them

HEROES

*Matt McAndrews, Grade 7*
*Strath Haven Middle School*

**Capture the Moment**
Her name tells of how
It is with her
Seeing life through a special lens
Puzzled by how the obvious is not obvious to others
A strong, supportive friend
Her quiet hides an artistic mind
She's like a rainbow that sees things in color
Imagining and creating the movie of life
Through talented eyes, she captures the moment

*Korin Bradley, Grade 7*
*Sandburg Middle School*

**Jesus' Death**
Tonight was the night.
My son told me it would come.

The sky dark with no light.
I could hear the wind hum.

My heart trembled with fear.
What was going to take place?

My cheek stained with a tear,
as I hurried with such haste.

I was racing through the mob,
and began to uncontrollably sob.

My poor baby was hurt,
they were treating him like dirt.

Next he was carrying a cross
and I stopped to take a pause

I caught the look in his eyes,
he finally died with a sigh

I left wailing so loud.
What else could I do?

There was no longer a crowd.
Who would take his place, who?

*Hannah Brubaker, Grade 8*
*Lancaster Mennonite School - Locust Grove*

**Don't Forget Me**
I see you like you see me,
So why can't it just be you and me,
And you not to like anyone else like you like me,
I know you won't have a friend like me,
So why can't it be,
Just you and me?
Because we are like apples on a tree,
And, I know you're my best friend,
And always will be,
So just please, don't forget me,
Because we are,
TOGETHER FOREVER!

*Jordan Barclay, Grade 7*
*Pennbrook Middle School*

**The Embarrassment of Life**
Parents…when they are meeting my friends
for the first time, acting like creepy monsters.
Friends…when they do crazy things in front
of me in public. Rowdy people in public…with loud,
booming, screechy voices. Siblings…when they tell people things
you did when you were little. Teachers…when they pick on me
in front of the class.
My niece Lilly…when she screams and
whines all over town.

Getting food on my clothes…
splattered everywhere, visible to see.
Dancing…when I don't know the moves
and I can't dance. Singing…afraid to show what
comes out from inside. When I don't know the answer to
a question…
I can hear the snickers from the back
of the room.
*Lauren Seiple, Grade 7*
*Big Spring Middle School*

**I Am…**
I am not afraid to share my opinion, I think outside of the box
I wonder if we are real
I hear ghost whispers
I see hope in the air
I want a cure for diabetes
I am not afraid to share my opinion, I think outside of the box
I pretend that nothing is wrong with me
I feel staring eyes
I touch hopes and dreams of many
I worry about death
I cry when I feel grief
I am not afraid to share my opinion, I think outside of the box
I understand that life is precious
I say God is true
I dream about murder
I try to be myself
I hope for world peace
I am not afraid to share my opinion, I think outside of the box
*Alexis Caltrider, Grade 7*
*South Side Middle School*

**Love**
Love is caring,
Love is kind,
Love is something we should all keep in mind.
Hopefully, love is around the world,
Love should run through both boys and girls.
Love is both my grandfathers in heaven,
The last time I saw you was when I was eleven.
Your love will and always forever be with me,
Because your love was very sweet and lovely,
Rest in peace, love, Tayler.
*Tayler Robinson, Grade 7*
*Barack Obama Academy*

**Forest**
I will explore a forest that's distinct
A place which is full of green and tall trees
Choose paths to explore before it's extinct
Because that hold nature's true mysteries

Sighting new wild animals would be cool
Finding a tiger could be very hard
But to go near him, I would be a fool
If so, I might end up in a graveyard

Though camping out there would be fun at night
Hearing wolves howling loudly for their mate
In dark creepy woods nothing in my sight
That is what I really don't like and hate

So my dream is to go there at one time
Even if I had to spend every dime
*Devarshi Gohil, Grade 8*
*Pocono Mountain East Jr High School*

**Let's Do Lunch**
Let's do lunch
Lunch
At home
Shall we make some lunch?
Hearty, slurping, delectable
Hot like a volcano or sweet as cherries
What should it be?
It should simmer like the sidewalk in the summer
And swish like a deep, vast ocean
Maybe some classic chicken noodle
Maybe some rich green bean casserole
No, no, no, no, it should be…
OH! I got it!
We should make,
Creamy broccoli
Yes, that's it we should make creamy broccoli soup
Let's do lunch
*Nick Vescio, Grade 7*
*South Side Middle School*

**Help Me Now**
I don't know which way to go,
my head keeps turning to and fro.
Keep away from the darkness,
turn to the light.
Please help me now this very night,
and help me do what is right.
Make me feel great tonight.
You are the light in the darkness,
that I have found.
You make me jump around and around.
I will stay in your light,
and I will not turn away this very night.
*Abigail Roberts, Grade 7*
*Lancaster Mennonite School - Locust Grove*

### Spirit

The horse's name was Spirit,
you can see why when he runs.
His mane, whipping in the air,
as he tries to fly with an eagle.

Not watching where he's going,
he is caught up in a trap.
Two-leggers with sticks
captured, with a fight.
He finds his chance and makes a move,
freeing other horses too.
He once was caught. But not again,
free and running with the eagle, his friend.

*Charles Rissmiller, Grade 7*
*Tulpehocken Jr/Sr High School*

### Winter

Winter is death in a dark hole
It feels like it never stops happening
But when it does
I feel sad, but happy

When spring starts
And we go outside, people
Think they're going to die
When fall comes back and
Everything dies
I can never believe
My eyes
Why does everything die?

*Brandon McAlister, Grade 7*
*Tulpehocken Jr/Sr High School*

### Sadness

Sadness is like a black rose.
It's very dark,
nobody comes back from the hole,
but deep inside their soul,
they feel a catastrophe,
you feel so sad.
You feel so mad.
You just want to
get out and about.
You're still stuck in this hole,
but you feel like a mole,
deeper and deeper till finally
you're out.

*Christian Gromlich, Grade 7*
*Tulpehocken Jr/Sr High School*

### Tiger

Orange and black stripes
Hunts, eats other animals
Big paws, white whiskers

*Damien Shaub, Grade 7*
*Pequea Valley Intermediate School*

### Lost to the Streets

We're losing the generation to the streets, too many murders in one week.
So many gunshots you can't sleep, waking you up with thought of
who's it gonna be?

One little argument and we turn to a trigger, what happened to this world?
Now it's all fights and violence, then the gun goes off and there's silence.

What happened to the dream?
16 and pregnant? No. 14 and slave to the corner? No.
What about 18 and educated? 30 and successful?
Live the dream…Live YOUR dream.

Little kids growing up in trash, learning to use drugs,
dying so soon, bodies turning to ash.

Parents used to call their kids and set a curfew,
Now it's just do what you want, survive if you have to.

A generation now belonging to the streets, what happened to the dream?
It's not too late,
There's still a chance to bring your kid in safe.

*Heather Weaver, Grade 8*
*First Philadelphia Charter School for Literacy*

### Test Drive

I approached a small white car.
I sat in the driver's seat and pushed the smooth round start button.
I slammed on the gas and heard the vicious, vigorous, vroom of the engine.
I'm going 140 M.P.H. on the track.
I came up to a corner, instantly I cut the wheel to the left and drifted all the way around.
It felt like I was going as fast as a jet plane, and yet the ride is smoother than sea glass.
I approach my favorite corner, so I sat on the brakes and followed through.
Once it started to straighten up I released the brake and put it at full throttle.
It propelled me like a bullet, and felt like a 20 lb. weight was on my chest.
I came to the end of the track and I decided to show off.
At the end of the track I sped up, going 120 M.P.H.
I pulled the hand brake and turned the wheel to its farthest.
I could feel a force push me forward.
I stood out of the car and was walking away through the thick,
Smelly fog of smoke from the burning rubber.

*Nico Albertson, Grade 7*
*William Penn Middle School*

### I Remember

I remember the vacations to Rays Town Lake
I remember riding my bike to the candy shop
I remember tubing with my cousins
And jumping off the cliffs
I remember sitting on the bow of the boat feeling the wind on my face
I remember sitting by the fire talking and laughing
I remember the delicious mountain pies
Even trying to make breakfast in the cramped camper
I remember going swimming
But my favorite memories are yet to come

*Rhiannon Peachey, Grade 7*
*Pequea Valley Intermediate School*

## Goodbye

Thinking of you,
My thoughts go on and on
Dreaming of you,
I can sleep all day long
Trusting you,
The trust I once had for you is long gone
Believing you, that would just be wrong
You were my best friend, my love
I actually thought we could last
Things switched up
Now you're my past.
As time changed and you played your games,
I benefited from it in a way.
You made me stronger with all the hits of your lies and deceit
You're out my life now I feel complete
Although I'll miss you as time goes by,
The time has come to say goodbye…

*Nerrisa Hurde, Grade 9*
*Motivation High School*

## Onset of Winter

As winter dawns,
I observe changes everywhere

Gray, gloomy skies surround me,
Short, long days trap me inside

Outside, chilly, whizzing winds embrace me,
Ice cold air stiffens my body

Barren, leafless trees are all around me,
Birds fly South in search of warmth

I see my own breath linger in the air,
It is a ghostly white

I put my hands by the fire for heat,
And think, when will it be spring

*Travis Ives, Grade 9*
*Holicong Middle School*

## Summer Riding

Summer is the time of acting crazy.
The once soaked ground is now barren and dried.
Trough winter, you're used to being lazy.
Now that it's summer, go have fun outside.

I like to practice wheelies on my bike.
It's the second lightest bike of its kind.
It's designed for the street and dirt alike.
This bike is so nice it will blow your mind.

My Honda dirt bike is so amazing.
I'm flying through the warm summer air.
I want to become involved in racing.
If I did, racers would say that's not fair.

I really love anything with a wheel.
To do all of this, summer is ideal.

*Brandon Reiner, Grade 8*
*Pocono Mountain East Jr High School*

## 9/11

The sky filled with smoke
The sound of bodies dropping into their fate
Firefighters fled into the building
Family members hoping their loved ones are alive
Our world won't be the same
All that is left was a dirty city
Our world is crumbling down in front of us
Why can't the world come together as one?
Violence will never be the answer
Let's try and stop terrorist attacks
Peace
We can rebuild our city of New York
This time make it bigger and better than last time
Everyone join hands to help
Hope
Even though lots of people died that day
Doesn't mean America died

*Erin Mathews, Grade 7*
*Indian Valley Middle School*

## Just Because I Am Black

Just because I am black

Doesn't mean I am a criminal
Doesn't mean I am one of Kony's victims
Doesn't mean I am a tough guy
Doesn't mean I am amazing at basketball like LeBron James

Why should it matter?
Why does it matter?
Why do you care?

Can't we just get along?

*Anthony Pagan, Grade 7*
*Prospect Park School*

## Riding in Autumn

Riding down the midnight trail,
On my grey and dappled horse,
With his black tail and mane,
We galloped down the mighty paths,
We jumped over logs and ran through streams.
Running for hours so carefree,
Feeling the autumn breeze,
Running through the colorfully fallen leaves,
Red, yellow, and golden brown,
So many leaves on the ground!
My wind-struck hair, I'm happy at last
I think I'm home today!

*Taylor Shildt, Grade 8*
*Bellwood Antis Middle School*

### Not an Empty Shell

I am not the me others want.
The shell that I take up holds me.
It gives me purpose, but it is only temporary
What I give, what I achieve,
That is forever.
I cannot be an image created by others.
What am I then,
But an empty shell?

I am free, I am me.
Not the me everyone wants me to be.
Why should I be the product of others' vision?
I cannot stand tall like a skyscraper,
I have my doubts.
I cannot charge with headstrong aggression,
I have my fears.
I can have some courage, some confidence, and some smarts,
But not all.
I respect other's opinions and advice,
But I am not their painting.
I am the artist.
I am me.

*Siddarth Narayan, Grade 8*
*Marshall Middle School*

### Working Out Is

working out is a tree
sometimes you will be
just as you please
then your leaves fall
never mind a rake
we implement a trainer
working out is an art project
your body is clay
the dumbbells are paint brushes wiping away
inside you is a canvas
you choose the paint colors
the brightness of fruits
or the greasiness of fries
your body is yours
you choose the disguise

*Kelsey Hess, Grade 8*
*Ephrata Middle School*

### Too Young, to Leave

Had so much potential,
But getting pushed too much too hard
Never allowed to say no or give up
Then one day as you were trying to get it Perfect
One little thing that didn't seem like a big deal
Put you on life support
And then God reached out his hand and you took it.

R.I.P. Whyatt

*Kaley Donmoyer, Grade 8*
*Northern Lebanon Middle School*

### Easter

Easter only comes once a year
When you look for a basket in an unseen place
The kids have no fear
That the Easter bunny will hide eggs in a hidden space

No one will be the same shape or size
The yard will be a rainbow of pleasant surprises
The kids are in the kitchen with many colored dyes
And once all of the eggs are found, there are a plethora of prizes

Once all have cracked open their eggs
They will file into the kitchen for the dinner that has been made
We will eat and sit down to rest our legs
And think of the memories that will never fade

As everyone goes home after this eventful day
We are all tired, so we decide to hit the hay

*Molly Storz, Grade 8*
*Lake-Lehman Jr High School*

### My Little One

When fall came round there were some changes near.
The wind blew seed up and into the ground.
The snow helped keep it safe and sound in here.
I waited in excitement to be crowned.

I knew the beauty that was kept inside
And knew when spring came round it would need care.
It sprouted and my joy I could not hide.
This little fragile plant I could not share.

But critters gathered close to watch it feed
And stared in awe as it grew big and strong.
My gardeners tended to its every need.
We loved him for with us he did belong.

Still every day a brother brings much fun.
I whisper soft, "I love my little one."

*Antonia Hassan, Grade 8*
*Pine-Richland Middle School*

### Forest on the Mountain

The vast mixture of tree types
Wild animals scattered freely in the valley
Peaceful chirps and trickles from
Soaring hawks to a hillside stream
Maybe an adventurous hiker roams the trails
Seeking to discover something abnormally new
Peck, peck goes a woodpecker on a
Tall solid tree trunk from a distance
Crawling about among the greens of life
Could be a caterpillar chomping on a leaf
Oh the humble forest on the mountain
Where mother nature lives in no state of danger

*Kyle Sweigart, Grade 8*
*Ephrata Middle School*

## One of Them Things

Sometimes they're hard.
Sometimes they're easy.
It ain't always perfect,
But yet it is.
You enjoy the time you have,
And wish the times you don't.
You dream,
You wish,
But together you unite.
Relationships.

*Sam Crone, Grade 8*
*Danville Area Middle School*

## A Shining Night

Tonight is a shining night;
it gives me great peace.
To see the stars;
to see my future.
As I look in the sky;
I see the North Star.
It is my guide in the night;
it is my hope for my future.
Bright as bright can be;
full of wonder.

*Mary DePrimio, Grade 9*
*Bishop McCort High School*

## Boring, Snoring, Poetry

Writing poems is really boring
As I write I feel like snoring
The clouds are dreary
I start to feel oh so weary
I don't know what to say
It is mostly about my day
As the yellow bus is rolling
Even that seems really boring
My day is finally over
I can see it's finally over

*Austin Johnson, Grade 8*
*Donegal Middle School*

## What a Skater Knows

Putting on your blades
Cruising with your shades
Out on a summer day
It's so hot, I can just decay
Acting like you're dancing
But all you're really doing is prancing
We all had our fun
I think this day is done
Tying up my bows
And that's what a skater knows

*Julie Stout, Grade 7*
*Easton Area Middle School 7-8*

## Words

Words float through my head night and day,
Words of this and that, I sometimes don't know what to say.
Some are simple and some are rare,
But no matter how much I stumble or ramble, the words are always there.
Words can hurt and words can heal,
They can annoy, they can anger, and some are as catchy as a fishing reel.
Without words our world would be so bland,
It would be like a beach with no seashells in the sand.
Words help people of all times and all ages connect.
A wordless world would be one huge wreck.
There is a myriad amount of words, and almost all of them are necessary.
Words needed and unwanted can be found in the dictionary.
Words describe what I see, what I think, and how I am feeling.
I can state how red the apple is and how the smell of the rose is very appealing.
Words are a fantastic thing,
If I put them together correctly, I can make a rhythm that I can sing.
Words are everywhere I look,
They are on posters, signs, and of course in books.
Without words I do not know where I would be.
Without words I would not be able to write poetry.

*Aurora Mills, Grade 8*
*St Luke the Evangelist School*

## My Competition

I've competed so hard
My life is just one big competition
My competition just doesn't stop
The competition is like a roller coaster that doesn't stop
you can't hop off anytime you want
You have to go along for the ride
It's a roller coaster that has bumps and loops

I have ridden that roller coaster so long
I wonder if it's ever going to stop
In the end the roller coaster will teach me something and hopefully bring me joy
The roller coaster ride is teaching me
You have to fight till the finish line
If you fall along the way
You have to pick yourself up and keep going

*Mary Miller, Grade 7*
*Schuylkill Valley Middle School*

## Oceans

The ocean is a mystery
It is not what it seems to be
It just looks like a bunch of water
But really it is a huge world, home to a lot of creatures
We can't even get to the bottom of the ocean
We know very little about the ocean
It's a big mystery, ready to be solved
There are many oceans, and they are huge.
People swim in them, and take its water to use.
We take a lot from the ocean, but really don't know what the ocean is
Until we finally know about the ocean, it is a huge mystery.

*Ethan Reed, Grade 7*
*Barack Obama Academy*

### The Sun

Bright, Beaming, Warm
The Sun gives everything light and warmth
Bringing joy and pleasure all around
As he hangs in the sky each day

Big, Lively, Uplifting
The Sun plays around as he peeks through the clouds
Looking down below on the objects that exist on his planet
Delivering happiness on rainy days throughout the sky

Powerful, Massive, Fierce
The Sun disappears behind his opposite
Shining though with a mysterious glow
When there is a solar eclipse taking over the skylight

Beautiful, Delightful, Magnificent
He says goodbye as he paints the sky with his graceful colors
Transforming the clouds to stars, the Sun temporarily departs
Then sleeps overnight and trades jobs with his friend,

The Moon

*Megan Price, Grade 8*
*Penn Middle School*

### Summer

I dislike fall because it gets cold,
And the green becomes red, yellow, and orange,
And winter begins to take hold.

I hate winter because of the snow,
I can't see the cactus on my porch,
Because of that my brain is so slow.

I really hate spring because of the rain,
It's always very gloomy and gray,
And that drives me completely insane.

I love summer because there's no school,
And the days are always warm,
I get to swim in my cousin's pool.

*Jairo Zamudio, Grade 9*
*Avon Grove High School*

### Farm

**A** pples falling from the trees
**B** ees buzzing through sunflower fields
**C** ows chewing on grass in the pasture
**D** ogs playing in the yard
**E** ating fresh-grown corn for dinner
**F** arming the fields near home
**G** rowing fresh sweet flowers
**H** ay bales stacked up in the barn
**I** ce cream dripping from the cone
**J** umping into the creek on a hot summer day

*Chloe Conroy, Grade 8*
*Ephrata Middle School*

### Poems and Why I Don't Write Them

I have trouble
Writing poems
I can't get the words to sound
Just right.
So I don't try
   Poems are defined
   By creative freedom
   To express feelings
So I will express mine.
Why all the rules about writing poems?
   Some poems rhyme
   Some make you cry
Or realize how stupid
Mankind can be.
   That's not why I wrote this
   But read it how you want
Hopefully you'll laugh
   Maybe grin
   Maybe not
At least you were privy to my thoughts
   On poems

*Margot Nelson, Grade 8*
*French International School of Philadelphia*

### I'm a Redneck

I am myself,
I hear big loud trucks and country music,
I see a farm with livestock all around,
I want my horses back,
I am one of a kind.
I pretend it's summer all the time,
I feel the soft grass under my toes,
I feel the wind blowing through my hair,
I worry about nothing',
I am one of a kind.
I understand the animals,
I say that I love the smell of fresh air and cowboys,
I try to never change anything about myself,
I hope I will find the right guy someday,
I am one of a kind.

*Danielle Demchak, Grade 8*
*Trinity Middle School*

### Fears vs Love

When fears are darkness, love is light
When death haunts you at the den of the night
Love is your savior
Shadows whisper your name
Light emerges to save you
The trees dance
The sky screams and cries
Love enchants the fear
Love is our savior,
We just need to listen to its song

*Bedelia Abel, Grade 8*
*Centerville Middle School*

## Homerun

Every soul in the stands staring
The solemn walk to the batter's box
It's like a sweaty sauna
The tired pitcher awaiting my presence
I took a practice swing
Practice, practice, practice
Fans were nervous because the game was tied
Here comes the first pitch
"Ball one," shouted the umpire
Then comes pitch two
"Strike one," shouted the umpire
Although I didn't swing
Here came the third pitch
My whole team depending on me
I watched the ball the whole way
CRACK, I had hit the ball
The fielder was retreating
It had soared over his head
I lifted my hands high
I was a hero to all of Bellwood
It was my first homerun
*Noah Burns, Grade 8*
*Bellwood Antis Middle School*

## County Fair

A day at the fair, what could be more fun?
As you stand in lines and cook in the sun.

An arm and a leg for tickets for everything you do,
Crowds, dirt, dust, rides, shows, food.

The demolition derby, a favorite event of mine
Is so cool to watch, except the three hour wait line.

Tons of candy apples are calling my name,
Cotton candy galore, I'm so glad I came.

Riding the rides at dark is best, with colorful lights,
Lots of friends, it's the best six summer nights.

Two dollar games you never win, cheap prizes are given,
Look at the guy behind the stand, half his teeth are missin'.

Fun and manure are in the air
So let down your hair, if you dare,
Let's all go to the county fair!
*Mariah Younker, Grade 8*
*Bellwood Antis Middle School*

## Who Will You Be?

Fifty days of middle school remain.
My last year at Pennbrook was not the same;
Moving onto high school, focus becomes a demand.
Higher expectations and more to understand;
No more lurking the hallways or omitting schoolwork.
Forget all the people who acted like jerks;
More math equations and vocab to remember.
Don't forget the things you acquired in September.
Excuses become worthless to an adult's ear,
And getting ghastly grades grows to be more of a fear.
Start paying attention to what you should learn;
Stop complaining about how your teachers are stern.
When making new friends and losing the old,
Are you going to be ordinary or stand out and be bold?
Being noticed in high school is an individual choice,
So decide if you want to fit in or have your own voice.
*Nicole D'Agostino, Grade 9*
*Pennbrook Middle School*

## Pay Day

Being a kid is always tough
'Cause parents tell you what to do
Like not dip your head in the chocolate fondue
Nothing is completely yours
"Home" is a jail with closed doors
Every day they say they love you
But we know it's a security review
We want to roam
And have no curfews to bring us home
I scream and shout and pull my hair
But they twiddle their thumbs and say they don't care
I've had it up to here with their lazy actions
While they sit there waiting for a reaction
So to all kids I need to say
It's time for kids to be shown some mercy
And have a pay day!
*KC Carrelli, Grade 7*
*Pennbrook Middle School*

## Choices & Decisions

There are many challenges in life.
You may never know which road to take.
Not deciding may cause strife.
Thinking about the day when you wake.

Making smart choices will treat you good.
Sometimes you can't say no when you really can.
Thinking it was impossible but you knew you could.
Everything is possible on this land.
*Kristen LaRosa, Grade 9*
*Pennbrook Middle School*

## Dawn Is Breaking

Dawn is breaking into a new day
To snowflakes outside my window
Drifting one by one slowly piling up
I have a flash of joy seeing the snow-covered streets
Untouched and full of black ice covered with a white blanket
Suddenly a squirrel runs by my window
As I climb back into bed admiring the perfect footprints
As another chases behind
Dawn is breaking as I settle back down for a calm snow day.
*Maggie Fleming, Grade 7*
*Strath Haven Middle School*

### Guardian Angel*

I've never heard your voice.
I've never seen your face.
Yet I know you exist.

In times of need,
When I look for light,
I know you exist.

When I can't think straight,
When I feel despair,
I know you exist.

Thinking there's no one to turn to,
Feeling like I don't fit in.
I know you exist.

Not knowing an answer on a test.
Not understanding an equation.
I know you exist.

Receiving the feeling of comfort
Or having the light bulb turn on,
Lets me know you exist.

Guiding me in the right direction,
And helping me succeed.
Thank you, my Guardian Angel.
*Breanna Dewalt, Grade 8*
*Danville Area Middle School*
*\*Dedicated to my pappy…You'll always be in my heart!*

### New Chapter, New Me

A concussion is something I never wanted to find.
It is like a pounding pain that never stops.
I found it one day after being kicked in the head,
And was never the same again.
Each day is a new chapter,
I never know what I'm going to find.
It tears me apart and makes me feel helpless.
I just have to know
How to put myself back together again.
It is annoying and very stressful
and want to give up sometimes,
But there is always a light at the end of the tunnel.

There the nuisance is,
Right there with me
Never leaving my side.
The contemplating we go through
Always takes my mind sky high
Each day is a new chapter,
I never know what I'm going to find.
Each day is a new chapter,
I never know what I'm going to find.
*Nicole DeIvernois, Grade 8*
*Pine-Richland Middle School*

### Bowling

Rolling down the alley hitting the pins
The ball spinning and rolling down the lane
The pinheads are winning let's beat them, win!
When we don't win the pinheads are in pain

The four-step approach is a good technique
Steps one two and three are at least value
Four is the best it is very unique
The ball is now spinning the pins just flew

The bowling pin's red stripes around the neck
The bowling alley, oily and light brown
The scores of the pinheads were up and down
The noise when the ball hits the pins is loud

When the kids win the game they scream and yell
And that's the game of bowling, farewell
*Jasmin Greydanus, Grade 8*
*Pocono Mountain East Jr High School*

### My Amazing Mom

My amazing mom means the world to me
Always by my side through thick and through thin
Without you I don't know where I would be
Helping me when I had scrapes on my chin

Always making sure I have what I need
Making me laugh when I'm upset and sad
With your kindness I am sure to succeed
Giving me everything you never had

A good cook, a good soul, and a good heart
Teaching me how to be oh so clever
I do not ever want to be apart
You're the world's most amazing mom ever

Mom just to let you know, we're stuck like glue
I don't have much to say, but *I love you*!
*Haley Price, Grade 8*
*Pocono Mountain East Jr High School*

### Something's in the Air

Something's in the air
It caresses lips, the crisp smell enticing
the mind, slowly taking over.
The smells of spring grow near
winter losing its grip on the world.
Tulips pierce the ground
spotting the earth with color.
Heavenly light pours through the clouds
seeping to the ground, awakening the sleeping world.
A warm breeze blows through the woods
carrying the scent of pine it encases the valley.
Spring spreads through the meadow like a gushing river.
*Bryce Taylor, Grade 7*
*South Side Middle School*

## Things That Scare You

Spiders…their tiny legs and hairy bodies.
Clowns…replacing their actual face with make-up.
Snakes…slimy bodies and hissing mouths.
Being buried alive…no way to get out, left to die.
Bugs…they can't hurt you, but still so gross.
Heights…so high, falling could lead to death.
Dark…you never know what's behind that door.
Dogs…so cuddly and sweet, don't be scared.
Lightning…kills people with just one touch.
Flying…could lose control and crash.

*Brooke Van Hove, Grade 7*
*Big Spring Middle School*

## Smiles

Smiles, smiles, everywhere.
Everywhere from here to there.
I smiled at my classmates,
Then they smiled back at me.
Then in an instant, my smile was everlasting.

I thought about that smile.
And found out how it works,
That one day that very smile
Will spread around the Earth!

*Francesca Noel Marren, Grade 7*
*Poquessing Middle School*

## Ominous Night

The birds and the owls make nighttime howls
The wind in the trees make the branches creak
As the nighttime moonlight reflects on the street
I don't get freaked…
I just turn over and go to sleep!

*Patric Dempsey, Grade 9*
*Motivation High School*

## Bagel to Go

At the café there was luscious smells around.
It was as hot as a desert.
As dirty as a dumpster,
But the food looked five starred.
The people there were like vicious hyenas.

*Jared Conti, Grade 7*
*South Side Middle School*

## Easter

Easter bunny,
Easter egg hunts,
Baskets, chocolate, and jellybeans,
Hiding places, fun times, memories,
Happiness is found throughout the celebration.

*Parker Myers, Grade 7*
*Holy Sepulcher School*

## An Artwork Come to Life

The lush, red drapes of a giant window open up
To a gold and wooden field
Only to find me right in the center, already present
I was just standing there, as still as a statue
Sensing the eyes of a million owls upon me
Made it the darkest night

Once the music started
My legs began to tell a graceful story
As I was leaping better than a frog
Twirling like a baton
And spinning as if I were my own merry-go-round
My arms were flying
Painting each stroke with elegance
The sun is beating on me, following me every time I
Expressed a feeling without words

I strutted into a unique rainbow
Knowing I would soon run out of paint
Just like every piece of artwork deserves
I finished it off with my beautiful signature
And by the time the velvet red drapes had to come to a close
Everyone knew the title of my creation.

*Nina Nguyen, Grade 8*
*Pine-Richland Middle School*

## Missing You

I miss having my head on your shoulder,
Also all the hugging that we did,
Plus us always fooling or joking around,
And when you put your arm around me,
When I was crying about losing my phone.

All I can think about is your voice in my head,
But most of all of what I miss about you,
Is when we were standing in front of the door,
And I put my head on your shoulders.

Then my hands went down to yours and…
All I had to do was flip my hands around and I did,
You took my hands in yours and we held it there,
When we were seen by her we let go like we were in trouble.

I go back to the night before that all happened and,
I can think about how I just put my head on your shoulders and,
You didn't argue with me, but you let me be because you liked it.

You confused me when I said, "I love you" and you say,
"When did you decide that because you never did before?"
I actually loved you as a friend but you changed my mind.

*Cecily Ingraham, Grade 7*
*Schuylkill Valley Middle School*

### Touchdown

I ran down the field as fast as I can,
the pass would be coming as I ran.
I put my hands out,
without a doubt,
that I would be getting a touchdown.
I caught the ball and went to town.
I ran fast towards the end zone,
I started to hear the guys behind me moan.
The crowd started to cheer
and then I couldn't even hear,
because I got a touchdown.
My teammates came running towards me,
I was as happy as my mom when she sees me.
My coach Bob
told me good job,
and
then
we won the game.

*Nevin Wood, Grade 7*
*Bellwood Antis Middle School*

### My Bracelet

Coming together in perfect order,
It's like a picture with a border.
Each meticulously chosen bead and charm,
Sit so beautifully on my arm.
I received this bracelet for my special day
From my cousin and aunt who love me in every way.
The charms dance and clink when they are twirled,
This symbolizes my thirteen years in the world.
Every day when I blink
All I see is black and pink.
The iPhone, lipstick, and the shoe
The purse and G charm are all so new.
This bracelet was such a surprise
The way it sparkles in my eyes.
All the gems tell I like bling.
A music note shows I like to sing.
No one else has the bracelet you see,
Because no one is exactly like me!

*Georgia Naples, Grade 7*
*J R Fugett Middle School*

### Leave a Rose

Regret would consume you as
you walk by.
Leaving grumpy like a
Scrooge would
make the situation worse.
Past loved ones whispering
like it was a conspiracy
and everybody knew
about it but you.
After getting tired of grave stares,
blank and straight,
doing nothing but that.
You stop and buy something from a man.
Hands shivering, tears falling, as you place a rose
in front of a loved one.
The man walked away
with care, leaving the
rose.

*Jasmine Lee, Grade 7*
*Garnet Valley Middle School*

### The War of the Grades

I enter this battle on the first day of school.
I lead my army of numbers and letters.
They ready their weapons of pencils and paper,
Then suddenly it starts.
The homework comes flowing in,
The tests and the books,
All kinds of schoolwork.
But my army is strong,
We get a B+,
But then someone drops an F- on us.
It seems like we'll never recover,
But good fighters never give up.
We battle harder than ever before,
The schoolwork didn't stand a chance.
Then suddenly the enemy retreats,
A report card then comes,
It's covered in A+ after A+.
I then declare this battle over for another year.

*Lydia Szymanski, Grade 8*
*Wattsburg Area Middle School*

### What Makes An Angel

She's an angel
She's just been through some stuff
What didn't kill her definitely made her stronger
She's gotten real tough
Now she'll fight longer
She won't leave in a huff
She's an angel sent here from heaven
She's just in disguise
Just an average girl
But an angel inside

*Heather Dietrick, Grade 7*
*Cambria Heights Middle School*

### I Remember

I remember the weeks at Cape Cod
I remember the week at Williamsburg
I remember the beach in the winter
And how cold the water was
I remember the time in South Carolina
I remember the really big blizzard
I remember Christmas without snow
Even bins filled with apples from our apple tree
I remember fun times as a family
But my favorite memory's yet to come

*Ben Good, Grade 7*
*Pequea Valley Intermediate School*

## My Angel

A hug, a kiss and a see you later
was what I got.
No knowing that later wouldn't come
A smile, a wave and a blown kiss
was what I got.
Not knowing that it was done
A laugh, a silly picture and another hug
was what I got.
Not knowing that she would be gone
A scream, a horrible crash and a tear
was what I got.
Not knowing why or how
A lost soul, a pain in my chest, and emptiness
was what I got.
Not knowing what to do or who to call
An angel, a beautiful angel, my beautiful angel
was what I got.

*Brittney Griffith, Grade 9*
*Avon Grove High School*

## The Rose

The flower that lay on a blessed hill
The berry bushes, its beauty confined
Its gorgeousness was beauty still
Its lovely red rays lay sadly undefined

Until one sunny day, a child would approach
And she would pick the flower from its place
The rose she attached to a silver brooch
A gift to mother towards the end of her race

And lo, the last thing her mother would behold
The rose's fair grace, numb her sting of death
Thanks all to her daughter's heart of gold
And after she passed, we recall her last breath

Precious, the daughter who loved her mother so
And the mother who died in the flower's glow

*Tara Steinheiser, Grade 9*
*Eden Christian Academy - Mt Nebo Campus*

## Reading

Reading, reading, reading. What can I say?
When I start a good book, I can't put it down.
When I start a good book, it's the best thing in the world!
Reading a good book is like having a chocolate cake all to yourself.
There are all kinds of books that you can read
"Crash! Boom! Snap!" There's cartoon books.
"…and they lived happily ever after." There's fairy tales
For some people, reading is their life.
As for me, reading is part of my everyday schedule.
When I'm bored, I try to picture my life as one big, long novel.
When I'm older with nothing to do during the day,
I think I might turn my life story into a book for others to read.

*Lindsey Cook, Grade 8*
*Donegal Middle School*

## Relaxing

The freshly cut grass,
The crystal blue pool,
With the hot sun rays
Beating down on me.
I see the two big maple trees,
Sitting beside the old ant tree.
By itself it lays there,
The old basketball net,
All rusty.
I see the new red pickup truck,
In the eggshell garage.
The pool swallows the sunlight,
There are no clouds in the sky.
The shadows of the fence,
And the diving board.
I can hear the flip flops hitting the ground.
The 32" TV blasting in their kitchen.
The breeze rolls in and makes the branches rumble.

*Emily Hinson, Grade 7*
*William Penn Middle School*

## Imagination is the Key to Creation

Anyone can find the key to the rooms full of creation!
A place to start might simply be the road to inspiration.
This road is not too hard to find,
In fact, it's everywhere!
It's in your kitchen, out the door,
Up and down or here and there!
Once you pick out what you like
And what you shall explore,
Your imagination becomes a key
To open any door!
The possibilities are endless,
You only need to dream.
The heart and mind make a great duet
In spite of what it may seem.
Your imagination cannot shrink —
It only ever grows,
So take that key and unlock a door
And find out where it goes!

*Crosley Kudla-Williams, Grade 8*
*Swain School*

## The Honeybadger

The honeybadger
Highly underestimated
Sneakily aggressive
Just about the only thing
A cobra will fear
Cobras are dangerous
The honeybadger can kill the cobra
Nobody will know when the cobra will strike
However, the honeybadger will be there
To claim the victory

*Lincoln Mimidis, Grade 8*
*Bellmar Middle School*

### The Dash

Have I fulfilled my life so far?
Or have I just wasted time?
Have I wandered aimlessly into the dark?
Or has someone been by my side?

These are the questions I ask
Along with the "What-ifs."
But my only one true task
Is to cherish not to miss.

I know friends come and go
But family is forever.
I would really like to know
If true friends actually stick together.

All of this comes to mind
When I think of the future or the past.
And what I want to leave behind
Is how life can go by so fast.

*Ashlynn Young, Grade 8*
*Spring Grove Middle School*

### What a Snowflake Knows

I twinkle
I sail—
Through the air I fly
Dancing across the baby-blue sky
I flutter
I sparkle
Absolutely unique
Graceful and beautiful
Elegant—
Sleek
I shine with the sun
And the stars at night
Cold and shining
A crisp and clean white
A wintery wisp
From my head to my toes
And that's just about all
A snowflake knows

*Jamie Kahn, Grade 7*
*Easton Area Middle School 7-8*

### Recipe for a Cheetah

Mix in speed and agility
Then combine in nine lives
Put on claws sharp as knives
Now glaze with gold
And sprinkle with spots
Plus make them look like random dots
Now bake at 300 and cool
Enjoy this wonderful creature
That might not be here in the future

*Kristalyn Bender, Grade 7*
*Pequea Valley Intermediate School*

### Civil War

I am in the civil war,
it is such a fright.
There's gloomy faces every where,
but my most dreadful sight,
is the ground.
A bed of dead soldiers,
a frame of loose rifles,
a red blanket of blood,
a pillow of nurses,
and the few soldiers left standing,
is the kitten trying to get comfortable.
Only a few can live to tell,
the bitter story,
of the civil war.

*Boni Trinter, Grade 8*
*Fred S Engle Middle School*

### Life

Life is a journey
Can be long
Can be short
It is cruel never forgiving.
Life can be sweet and nice
It is light in the dark
Life goes both ways but life
Is a
Mystery and that is all
You see
Life
Will never
Be
Fair.

*William Rose, Grade 7*
*William Penn Middle School*

### What a Swimmer Knows

What a swimmer knows
Bathing suit
Mask
That's your task
Dip your toe
In you go
Throw the stick
Not a fit
Dive on in
Let's go for a swim
Dry off
Pack all your things
You had your fun
Now the day is done

*Samantha Moessinger, Grade 7*
*Easton Area Middle School 7-8*

### What a Dancer Knows

Toes pointed
head up
wooden floors
strive for more
ballet, tap, jazz, and lyrical
hoping and praying for a miracle
waiting for the show to start
wishing I could slow down my heart
I have to do my jump on time
this moment is mine
I have been waiting in line
for my time to shine
put the glitter on my eyes
I feel like a feather free to fly
when on stage time goes by
the audience cheers
my fears disappear

*Brandi Quasney, Grade 7*
*Easton Area Middle School 7-8*

### Patience

I was once told
Patience is a virtue.
My mother would say
A little patience never hurt you.

I always hated waiting
It seemed everything took so long.
I also hated painting
Or listening to long songs.

For all these things take too much time
I never wanted to be behind.

But over the years when I had time to grow
I learned some things and now I know…

Patience truly is a virtue.

*Jenicka Schmidt, Grade 8*
*Danville Area Middle School*

### Dark Days

Days like this are gloomy.
Dark,
Often wistful.

Startled.
Listen to the wind's melody,
Listen.

Cautious.
Be aware of what's there.
Be aware,
What's lurking in the darkness…

*Ashley Smith, Grade 8*
*Saegertown Jr/Sr High School*

## My Friends

Together through
Thick and thin
Always here
When stuff happens

Friends
Oh my friends
So respectful and kind
Even when we are going
Through tough times

Always accepting
Always caring
Not only for me
But for everyone they can

All through life
We will stick together
No matter where
Our dreams take us

Friends…

*Madison Pacana, Grade 7*
*Pequea Valley Intermediate School*

## Wings

Held to the ground,
pinned by my wings.
All I want is to fly
and forget all these things.
But instead I am left
in the bottom of the well.
I attempted at flying,
but instead I just fell.
Hold me no longer,
because I am free.
Free as the bird
you held inside me.

*Isabella Gonzalez, Grade 7*
*21st Century Cyber Charter School*

## Singing

Singing is my passion
Singing is my life
I write songs
And rap them out
In the lime light
I don't play
When it comes
To my singing
So back off
And I'll show you
How to do it
Right.

*Amira Weathers, Grade 8*
*Barack Obama Academy*

## Leaving Footprints

As you are walking on her heart, leaving footprints in that freshly cut green grass,
You are planting a seed, that will grow into a flower.
A flower that will stand strong, no matter what she goes through,
Rain, snow, sleet, hail. The lies, the deceit, fail…
To break her delicate stem. To pick her apart, petal by petal.

As you are walking on her heart, leaving footprints in that freshly cut green grass,
You are fertilizing her future, applying pesticides to her past.
Guiding her way through what used to be a garden,
A concrete garden of skyscraping weeds and hate.

As you are walking on her heart, leaving footprints in that freshly cut green grass,
You are watering her dreams, teeming with hope as her bud blossoms.
Reaching for the sky 'til she can't reach anymore.

Now as you are stomping on her heart, leaving footprints in that dirty, dry soil,
She lets you stomp as hard as you want, but…
Her roots are too deep to feel you, her stem is too strong to break,
And her colors are too vibrant to change.
You took her weakness for granted.
She will forever — be THAT flower,
While you are that dormant seed that will never become one.

*Angelica Murphy, Grade 8*
*First Philadelphia Charter School for Literacy*

## The Mystical Ocean

I know the ocean…
All the dolphins clicking to others,
Waves rolling and breaking inshore,
Fish swimming through the stinging anemone,
People splashing and morphing the sand with each step they take.
I know the ocean…
Jellyfish floating gracefully, parting the water,
The anglerfish flickering their lights on and off in the deep,
The coral greeting me as I swim by,
The schools of fish ripping through the water.
I know the ocean…
All the salt leaves a scent in my hair as I exit the paradise,
Fish washing up on shore,
The aroma of the greasy boardwalk pizza and fries not far away,
The ocean mist being carried off the waves spraying, my face.
I know the ocean…
Scuba divers fascinated and taking in the sights,
Submarines attempting to reach the bottom of Mariana's Trench,
The yellow beach sand so warm around my feet, burying me deeper,
The newborns swimming with their mother as they take a glance at their home.
I know the mystical ocean.

*Jessica Fry, Grade 8*
*Ephrata Middle School*

## Time

Time feels like it's slowing down when you hit a mine.
And your life flashes in your mind, time flows like a river or a slug, slow and steady.
In nature time is slow peaceful and silent, time is what helps life survive, thrive, and evolve.

*Andrew Gallo, Grade 7*
*Pennbrook Middle School*

### Standing Alone

Just standing there all alone,
though many are around.

All entranced in their own world,
running all around.

Despite the joyful atmosphere,
I stand there not happy at all.

Trying to put a smile on my face,
unsuccessfully trying so hard.

All I want is for someone,
to talk to me.

It's hard for me to be ignored,
I don't know how they do it.

When I'm the only new kid there,
just standing all alone.

*Sarah Hartman, Grade 7*
*Lancaster Mennonite School - Locust Grove*

### Special Tree, Brilliant Tree

Special tree, brilliant tree,
come toward me.
I want to climb you to the top,
without having to stop.
You reach on forever,
without halting, never.

Special tree, brilliant tree,
come toward me.
You reach to the stars, past the cloud-strewn sky.
On you, I'd like to spy.
Oh, special tree, oh, brilliant tree,
please, come toward me.
I hope you never die.
I wonder if you see the planet with an enormous eye.

Come to me, come to me,
special tree, oh, brilliant tree,
and you will see my world.
I wish I could see yours.

*Jacob Rogers, Grade 7*
*North Pocono Middle School*

### Someday...

Someday I want to be yours again.
Someday I want to be happy with you.
Someday I want the pain of you to go away.
Someday I want to hear you say "I love you" and mean it.
Someday I want you to stop hurting me.
Someday I want to be with you forever.

*Morgan Hollenbaugh, Grade 7*
*Pequea Valley Intermediate School*

### English Teacher

I love Ms. Seiler.
She's cooler than Tyler.
You don't know why it's true?
Well, I'll tell you.
She took us to a movie and we had much fun,
Because in the end, the heroine won.
We talked about stuff,
And it was more than enough
To satisfy our hungry brains
That were suffering great pains.
But just eighth period couldn't supply,
All the info that I needed, so I decided to try,
Coming second period every Wednesday.
I walked in smilin' and she said "Hey!
We will have a great time,
Writing stories that rhyme!"
I said "Cool!"
Then I wrote about the pool.
My book came to life,
And taught me cool words like "strife."
Ms. Seiler, you rock!

*Marcus Curlee, Grade 7*
*Pennbrook Middle School*

### An Easter Poem

"Lord, take this cup from Me, yet not My will, but Thine.
I will go upon the cross and make the world's sin Mine."
In the darkness of that hour while Jesus softly prayed,
He was thinking about me and how I must be saved.
He willingly was beaten, scorned, and whipped, and bruised.
Did you ever stop and realize that He took all that for you?
Nails held Him in body, yet love held Him in soul.
Though we do not deserve it, that love lets sinners go.
He lived His life to die. He died His death for sin.
The sin that we should pay for, was paid in full by Him.
But my Lord isn't dead. In truth, He lives today!
He conquered death itself, and is risen from the grave.
I still fall short quite often, but my heart can always sing,
"amazing grace, abounding love;" for death has lost its sting!
Before I knew my Savior, I longed to be set free.
But now I am forgiven and sin no longer holds me.

*Katelyn Fisher, Grade 9*
*Commonwealth Connections Academy*

### Lost Forever

Life is short, death is long
But if I live forever, I will never belong.
I've been cursed to be eternally alone.
For you I have no world of my own.
For your face I fought all, no matter how large or tall.
But when I saw you walk away, left me in a land without rain.
For what he had that I didn't, I don't know.
Now I sit in a chariot of metal and stone.
Lost forever, in a land of not my own.

*Kyle Tadda, Grade 9*
*Mcdowell Intermediate High School*

## The Wait

Wanting, waiting for the snow to melt.
It's been far too long since I've felt
the nice warm sun on my back.
Oh, how I miss the rough sand between my toes.
But for now, I settle for the sweet lovers chocolate
and the warmth of my coat cradling me
as the school bus rushes me to school,
through snow and sleet.
Five more months until I smell the salty air
and the sticky chlorine in my hair
and the sweet, cool boardwalk ice cream.
But for now I sit,
Wanting, waiting for the snow to melt.

*Cassandra Vaitl, Grade 8*
*Ephrata Middle School*

## Savanna

Loving, funny, easily bored
Who loves golden retriever puppies
Who wants games on an iPod touch
Who likes cheesy meat lovers pizza
Who doesn't like to read big chapter books
Who fears jumpy scary movies
Who tries to have sleepovers every weekend
Who is proud of being one of the tallest seventh graders
Who wonders about her friend's feelings (happy, sad)
Who worries if she will pass failing classes
Who believes in unicorns with glitter
Who wishes to live in a mansion
Who dreams of going to a real Lakers game

*Savanna Claxton, Grade 7*
*Pequea Valley Intermediate School*

## Life from My Perspective

For some people winning is the name of the game,
For others it isn't always the fortune and fame.
You must be tough to make it,
Even if it means to fake it.
People that work hard every day,
Also enjoy some time to play.
Although most people get by in this world,
It could be tough for a teenage girl.
But if I try really hard, and stay confident and bold
I just might end up winning the gold.

*Anna Sees, Grade 8*
*Danville Area Middle School*

## Oak

There was a kite who loved to fly
On a windy day the kite string broke
In the clear blue air she danced so high
Then — as wind drew breath — found rest on oak
Year after year she longed for sky

*Obi McGrath, Grade 9*
*Shade Mountain Christ School*

## Reflecting

A girl at home singing,
Reflecting on her past.
That has passed her by so very fast.

As she sings la la la,
She thinks of what she could be like.
Instead of what she is today.

Singing to her gets the things out of her head that never go away.
Words that are like thunderstorms on a rainy day,
Or actions people do that are hurtful in many ways.

Just singing a few words makes her feel happier inside.
Which makes her feel that ocean is right by her side.

The feeling of the ocean makes her feel calmer,
Washing out all the bad words and actions out of her head.

A girl at home singing.
Now singing of joy,
Instead of the demons that haunted her in her head.

*Meredith O'Neil, Grade 8*
*Pine-Richland Middle School*

## I Used To...

I used to love you more than I do now
But now I am not exactly sure
I always have you on my mind
But I never cry about it
I once believed in second chances
But now I think they don't exist
If I could ask you one more question
I would ask you "Why did you put me through that?"
I never meant to make you feel bad
But I might just feel the same
I can't have you back
But I can try and let you go
I won't stick around
But I might stare as I pass through
I used to feel butterflies in my stomach
But now I never think about you anymore

*Kelly Manning, Grade 7*
*Pequea Valley Intermediate School*

## Tear Drops

Tears are like rain on a window
they trickle down
like tears on your face.
Rain holds memories
of kids running and jumping in puddles
like your tears
There are memories you hold dear to your heart
so live your life full of tears.

*Julia Richards, Grade 8*
*Spring Grove Middle School*

## Snowboarding

I meet my friends and go into the park
But first I will need to strap into my board
We are at the top and ready, set, mark
I slice through the snow like a silver sword
As my iPod is blaring I speed up
Passing other skier and snowboarders
I meet more of my friends and say what's up?
After that we eat our food orders
Fly down the slope with a lot of great fun
We want to go eat and that will be fine
Then I will go buy a cinnamon bun
With all my friends and have such a good time
Before we eat we unlatch our boots
Then we will go in the lodge for some hoots

*Jensen Berman, Grade 8*
*Pocono Mountain East Jr High School*

## The Athlete I Should Have Been

The athlete I should have been is big and buff
He has huge muscles and he's extremely tough

He can hit baskets on the court with a SWISH!
Do you think you can guard him? Ha, you wish…

"Do you think your team will win this year?" the reporters say.
"It's not just about winning; I come to have fun and play!"

The athlete I should have been is rich, not poor
He loses track of all his wins as he dominates the floor.

The athlete I should have been plays pro but gets injured one day
Maybe I should just play for fun instead of going all the way.

*Jifu Li, Grade 7*
*Strath Haven Middle School*

## Cat Time

Could I join my kitties for some me time?
Every gentle cat comes to me with love.
To live in a cat-less world is a crime.
They so know the ways of heaven above.
A cat will pounce and play with bits of yarn,
And if it feels like it, do tricks with words.
They will however hunt down mice in barns,
And chase and kill fat hens and little birds.
Yet still cats are so sweet with fluffy fur,
And gleaming yellow, green or orange eyes.
They love to have you pet them, then they'll purr,
But if you would ignore them, hear their cries!
A cat to me is really my best friend,
And may its lovely spirit never end.

*Delaney Henasey, Grade 8*
*Pocono Mountain East Jr High School*

## Old Pennies

Pennies which have rested on the dresser forever
have tarnished from time and began to decay
They lay in the same spot for months now
aging a little each day

As the days turn to weeks
eventually, the pennies are shoved aside
making room for shiny new copper
leaving the tarnished hidden from sight

And so the old pennies just lay in the shadows
sobbing for the unjustness presented
They look to the gleaming coins that replaced them
wondering why their value was neglected

*Lisa Tripon, Grade 8*
*Pine-Richland Middle School*

## A Night on the Beach

The stars shine so brightly in the night sky
The moon looks like a gigantic glazed bun
Planets twirl and look oh so very spry
Playing on the beach is a lot of fun
On a beach at night is oh so peaceful
The sand caresses my toes every day
Watching stars makes me very cheerful
I would not spend the day another way
Listening to a seashell makes me sleep
As I look up I see a plane fly by
Away from the beach always makes me weep
Go lay down and look at the bright night sky
Staying on the beach is the life for me
I will spend time there with my family

*Brandon Plastino, Grade 8*
*Pocono Mountain East Jr High School*

## Sky

Staring above at the endless night sky
Hearken, the mysteries, the vast and bright.
Stars tell their stories, but to you and I,
Are twisted by time, unseen by sight,
Begging us to understand the unknown.
In them, I see epic tales of dark and light.
They shine, and millions of years ago shone.
A telltale heart, a wholehearted night,
Some things, yet best forgotten, live above.
While the night sky expands into everything.
It holds together clouds, and houses doves.
Space's pen, always observes, always writing,
While its beauty is hard to understand,
It shows, and shares, a timeless loving hand.

*Abbey Helvey-Roth, Grade 8*
*Pocono Mountain East Jr High School*

## School

As I sit in this room,
I tend to think back on things,
The good things.
The good times with my teachers and friends.
The laughter,
The happiness,
The proud moments…

I also think back on the bad times.
The heartbreak,
The silent sobs,
The despair.
The hopelessness.

This room makes me think.
Think about my choices.
My decisions in my life,
My actions and my reactions.
This room makes me think about my life.
About everything good and bad in the past,
And about everything I will make it become in the future.

*Janelle Oakley, Grade 8*
*Blue Ridge Middle School*

## Unexplained Lies

The only true painful lies,
Are the ones never said and never explained.
Why would you lie to begin with?
These unexplained lies were what I wanted to hear,
But they were just sweet nothings,
Whispered in my ear.
I deserve more,
But this is the end,
Walk out the door,
Don't think of turning around,
I won't be found.
I can't take these lies,
This will be,
Our last goodbyes.

*CelinaRae Starvaggi, Grade 8*
*Wattsburg Area Middle School*

## The Memories

As the sound dances around in my ears
it reminds me of the memories made
the laughs I've learned to love
the tears I've learned to dread
the sound suddenly drifts to my heart
the heart that has taken those laughs and those tears
those memories made
the heart that has been broken
the heart that is now healed by this sound
But what is this sound?
This sound is none other than the music that consumes my life.

*Carlynn Adams, Grade 8*
*Centerville Middle School*

## Dance

In the studio is a neon green room
With mirrors in the front of the class
Fans in the corners blowing on full blast
Cooling me down
From sunrise to midday
I can see the shadows following me
As I dance
It shines through the big double doors
Sunlight reflects off of my water bottles
As I dance and move around
I can feel the beat
As it vibrates on my feet through to my head
I can hear the dance teacher yelling 5-6-7-8
I wonder why some people don't give it their all
When they dance
This place makes me so happy
It makes me feel like I belong
I was born to dance
It takes my worries away
Makes me feel free
Strive, strive, strive

*Lexus Sinkiewicz, Grade 7*
*William Penn Middle School*

## Only Just a Dream

I dream of a place where only I exist,
my worst fears are gone,
and all the troubles I face have vanished.
People are only a vision,
and I am free.
I have no worries,
I can live my life the way I want,
The nice breeze washes over me,
I smile and twirl,
As I'm twirling, every bad thought has left my mind.
Every tear has dried,
Then I feel a shake,
Everything comes back to reality,
My tears, thoughts, and fears are back,
I wonder why and I shout,
Then I realize, it was only just a dream.

*Nguveren Zume, Grade 7*
*Shippensburg Area Middle School*

## Usain Bolt

Usain Bolt is as fast as a cheetah,
His shoes are on fire,
When he runs it's like a lightning bolt in the sky,
When he runs it sounds like thunder,
When he runs you can see dirt dancing in the air,
He always has fun,
And he is always number 1,
When he got hurt he said,
This is not going to be the end.

*Peter Attia, Grade 8*
*Centerville Middle School*

## Morgan's Ladybugs

I just can't take this anymore.
Reality hit me hard and now,
Seeing you like that made me realize something.
I realized that I will never get to see you again.
I will never see you walking thru the Holicong hallways.
I will never get to see your welcoming smile.
I will never get to see you at freshman day or dance.
I wish that I had one more chance to see you again.
Just one more chance to talk to you,
But, I don't.
My heart aches knowing that you are gone,
I didn't know that it would affect me this much.
I try to hold back tears once a day.
I can honestly say that you are my inspiration and hero.
You fought harder than I have ever seen anyone do.
You make all my problems seem like nothing.
You were diagnosed and you lived on.
You make me want to be a better person.
I may not have known you too well,
But you will always have a place in my heart.
Fly high Morgan.

*Yelena Wermers, Grade 9*
*Holicong Middle School*

## Rises Above the Rest

The air stands still as I wait for the gun.
Deep breaths, full of motivation and thrill,
Tug at my heart as I begin to run.
All I feel at that moment is the shrill
Screaming of the bright red ground beneath me
And the sticky heat surrounding my face.
As I go on, I begin to feel free,
The ground tries to keep up with my hurried pace.
My body starts to strain through concrete air.
The finish line looks increasingly near,
I feel as if I have nothing left to spare.
But as I think that, my goal becomes clear.
After all the years, one sport is the best,
Track is the one that rises above the rest.

*Madilyn Kimmel, Grade 9*
*Linden Hall School*

## If Happiness Was a Color

If happiness was a color,
It would be yellow
As bright as a sunrise.
If happiness was a taste
It would be just like angel food cake.
If happiness was a feeling
It would be as jumpy as a frog.
If happiness was a smell
It would be delightful as a bouquet of tulips.
If happiness was a sound,
It would be happy as a child's laugh.

*Paige Mendenhall, Grade 7*
*Pequea Valley Intermediate School*

## China Plane

As I glide like an airborne fish,
Through a sea of fluffy clouds,
I stare at the backs of the black leather seats,
And see dust mites swirling in the sun.

The blazing sun sheds white light,
Glittering on the metal walls,
Reflecting off the dull dark chairs,
Streaming through the half-closed blinds.

I hear the buzzing, vibrating, plane,
Squeaking seats, snoring sleepers,
And the whirring of the cold fan, tickling my ear.

When will 13 hours come to an end?
Why is the bustling capital not in view?
Why is the sparkling city not greeting me home?

My eyes twitch irritably in the boring air,
My feet are restless, itching to run, and flee,
Away from my cramped position in the seat,
Leaving behind, a grumpy mind.

How much longer is this tedious flight?
How much longer is this tedious flight?
How much longer is this tedious flight?

*Xinqiao Zhang, Grade 7*
*Saucon Valley Middle School*

## Secrets

Words spread like mold
Their words are ice cold
It isn't fair what she's told
All I can say is hold on
But there's nothing for her to hold

She's letting them eat her soul
Her soul, they all stole
The wind tells her their secrets
And the leaves dance upon it
She tells them, revenge she seeks
The trees reply, "Don't believe what they speak"

The child looks down
And tries to hide her shame
The clouds begin to frown
Then begin to rain
The sad and lonely child has only stooped to their level

She hoped to be forgiven
And she was
'Cause a friendship like that could never be broken
But mostly because
Their biggest secrets have already been spoken

*Jordan Altice, Grade 8*
*Donegal Middle School*

## A Perfect Sight

The most beautiful sight
Trunk Bay, glistening bright
Water shining with perfect glow
Everything quiet, feeling so slow
Seagulls floating in the air
Enjoying all without a care
Waves gently kissing the sandy beach
Water cools the sun baked reefs
Clouds hovering in the sky
Like cotton balls floating by
Gorgeous green giant peaks capture the Bay
Dotted with blooms that color the day
Trunk Bay is a living postcard
Everything calm
Everything warm
Everything right

*Elizabeth Hassett, Grade 8*
*Pine-Richland Middle School*

## Nature's Music

The human ear can hear so much.
So much more than the palm can touch.
You just have to listen
To hear the wind whistlin'
A remarkable song
That we both knew all along.
A song of passion
And songs of great compassion.
But most of all
I love when the bluebirds call
And sing a beautiful melody
As songbirds of serenity.
Because nature has its own music.
Better than any song on acoustic.
You just have to listen
And the whole world begins to glisten.

*Shaelyn Hand, Grade 7*
*Villa Maria Academy Lower School*

## Blind

I'm on my way up.
As I'm about to get off,
The lift stops.
There is a man in front of me,
He takes his jolly old time getting off.
One of my friends yells
"Hurry up!"
He slowly gets off,
And immediately falls,
As he gets up,
I see what is written on his jacket.
"BLIND SKIER"
I feel horrible,
And immediately apologize.

*Jacob Knauer, Grade 7*
*Strath Haven Middle School*

## Breathless

The frozen lake has cracked,
The blooming flower taken by the wind.
Breathless, the pain inside indescribable.
Like a dancing flame among the ambers.
The river flows with no path,
No end to be seen.
The rose has wilted,
The love no longer there.
Just before I reach the light,
I trip and fall again.
Hiding away,
Unsure of what to do next.
Breathless from running,
Not wanting to go forward.
The halo gone,
A time to walk alone in the dark forest.

*Alexis Murphy, Grade 8*
*Pine-Richland Middle School*

## The Quiet Joys of Life

The things we love the most
We forget the moment they pass.

The tangerine hue
Of a setting sun,

The beauty of
Winter's first snow,

And the warmth
Of a lover's hand.

Strange is it not?
That we forget the simple joys of life
Once they pass; only to be
Recalled in a time of loneliness.

*Liam Clark, Grade 9*
*East High School*

## Think

When you walk down the hall,
What are you thinking?
When you see me and smile,
What are you thinking?
When you say my name,
What are you thinking?
When your heart skips a beat,
What are you thinking?
So many questions,
That I'm too scared to ask.
I just want you to see,
What's going on in my head.
All I can do is think,
About what you are thinking.

*Tiauna Schweitzer, Grade 8*
*Wattsburg Area Middle School*

## I Will Love You Forever

I will love you forever, Aunt June
I miss you being here with me
Without you nothing is the same
I miss you coming to my dance recitals
My softball and basketball games

So many memories that we had
That I will never regret
Looking back now makes me sad
But I still don't want to forget

You and I had a special relationship
That I know will never go away
All our stories and fun times
That I think about every day

But now you are in heaven
Which is so far away
I hope we meet again someday
There is so much I have to say

I wish you could be here a little longer
I never got the chance to say goodbye
But you taught me to stay strong
And to keep my head up high

*Courtney Chiodo, Grade 8*
*Penn Middle School*

## Basketball

When you start out
It's a little hard to dribble that ball
But dribbling the ball isn't all
You will need to shoot and drive

You will be successful with a little hustle
To do that you need a lot of muscle
With muscle in store
You won't have any problems to score

Basketball is war
When you start the sweat will pour
The ball will sometimes whistle
Through the air like a missile

The big bouncing basketball
Will sometimes cause you to fall
But if you keep your head in it
The game will never be dull

Just be Kobe Bryant
And you will have no struggle
But make sure you stay in the huddle
Basketball is my life.

*Emily Dabbs, Grade 8*
*Richland Sr High School*

## Losing the World

Everybody is busy
And people don't care
It's all about the money
But not the smoke everywhere
This pollution has gone crazy
And I guess so have we

Just think for a second
What have we done?
Now our sons and daughters
Will not be able to breathe in the air

But it doesn't have to be this way
If we all work together we can change
The world

If every day
Put in a minute of effort everybody
If just one took the bike to work
If just one recycles just once
We would make the world closer to a
Wonderful place.

*Somanshu Ghotra, Grade 7*
*Indian Valley Middle School*

## Broken

I've thought so many times
Of what path I would take
But believing in you was a huge mistake
You lied,
You promised,
You tore my heart.
The lies that you made,
They tore me apart.
Life isn't a game,
You're not a player,
This is my heart,
Don't be a slayer.

*Emillie Shaffer, Grade 8*
*Wattsburg Area Middle School*

## Welcome to Me

Welcome to me
I'm 3% girly
6% smarts
15% I am music and arts
10% Christian
5% writing
35% I'm karate and fighting
I'm 20% bookworm
And my gymnastics earn a 7.
But as well as all this
I'm 20% opinion
Welcome to me

*Dorlisa Frank, Grade 7*
*Pequea Valley Intermediate School*

## Spring Has Finally Arrived

The snow starts to melt
The sun appears high in the sky
Temperatures rise quickly
Plants start growing from the earth
That will soon bloom flowers

The animals come out of hibernation
They can finally be outside in the warmth
To greet and mate with others
Coldness and starvation will disappear

No more sweaters or long pants
It's time for T-shirts and a dress
Get the pools ready, close down ice rinks

All these changes lead to one answer,
Spring has finally arrived

*Priscilla Tran, Grade 7*
*Landisville Middle School*

## Our Path

Molded, mended, made better
We are the clay
Preplanned
To be shaped into
The bright future
Of which we shall run
Templates hold us tight
In our place
Noses turn upwards
When the quota is not stuck to
Conventional, rational
We are to be wise
And responsible
Our path is predestined
We are a success
We are the future
Of which they molded

*Hannah Trichon, Grade 9*
*Holicong Middle School*

## My Obsession

my phone has not nor will leave my side
crazy?
maybe, but oh well.

when it's taken away, I run and cry
it has its own pillow
on my bed.

while I sleep, it charges
near my wonderfully big head.
maybe I
am obsessed!

*Katelynn Sample, Grade 8*
*Saegertown Jr/Sr High School*

## What a Cheerleader Knows?

What does a cheerleader know
Jumps, flips
Yells and screams
Very loud
Feels the players
With spirit untold
They know how to pump you up
When you're down
In the dump
They dance, they cheer
They have no fear and
They will always
Cheer until the end
They work as a team
When they scream
But they will
Always go
Until the win

*Destiny George, Grade 7*
*Easton Area Middle School 7-8*

## The Hero

He has the basketball
with the game on the line
Time slipping away
5
He takes the dribble
4
He gets double covered
3
Pulls up to the 3 point line
2
Pump fake
1
The shot is off
Complete silence
Swish
Game over
Knicks win
With J Lin the hero

*Jason Marmorstein, Grade 7*
*Strath Haven Middle School*

## Dance

As I was looking at pictures
Something reminded me of the past
Being someplace I belonged
Everything was amazing, I loved it.
I had that feeling a long time ago
All of the sparkling outfits
All of the cool moves
And the cool shoes.
I wanted to do it again,
But I couldn't.

*Harlee Lewis, Grade 7*
*Bellwood Antis Middle School*

## Colors

Red, orange, yellow,
The colors paint the sky.
Blue, black, purple,
The colors come alive.
Like the colors of the rainbow,
Or the colors of the moon,
They all dance around us.
Red, yellow, orange, green, and blue.

*Tamra Arroyo, Grade 8*
*Donegal Middle School*

## Basketball

The clock starts,
Running up and down the court,
Moving around to get a chance to shoot,
Gently, the ball leaves the players hands,
Gasping for air the stands are quiet,
The ball falls into the basket,
And the crowd goes wild.

*Morgan Thomas, Grade 7*
*Cambria Heights Middle School*

## Beginning to End

Life is the last thing you see
before you leave.
Hope is just a simple, yet
powerful wish.
Fate is something you cannot
control.
Death is unpredictable.

*Alexa Manko, Grade 7*
*Moon Middle School*

## Sunburn

Sun
Hot, bright,
Lighting, blinding, tanning
Long time; hot outside,
Blistering, burning, damaging
Red, angry
Burn

*Kaitlynn M. Donovan, Grade 7*
*St. Luke School*

## Seasons

Winter
Snowy, dark
Sparkling, amazing, shuffling
Icicles, mountains, beach, sun
Shining, burning, heating
Vibrant, hot
Summer

*Kelsey Badel, Grade 7*
*Garnet Valley Middle School*

## Truth

Life is fragile.
That's what they say.
It's true.
It's a delicate, beautiful, intricate glass vase.
Its ornate twists and depictions,
Easily cracked,
Easily broken,
Easily shattered.
Someday its end will come; no matter how well preserved,
It will give up souls to death.

Death is resilient.
They don't speak of it as often.
It's true.
It's a solid, sturdy, dense piece of rock.
Its textured sides and sheer strength,
Cannot be cracked,
Cannot be broken,
Cannot be shattered.
Death is for an eternity; no matter how much one attempts to avoid it,
Death is undying.

*Julie Raiff, Grade 7*
*Mellon Middle School*

## In the Forest

As I walk through the forest nature surrounds me
A breeze rolling through the trees
A lonely Brooke trout swimming down a shallow stream
Nature is everywhere in the air and sky
In the dirt and mud
The crackling of the leaves under my boots
The howls of a lone wolf
It embraces me as I take a morning stroll through the forest
The warmth of the sun on my back
It warms my body as if I am being hugged by a giant ball of fire
The songs of birds fill my ears and I enjoy listening to their beautiful music
The croaking of a bullfrog as I pass a pond
Buzzing of bees around my head
It is as if nature has curved a path for me though this dense ecosystem
It is as if nature has given me this path to experience this beauty
As I continue my walk the trees separate and a large valley appears
From my vantage point I see a family of deer
They gracefully jump around and eat the grasses
A single tear falls from my eyes and all I could say was
Nature is so beautiful

*Patrick Thomas, Grade 9*
*City Charter High School*

## Water Is Fear

It rushes and flows. It will destroy all in its path.
You panic and struggle, but it's no use.  You can feel your lungs
Contracting. You need air. You kick and try with all of your might, but
It is no use. You feel your body go numb and you feel like your soul
Fades away. Fear is water.

*Alan Chess, Grade 8*
*Saegertown Jr/Sr High School*

## Cats and Dogs

Cats
Quiet, stealthy
Tracks, stalks, pounces
Intelligent, cunning, hard headed, smelly
Drools, chases, plays
Incredibly stupid
Dogs
*John Kleinfelter, Grade 8*
*Northern Lebanon Middle School*

## The Bad Times

Black
Sad, confined
Working, listening, dying
Slaves, chains, relax, fun
Watching, owning, beating
Happy, lazy
White
*Matthew Vines, Grade 8*
*Northern Lebanon Middle School*

## My Passion

Soccer
Passion, fierce
Kicking, scoring, winning
Ball, foot, stick, cage
Slapping, shooting, pushing
Violent, talent
Field Hockey
*Madison Lerch, Grade 8*
*Northern Lebanon Middle School*

## September

September creeps
around the corner
hauling school with it.
It stops your summer
fun cold in its tracks.
It brings dread, it brings school.
*Dante Dignazio, Grade 7*
*Garnet Valley Middle School*

## The Bird

I am a bird,
I fly up high,
I spread my wings,
in the open sky.
Now I will fly down and play,
on this very beautiful summer day.
*Hannah Glick, Grade 7*
*Pennbrook Middle School*

## The Follower*

I am from neighing back and forth
And always wanting food
From pinning ears, to racing to stalls
And hooves' pounding on the ground

I am from feeding no matter the weather
And walking far and near
From chasing, kicking, shoving
And following when you are here

I am from the sound of horses trotting
And hoof prints on the ground
From jumping, walking, working
And finally calming down

I am from brushing, combing, and relaxing
And eating a midnight snack
From hearing the wind blow past our faces
and neighing forth and back…
*Mollie Rohrer, Grade 8*
*Ephrata Middle School*
*\*Dedicated to my teacher, Mr. Miler, for all his help this school year.*

## The Top of the Mountain

In the year 2013, I have a chance for a once-in-a-lifetime opportunity.
Attending Summit could be the peak of my scouting years.
A National Jamboree with scouts from each of the fifty states.
And many opportunities to explore…
Soaring through the air like a bird while on a zip line;
Rafting through raging river rapids in the New River Gorge;
Climbing to new heights I will boldly go;
Swish! My arrow pierces the bull's eye on the target
Decisions, Decisions, Decisions,
Should I go or shouldn't I go that is the question?
I would probably have an amazing time gaining new friends and experiences.
But if I didn't go, I would probably just be sitting on my couch watching TV thinking,
"Man, I wish I was at the Jambo with my fellow scouting colleagues being physically active."
I think I will go.

*Rick Herbert, Grade 9*
*Pennbrook Middle School*

## Running Free

I feel the grass, soft, under my bare feet,
wind whipping through my hair, mud between my toes, glasses forgotten at home.
A bow on my back and mud smeared on my face a Native American I pretend to be.
Fun, hide, skip, dive
FWOOP!
An arrow strikes its bulls eye in a tree.
I sit by the pond and pretend to fish, my imagination running wild and free.
I can be anyone out here anyone I want to be, from a vampire, and a bat
to a tiny little bee.
I love to run around out here, free.
Being anything I want to be, anyone I wish to be.
Everyone who's part of me.

*Milly Gorman, Grade 8*
*Bellwood Antis Middle School*

## Apology

We say things we don't mean.
We do wrong things.
We get blamed for the wrong reasons.
In the end,
We say two simple words:
"I'm sorry."
Whether we mean them
Or not,
We say them anyway.

We say the two simple words
To our family and friends.
Sometimes to people we don't like.
Usually they aren't meant.
From our point of view,
We believe we don't have to say them.

We should always mean them.
Whether we believe we should or not.
We always should say,
"I'm sorry" with sincerity.
*Kaitlyn Hafer, Grade 8*
*Coventry Christian Schools*

## The Piano Player

The piano player found inspiration
From every composer in the nation.
She learned songs throughout the day,
So she can sit down and play.

Her fingers moved up and down the keys,
As she did this with great ease,
All alone in the room,
The music had no gloom.

She wanted to be the best,
That was her only quest.
It would be her dream come true,
However she knew,
It would be very hard to get there.

So every day,
The piano player was willing to play,
Until her dream was alive,
And she survived,
To be the best she could be.
*Karlie Lobitz, Grade 8*
*Lake-Lehman Jr High School*

## Brothers

The sun falls down like a wounded soul,
its blood turning all skies pink.
His brother moon rises in black,
as a ghost form of this day's past.
*Billy Derksen, Grade 7*
*Garnet Valley Middle School*

## Lost Love

Tap tap tap went the finger of a man,
Who looked in the hospital room.

His heart filled with care,
Was very unprepared,
For what was yet to come.

Tap tap tap went the rain in the night,
As he watched beside his bed.

The windows were bare,
But he didn't care,
As he silently fell asleep.

Tap tap tap went the feet on the floor,
As he sat and waited to hear.

Much sorrow filled the air,
And his heart was left bare,
As he stood with tears in his eyes.

Tap tap tap went the finger of a man,
Whose heart was broken in two.

He tried his best to suppress the stress,
But the man and his heart were no more.
*Danielle Wieczorek, Grade 8*
*St Luke School*

## Birthdays

It comes but once a year,
A time to celebrate,
A time to laugh and cheer,
A time that you anticipate.

There are presents to get,
Like a bicycle or canoe!
Maybe a tea set,
Or a toy truck that's blue!

The cake is the best part
(For some people at least).
It can be shaped like a heart,
Or a monstrous beast!

Birthdays are fun,
And special, too,
But once they've begun
They are over too soon!

They come once a year,
Time to celebrate,
Time to laugh and cheer,
On your birthdate!
*Jeana Luciana, Grade 8*
*Redeemer Lutheran School*

## Parasailing…

The wind was what glided us along
Far above the ocean
You can hear the sea,
Humming you a song
But the wind stops and you go down
Down into the sea with the jellyfish
But when the wind kicks back on,
You are jerked up and up and up again
The sea breeze blows in your face
Your gliding is at such a relaxing pace
Sad to see,
But you are being pulled in gently,
Back to the boat as if a fish on a hook
You're on your journey back to land
The sea rocks you back and forth,
Careful not to get sick!
*Shaniah Miller, Grade 7*
*Bellwood Antis Middle School*

## Country Summer

Morning sunrise
Birds chirping
School houses silent
Mothers pushing baby buggies
Children running barefoot
Sun kissed skin
Rope swings dangling over the ponds
Picnics in the church yard
Malt shakes and sundae socials
Farmer's fields being plowed
Wild flowers in Mason jars
Sunset skies
Cricket's nightly lullaby
Fireflies dancing
Stars shining
Warm summer nights
*Brooke Butina, Grade 8*
*Beaty-Warren Middle School*

## What Does a Book Know?

What does a book know?
Shelf edges
Folded edges
Sentences stream
Shelf beams
Back pack bottoms
Read top to bottom
Pages turning
While kids yearning
In a library
On a table
Telling a fable
Back on the shelf
It goes
*Justin DePhillipo, Grade 7*
*Easton Area Middle School 7-8*

### I Am From*

I am from a world full of sadness,
and desperation beyond my control.
From only three meals a week,
to no home to go to and sleep.

I am from a world of hate toward me,
And no family left to keep me safe.
From no cures to my illnesses,
To no clean water to take a drink.

I am from a place full of abuse,
And terror to wake up and leave my dreams.
From no one there to love me,
To crying myself to sleep.

I am from singing myself lullabies,
and telling myself that everything will change.
From never learning to laugh,
To wishing I knew there was someone there.

*Shaniece Ebelhar, Grade 8*
*Ephrata Middle School*
*\*From the point of view of a third-world country child*

### Despair Lurks

After a friend leaves
Amid a pile of broken dreams
At the core of an aching heart
Near the pain of a failed start

I am always there

From within the minds of bent perspectives
During the strain of wrong objectives
At the time of a forced choice
Out of the pain of a lost voice

I am always there

From within a tortured soul
Around every ghost and ghoul
Beyond the sting of unkind words
At the time when your voice simply isn't heard

I am always there

*Noah Allen, Grade 7*
*Indian Crest Middle School*

### Someday

Someday we will play the new Super Mario Bros.
Someday we will play catch.
Someday we will play basketball.
Someday we will ride on our four-wheeler.
Someday we will go to the beach.
Someday I will get to see you again.

*Nate Shantz, Grade 7*
*Pequea Valley Intermediate School*

### Peace

Peace the object most desired
Yet the one never reached
The continuity of the thunder rattles the path
But never breaks it
The thunder overwhelms the world
As soon as one storm settles another ascends to its place
Thunder teaches hate
Hate teaches prejudice
Prejudice teaches the children
The children fire the bullets
Will the thunder terminate?
Will the hate halt?
Will the prejudice perish?
Not without the path, the part of peace
The broadest path yet, the one less traveled
But it isn't enough that we see this path
To end the thunderstorms, we must walk the path
Because peace is not a poem
Peace is not a song
Peace is not just a dream
It is a dream to be acted upon

*Liam Kelley, Grade 7*
*Indian Valley Middle School*

### Basketball Game

We are down by one
Our winning streak is in a doubt
There are two minutes left in the game, we're nervous now
They have the ball
The shot goes up
Miss
We rebound, run down the court
The basket ate the ball and made a swoosh
We're up by one
We have butterflies in our stomach now
48 seconds left we shoot again, score
Up by three
10 seconds left
9 8 7 6 5 4 3 2
Time out, 1 second now
The loud buzzer buzzes like a bee

*Elizabeth Whaley, Grade 8*
*Bellwood Antis Middle School*

### Pasta

5 quarts of water, 1 teaspoon of salt
Full box of pasta, if too much it's not your fault
Into the pot, to a rapid boil
Cook uncovered, use no foil
Stir quickly, cook until done
Drain off the water and let it run
Scoop it out and fill your plate
Add some sauce and some meatballs
And it will be great!

*Devin Davis, Grade 7*
*Pequea Valley Intermediate School*

## Things a Flyers Fan Knows

Everybody must know Bobby Clarke
And maybe a defense man named Mark
Lindro's fame
A five—overtime game
Everyone must know Mr. Parent
Only the lord saves more
Since then, goal tending's been quite poor
Claude Giroux has beautiful finesse
I must confess
A new goal tender to end all fears
But watching him brings me to tears
A blockbuster trade for this goal tender
I hope these Flyers have a good mender
*Michael McHenry, Grade 7*
*Easton Area Middle School 7-8*

## Untruthful Love

Secrets hide behind closed doors,
Trying so hard to get inside,
I try no more and step away,
Tears fill and blind my eyes.
Once the door opens,
I see there are lies,
To protect me,
To hold me,
Why?
You step out as light,
Then fade to less,
But the smile's still so bright,
How does love last when love has lied?
*Cheyenne Angelo, Grade 8*
*Ephrata Middle School*

## Pet Dog

I want a pet dog so badly
But my brother is scared of them sadly
I wish I could trade him away
Give him to the store
I would love that for sure
But instead he has to stay
My parents say dogs are a lot of work
I say I'd do it
They say they've heard that before with the
Hamster, the cat, the monkey, the giraffe
"There's no way you're getting a dog
So forget it
And quit begging"
*Gayatri Joglekar, Grade 7*
*Pennbrook Middle School*

## Life

Days are limited
Has miseries and sorrows
But clearly worth it.
*Victor Aung, Grade 7*
*Southern Lehigh Middle School*

## You Are Not a Dream You Are Real

You are strong, you are romantic, you are caring
I can't bear the feeling of you not at my side

You hold me close to keep me safe, your touch is as soft as a sheet
The tragic thing that comes upon this, is that you are just a dream
A figment of my imagination

In real life you are a cheat, you abuse, you mistreat
No flowers, no chocolates, just an empty box full of scraps
You may be cunning, you may be strong, but you touch brings me pain
The only thing you gain from me is the broken pieces from my heart

You enjoy the tears running down my face
You enjoy the fact that my sadness is like a sinking ship
What we had is now over and the feeling we had for each other are gone
I regret the hope that I had for you
For you to be my dream, not what's real

*Stacy Arciniegas, Grade 7*
*Tulpehocken Jr/Sr High School*

## A Typical Middle School

Buses pull into the parking lot, students file into the building.
The first bell rings.
Teachers yell, "Get to homeroom!"
First period bell
People rush into the hallways on their way to their first class.
Second period…s l o w l y…ticks by.
Third, fourth, fifth periods
Finally! Lunch and recess!
We eat and go out for some fresh air, we can socialize with friends.
The rest of the day is short. Two periods.
Yay! The school day is over!
We quickly pile onto the buses and they drive away.
We take some time to reflect on our day and look forward to the next.
*Joshua Luo, Grade 7*
*Strath Haven Middle School*

## Utopia

Of everything thing we dream
We dream of peace
Created we are from the Great God Almighty
Bringer of peace, bringer of justice
Peace we bring with our dreams
Our utopia, for our peace
A benevolent God we serve, for He saved us from our sins, now we save Him
Our Utopia
United we are free, together we are one
We watch as sin is taken, we see a Utopia rising to be
Our Utopia
A benevolent God we serve, through thick and thin we always trust Him
For our Utopia
*Ryan Thomas, Grade 7*
*Cambria Heights Middle School*

## Lead to Your Drought

When I am feeling sad I
Cry, cry
What else can you do?
You want to let your feelings out.
Sigh, sigh.
Because when you cry too much,
It leads to a drought
*Rebecca Boisvert, Grade 8*
*Northern Lebanon Middle School*

## True Beauty

People are windows.
Sometimes they are open
and sometimes they are closed.
The picture on the outside
may surprise you
but if you open it,
you can see the true beauty.
*Maile Chang, Grade 8*
*Saegertown Jr/Sr High School*

## Summer

Summer
Hot, sunny
Beach, fun, friends,
Sand, ocean, cold, freezing
Icy, snow, sledding
Snowman, skiing
Winter
*Taylor Berger, Grade 8*
*Northern Lebanon Middle School*

## Earth

Sky
Blue, bright
Breezing, blowing, flowing
Clouds, airplanes, people, animals
Comforting, warming, supporting
Green, soft
Ground
*Rebecca Boltz, Grade 8*
*Northern Lebanon Middle School*

## Green

Calm is green.
It smells like moss.
It tastes like wilderness.
It sounds like turkeys gobbling.
It feels like spring.
It looks like a frog.
It is very calm, like a deer feeding.
*Dustin Crum, Grade 8*
*Saegertown Jr/Sr High School*

## The Conversation

A lustrous, milky ocean and graphite
Is all that is needed
The reigns are released
So the magical journey begins
Using only the sparkling twenty-six
Anything is possible
Clusters that have never dared to come together appear
Ideas start to fall hard
But they are swept off their feet
And transformed into unique phrases
The sword drops a couple times
But it is levitated upward and quickly corrects blemishes
The kingdom cheers as the perfect combination is finally achieved
The enchanted letters string themselves together forming lines
As they animate themselves
The verses painting a vivid mini story
At last, the completed stanzas have engulfed the ivory desert
Now evolved into something with which the world has never danced
Only dressed with the magical twenty-six
All thanks to the milky ocean's conversation with the charming graphite
*Pooja Gandhi, Grade 9*
*Holicong Middle School*

## The Future

It seems so far and out of focus but with every step it is becoming clearer.
Sometimes I begin to wonder…
What will it be like?
How will it work?
What will I do?
It is a small candle in the dark of night.
It shines brightly enough to illuminate a few steps in front of me
But for the distant future we are in the dark.
It is a pattern.
You can try to predict it but you never know what will happen until it happens.
It is an empty calendar.
You can see the dates coming up but only you can fill them in.
It is a blank canvas.
Life gives you the colors and you decide what to paint.
It is a seed.
You plant it and then care for it when it is small,
Over the years you get to watch it as it becomes the biggest tree in the forest.
Will you turn left or will you turn right?
In the end it's up to you,
What do you want your future to look like?
*Ana Burns, Grade 9*
*Fox Chapel Area Sr High School*

## One Window Is All I Need for America

One window is all I need to see the American Flag
To say the pledge; loud and true
To see the shining sea; deep and blue
For saying thanks to the men who died
To keeping the American pride
And to seeing those stars and stripes dance across the bright blue skies
*Mariel Stoltzfus, Grade 7*
*Pequea Valley Intermediate School*

## The Coming Storm

I like to believe,
there's a place by the beach,
where happiness is what you can receive,
yet there is no limit to speech.

But passes a day,
when the sky was all gray,
and the sun and the ocean fought.
No, not a lesson was taught.

The sun smiled down,
the ocean frowned.
And as we know, the sun won,
and the universe all became one.

If there comes such a day,
when we are taken away,
by the envious ocean blue,
just remember there is nothing you can do,
yet let our lives renew.

*Cassie George, Grade 7*
*Tulpehocken Jr/Sr High School*

## Hockey

Loud and rowdy,
skating on ice,
skilled at the game,
no time to be nice.

The pounding of bodies hitting the wall,
teams gracefully sliding,
like a beautiful ballet,
then punches and fighting.

The calm broken,
helmets and sticks flying,
faces get bloody,
then they start playing.

Passing,
Shooting,
Scoring,
Missing.

*Ashley Hoover, Grade 7*
*Pequea Valley Intermediate School*

## Hard Work and Success

Hard work
Dedication, determination,
Participating, caring, wanting,
Effort, team, winning, dreams,
Achieving, accomplishing, defeating,
Proud, courage,
Success

*Madison Hiegel, Grade 7*
*St Luke School*

## Sophia

Her name is Sophia
She was born on December 30th
She had beautiful sky blue eyes
She had strawberry blonde hair

She was born on December 30th
She smiled at me and waved her hand
She had strawberry blonde hair
Everyone came in to welcome her

She smiled at me and waved her hand
Her hand, tiny and soft, rubbed my hand
Everyone came in to welcome her
She was precious

Her hand, tiny and soft, rubbed my hand
She had beautiful sky blue eyes
She was precious
Her name is Sophia

*Sydni Stearns, Grade 7*
*Garnet Valley Middle School*

## A Nursery Rhyme

I wish you would stay forever
I know you can't this time
But you're my Georgy Porgy
And I'm your nursery rhyme.

Go on and leave the nest
My sleepy Little Boy Blue
To outgrow these childish dreams
And begin your life anew.

Don't forget our precious tales
While I'm home in my lonely shoe
No spider to share my tuffet
As I bid you a sobbing adieu.

One day you'll return to Mother Goose
Speaking in singsong tone
Reading aloud as I once did
Only now it's for your own.

*Jenna Maida, Grade 9*
*Holicong Middle School*

## Stars

Stars are so pretty and bright.
They give off more than a dash of light.
Some are big,
Some are small,
I like to stop,
And stare at them all.
Lighting up our Earth at night,
And allowing us to sleep all right.

*Hannah Day, Grade 7*
*Bellmar Middle School*

## Together

We were here from the start
From morning to midnight
From dawn till dusk
We went together hand in hand
Side by side standing still
Till the end
We watched the sun eclipse the moon
Together we sang a melodic tune
We watched the sun in the bright blue sky
Bound together side by side
Every day until the end
Will you always be my friend?
I heard a crack and you were gone
You broke your promise
Like you broke my heart
But you will always be my friend
All together till the end

*Paulina Fournier, Grade 7*
*William Penn Middle School*

## The Mighty Eagle

The mighty eagle is the king
The mighty eagle is amazing

You do not want him as your enemy
You joke about this, but soon you'll see

The mighty eagle is our nation's bird
To mock him would be absurd

The mighty eagle is a sight
But you only see him in flight

The mighty eagle is the one
The one who stands for us until war is won

Even when he must sleep night it is nightly
He will always be the eagle, who is mighty

*Karson Lorey, Grade 7*
*Northgate Middle/High School*

## Life in a Cavern

YOUTH
Emerge from a tunnel
Into a cavern
Walls lined with jewels and gems
TEENS
Feel the cavern walls shake
Jewels mined from the silt
And view the cavern collapse
ADULTS
Dug from the rubble
Spirits and hearts broken
Enter the world of life

*Sean Ferry, Grade 8*
*Wattsburg Area Middle School*

### Friends

Friends are there to listen even when
You have nothing to say
Friends will make you smile when
You don't want to
Friends laugh with you not at you
Friends will never let you down
Friends will tell you the truth
Even though it hurts
Friends are with you through
Thick and thin
Friends are a team whether you win or lose
Friends will never quit on you
Even though you feel like
Quitting yourself
Friends are the best people to
Make memories with
No matter how far apart you are
Friends stay close to your heart

*Lauren Brawley, Grade 7*
*Cambria Heights Middle School*

### State of Being

I feel the earth slide from under my feet
I feel as though I'm at a defeat
I feel like a lesser
I feel all the pressure
I feel a great depression
I feel as though I'm just a regression
    But when it's all done
    I know I'm number one
I feel as free as a bird
I feel at a loss for words
I feel like I just could twirl
I feel at one with the world
I feel like I can take any chance
I feel like I should just dance
    And when I slow down
    I take a look around
I know I'm more than just perfect
I know it was all worth it

*Ashley Dutrow, Grade 8*
*Bellwood Antis Middle School*

### The Power Comes from Within

The power to win
Must come from within.
As for worry and fear,
Irrelevant.
Whether quick and strong
Or big and tall
It does not matter.
For the only way to succeed
Is to leave behind all thoughts,
And focus on one goal.

*Zach Collester, Grade 9*
*Holicong Middle School*

### The Present

Forget yesterday ever happened,
Don't remember tomorrow is another day,
Throw your mistakes in the trash,
And live without another delay,
Live every day to its fullest,
Never go back to before,
Start your day with a smile,
And live like you never lived before,
Try your hardest every second,
Don't get hung up on the bad,
Prevent the darkness from getting to you,
And live with regrets no more,
Live every day like you're dying,
Don't hold back your dreams,
Drop your fears out the window,
And live your life worry free,
Yesterday was history,
Tomorrow is a mystery,
Today is a gift,
That is why it is called the present.

*Lauren Miller, Grade 9*
*Holicong Middle School*

### My Horse and I

Across the prairie
We race away.
On my trusty ole horse
I'll ride all day.
Her mane is thick,
She gallops with pride.
She takes me all over
The prairie side.
Under the deep blue sky
We'll never say goodbye.
We'll catch the sun's bright gleam,
And there we will dream.
We'll stop where the wildflowers grow,
Never a care to bestow us,
Never a worry to slow us,
Down where the stream flows slow.
We'll catch the fragrance of flowers
And lounge there and rest for hours.
We'll launch a dream, my horse and I,
Under the wide, blue sky.

*Amy Peachey, Grade 8*
*Rock Haven Christian School*

### What the Sun Knows

The sun knows
    how to shine
        very bright
    and create sunlight
when to rise and when to set
    working up a sweat.

*Isabella Baratta, Grade 7*
*Easton Area Middle School 7-8*

### Trust

Trust
Doesn't always apply.
Loving home…not for me
No comfort, no support.
Horrors…hurt.
Unspeakable fear
Pain
Can't tell…will I be believed?
Facing rage and fury
Inches away
Going to court doesn't
Take away the hurt
Or solve everything
Trying to just be me
By myself
Isn't easy
But life goes on
And I'm going to live it!

*Destyni Jones, Grade 7*
*Sandburg Middle School*

### Dream

This world is not real.
I am standing alone.
In a world of darkness.
This place is not home.

Where all wishes are granted.
And where I am set free.
I can do anything in this dream.

People can talk.
But I don't really hear.
I can see people that are near.

This world is a dream.
Just for me.
I can do anything.
If I set my mind.
FREE!

*Dayton Gowin, Grade 7*
*Towanda Jr/Sr High School*

### Life

Life is everlasting and full of spirit
It lifts you up or you hit rock-bottom
But no matter what happens
You're the one who will change it.
You write your own future.
You walk the path to success.
You might fall into a hole,
But in the end the things you
Accomplish are going to be
The only things that matter.

*Heather Brown, Grade 9*
*Avon Grove High School*

**My Favorite Place**

The rocky black top that holds most of my memories
And the woodchips that fly after me when I run
Leaves that wonder about leaving me in a trace

The blinding sun that shines right through me
My long breathless shadow copying my every move
And swings that burn me in the hot sun

The chirping birds that seems the quietest of all
That noise the swings make in the calm afternoon breeze
Yelling loud screams of laughter and tears mix the air
My friends and I when we laugh and cry for no good reason

Will my special place ever change without me there?
Does anyone notice it's company like I do?
Does it know it's my real home?
Will it miss me when I'm gone?

I'm at peace when I lie in the grass
It always finds a way to make me smile
But when I'm all alone my place interests me the most
When I'm here I know I'm safe, forever

My freedom
My freedom
My freedom

*Julia Reinhardt, Grade 7*
*William Penn Middle School*

**Songs of the World**

The world has many songs to sing
With profound meanings of their own
They travel across the arid hills
Bearing stories of different sorts

The world has many clothes to wear
Made of diverse materials and threads
Weaved, sown, knitted, patched
They are the finest work of the hand

The world has many voices to speak
Whispering softly far and wide
Mingling together into one tune
That tells of every joy and hope

The world many battles to fight
And wars yet to be won
For this world is not a peaceful place
Struggles here are born and reborn

The world has many songs to sing
Each beautiful in its own way
They blend together into one voice
And unite to face the war

*Rebecca Lauver, Grade 8*
*Lancaster Mennonite School - Locust Grove*

**Life Is an Ocean**

Life is an ocean
where you never know what's coming next,
whether it's a big wave or small

There are plenty of
ups and downs every day

After a perfect day, bright and sunny,
a hurricane may occur

Life can be an angry monster
crashing down on you
and you feel like it is impossible
to get back up when a wave knocks you down

Or life can give you the perfect waves to ride
and you feel like you're on top of the world

Life is an ocean, whether it
crashes on you
or brightens up your day

*Nicole Loan, Grade 7*
*Garnet Valley Middle School*

**The Hunger Games**

**T** he
**H** unger games.
**E** ach district

**H** as to pick two
**U** seful people that
**N** eed to battle to the death to
**G** et the capitol amused
**E** very year. The only
**R** ule…Stay alive.

**G** igantic arenas are used for the 24 tributes
**A** nd only one person comes out alive.
"**M** ay the odds be
**E** ver in your favor"
**S** ays Effie to the tributes of district twelve.

*Mikala Hardie, Grade 7*
*J R Fugett Middle School*

**Path of Life**

When you want something, sometimes you
have to swim deeper, you can't just give up
just because things don't come easy you have
to overcome the obstacle, face your fears in
the end it's worth it! Life is always filled with ups
and downs, if you believe in yourself you will always
succeed and come through with value friendship, love
and faith never underestimate yourself believe
in yourself and follow your own footsteps!

*Kiara Ulrich, Grade 7*
*Cambria Heights Middle School*

### Rush

The quiet hum,
The icy clear.
A crystal cover,
Fills the air.

The night turns over,
A silent lover.
Reveals a secret,
Never told before.

A waking dream,
No need to rush.
Just close your eyes,
A calming hush.
*Jamie Paugh, Grade 8*
*Danville Area Middle School*

### Sunlight

Sunlight, sunlight, shimmering bright
in my eyes that just lost sight.
What rays or beams
could blame the sun at its height?

In what hides behind the clouds.
Burning yellow, is it proud?
On air dark as night?
Where does it get its light?

And I bet its figure is mighty tall.
Is it as round as a ball?
And it rises and sets.
Could it ever become upset?
*Camryn Howarth, Grade 7*
*Garnet Valley Middle School*

### Time Has Changed

Roses are red violets are blue
Time has changed for me and soon for you
When I first looked into his eyes
They were blue as the sky.

When I first inhaled his smell
It was as delightful as a ringing bell
But now since time has changed
He does not know that I remain.

This man that I hope will be mine
Always kept me in line
He made me smile every day
And we had lots of laughs along the way.
*Madison Powell, Grade 7*
*Landisville Middle School*

### Quiet Place

I'm seeing myself in a pool,
the crystal clear clean water.
Around that, the trees lined up one by one.

In the blue, bright, clear sky
the sun overhead brings little shadows.
The sun makes the water glitter.
The small waves soundly hit the ladder.

I always wondered if
the trees will come down,
or if the water freezes in the winter
I always wondered why it is so small.

My happy feelings
relaxed yard —
when I'm alone.
I feel like a whale
in the blue sea
thinking of nothing.
Water water water.
*Billy Aungpe, Grade 7*
*William Penn Middle School*

### Paul McCartney's Concert

Everyone is jeering
Everyone is laughing
Everyone is crying
For Paul McCartney
Everyone screams!
Everyone starts cheering!
It's time to meet
Paul McCartney
Oh what a feeling
To meet a star
In real life
Paul McCartney
Amazed as they can be
They cannot forget
No one can meet
Paul McCartney
But what a surprise!
He brings a fan up!
She is crying
We all knew she was
At Paul McCartney's concert
*Luke Hollingshead, Grade 8*
*Bellwood Antis Middle School*

### Love

Somebody to love
somebody to care
someone to love me
for who I am
*Travis G. Rhoad, Grade 8*
*Northern Lebanon Middle School*

### Companion

She was there every day,
Never daring to leave me.
My protector since the beginning,
A happy, loyal companion,
That will always be in my heart.

She was there every day,
The one who I could always count on.
We were bonded,
Like sisters,
Of a different species.

She was there every day,
Emotions so connected,
Nearly the same in personality.
A fluff ball of joy,
Who was the only real listener.

She was there every day,
Even when she was old,
And still the best in the world.
So when the day came,
There wasn't a tear, not shed.
*Ana Clayton, Grade 7*
*William Penn Middle School*

### Beach

White sand
like vanilla ice cream
warms my feet
as I walk through.

Soft ocean winds
carry cries of seagulls
blowing
cooling my face.

Bright blue sky
aqua green water
puffy white clouds
surround me.

I feel relaxed
warm at heart
wanting to stay
forever more
at my
big
beautiful
beach.
*Samantha Churchill, Grade 7*
*William Penn Middle School*

## Cha Cha

Graceful beauty with a flash of spirit.
Cantering down the triple in-and-out,
Landing so soft you can barely hear it
Launching herself to hear everyone shout.
As she trots around with athletic strength
An amazing mover, so effortless.
Her sculpted muscles stretch to such a length
Though she powers around with awareness.
She does not even try, it comes with ease,
Naturally fit and so quick to learn.
She runs past me, and I feel the cool breeze,
In a lively and energetic turn.
I love her so much my main muchacha,
I love you forever, you're my Cha Cha.

*Meghan Gray, Grade 8*
*Pocono Mountain East Jr High School*

## Gone

I can't even look at you in the face
Trust me, we all know what you intended
How could you move on at such a fast pace?
Wishing everything with you had ended
How don't you feel guilty, can you tell me?
To many, your soul is shady and dark
Now can you see you are finally free
I would love to know that it left a mark
There is no longer anything to say
I do wish you could vanish from this place
Questions soaring through my head every day
You made a mistake that you didn't face
That dreadful noise talking in your head
To me my feelings for you are now dead

*Estal Concepcion, Grade 8*
*Pocono Mountain East Jr High School*

## Asian with Slanted Eyes

Just because I am half Asian

I am not a Nike shoe maker
I am not a rice farmer
I am not a genius

What is culture?
What is "different color?"
Why are you so judgmental?

Just because I am half Asian; don't judge me.

Why are you so judgmental
Just because I am half Asian?

*Shelby Edwards, Grade 7*
*Prospect Park School*

## Mysterious Travels

The vastness and wideness of space and time
All the way out to the bright moon and mars
Going up there, I wish it was my case
Having an adventure among the stars
The time has been so slow, around the clock
Stars burning, exploding, wouldn't it be nice?
Galaxies whirling causing a mind block
Outer space is truly as cold as ice
Something beautiful as trees and the bees
A ship would board to find new planets
Think of how lovely are the foreign seas
It will be a long, long trip, so can it!
Through the sparkling space and time for you
Why not let it be a travel for two?

*Tiffany Ridder, Grade 8*
*Pocono Mountain East Jr High School*

## Goldfish

Tiny goldfish swimming in the big bowl
Colorful fish shining all the day long
Smaller than most things but have a big soul
Because of your size you're not very strong
Swishing your small fin, so you are moving
Swimming around the little treasure chest
Bubbles floating to the top are soothing
When your fish friends come you have fish fest
Colorful pebbles beneath the small fish
Feeling dizzy from swimming in circles
You want to escape, but can only wish
You can only see a lot of purples
Goldfish like to float up in small bubbles
Being a gold fishy has no troubles

*Sydney Swiatkowski, Grade 8*
*Pocono Mountain East Jr High School*

## The Pitch

You're standing, watching,
Waiting for the sign to come
It comes, the perfect pitch
You get set, knowing you're going to dominate the batter
You check the runner at first.
Stalking him like a leopard ready to pounce
You cool down and step off
Regaining the urge of aggression
You get your sign again
Get set up
And finally throw the ball
Releasing all of your built up aggression and power
The umpire calls a strike
And you then get ready to do it all again.

*Matt Benicky, Grade 8*
*Bellmar Middle School*

## Can You Sleep at Night?

Louder than a blaring horn
Louder than a huge tractor trailer
Louder than a small air horn
Or an explosion louder than a tractor
Or a motorcycle

Louder than an airplane
Louder than a truck
Louder than a jet
Louder than a gun
Louder than a crashing race car
Louder than a building falling
Louder than a door slamming
That's how loud my father
    SNORES!

*Kyle Doan, Grade 7*
*Pequea Valley Intermediate School*

## Blackberries

My mouth salivates
The fruit squeals between my jaws
My throat swallows it away

Sweet at first
Then turns bitter
And lasts until replaced

Collapses between my fingers
Melts in my mouth
Juice drips down my chin

The sweet smell wafts
A ball of ruby and black
With tiny hairs protruding

*William Field, Grade 8*
*Shipley School*

## The County Fair

**T** ime to remember
**H** orse pulls
**E** ntertainment

**C** ows
**O** ld tractors
**U** nbeatable games
**N** ew friends
**T** ime with family
**Y** ummy food

**F** un
**A** mazing shows
**I** ce cream
**R** ides

*Brandon Davis, Grade 7*
*Cambria Heights Middle School*

## Society

The world of advancement
made of clay and cement
filled with deception and dread
lawyers, liars mean the dead
all happiness covered or wiped from here
ask yourself: what lies near?
From what I see is a spec of smiles
but the rest is dread for miles
we revolve on what we want
fun, excitement is what taunts
but there is happiness in wisdom you see
for wisdom lasts for eternity
the only thing you need to do
to see happiness is do…
be wise for humanity
and maybe all will laugh for eternity.

*John Zhendrich B. Ordoña, Grade 8*
*Northern Lebanon Middle School*

## A Hidden Leaf

A tree with ruby leaves
Sways around the wind
The leaves rustle and rasp
While one leaf flutters…
But it shouldn't have,
For it isn't autumn
Not here, and not yet.
If you saw the colorful leaf
You would see the ruby redness
Below a golden middle
That fades to a dark amber
And ends at a tip of softest green.
If you saw the leaf,
You would see this,
But you can't.
Not here, and not yet.

*Gabrielle Barone, Grade 8*
*Mount Nittany Middle School*

## March Madness

I fill out my bracket with high hopes,
And pray in the end that I won't mope.
Upsets can occur in the first two rounds,
Leaving only the beat teams around.
The sweet sixteen are left to play,
Then half are forced to go away.
With only eight left to the battle,
Four must bear down and get on the saddle.
Now with only those teams to beat,
Each group is forced to play neat.
Two still remain on the court,
Marking the end of the NCAA sort.
Kentucky ends up winning it all.
They take the nets for the locker room wall.

*Joe Wermuth, Grade 7*
*Pennbrook Middle School*

## Ode to Sleeping

To feel the warm touch of silent sleep
Is to let my stress melt into my bed
My senses soon falter, the doze so deep
That the troubles of day so sweetly shed

My rest at night is fantastic indeed
A chance to start anew each somber night
I devour each hour with ravenous greed
And climb into bed with quiet delight

I cling to my sleep when grim threats arise
And struggle against them 'till all is clear
Times I fail I passionately despise
When I lose this peace I hold so dear

Why must I lose this glorious respite?
Even now I lose it with this poem I write.

*Will Newell, Grade 9*
*Pine-Richland Middle School*

## On the Beach

Her days star like all the rest
The warm sun beaming down on her skin,
The beach is crowded,
Then it becomes empty.

Once the rain starts,
Everyone leaves,
Just like all the rest.

She wanders along the rocky shore
And the empty coast,
She things about all the times
She's be wronged and broken.

She tries and tries,
Yet she is never good enough,
And she'll never know why.

*Sloane Hudok, Grade 8*
*Pine-Richland Middle School*

## The Race

I dive in the water, oh it's cold!
The sensation never gets old
Arms glide
And legs like a jet
Powering through the wet
Flip turn, push off, go, go, go!
Who's going to win? I don't know

The race is done
The swimmers exit the pool
You know what would've been cool?
If I'd ended as number one

*Sydney Glisan, Grade 7*
*Pennbrook Middle School*

## Seagulls

They dip and dive
They fly and swoop
They spin, fall, thrive, and loop.

They are simple creatures
Living in the sand,
Playing in the water,
Taking over the land.

They can take your food,
Steal your stuff,
Leaving like a small white fluff.

They are simple creatures
Floating in the water
Soaring in the sky
They are definitely not shy.

A seagull is like a friend
Who never stays for long
Always busy, moving along
They are simple creatures
Seagulls
*Angela Young, Grade 8*
*Bellwood Antis Middle School*

## Music Is

Music is a part of me
It runs through my veins
It combines with my blood

Music is my life
It takes up my whole day
It helps keep me sane

Music is my passion
It is my future
It is what I do

Music is my friend
It is always there for me
It picks me up when I am down

Music is my love
It is nice and understanding
It is my favorite thing in the whole world

Music is a part of me
It beats with my heart
It is also in yours
*Erin Sweigart, Grade 9*
*Ephrata Sr High School*

## Bulletproof Love

My love for you was
Bulletproof,
But you're the one who
Shot me.
My faith in you was
Strong as steel,
But you're the one who
Forgot me.
My hope in you was
Slowly fading
Because you're the one who
Left me.
My tears I cried for you were
Wasted
Because I let you get the
Best of me.
*Julia Reid, Grade 7*
*Big Spring Middle School*

## Prince Charming

His eyes are blue as sapphires
His smile sparkles like the sea
His lips as soft as butter
When he kisses me
His kisses gentle as snowflakes
Falling on the ground
How he makes
My world turn 'round
His hair as soft as a kitten's fur
His laugh, how I stutter
My Prince, makes my heart flutter
And as I try to find this boy,
As long as it may seem
I rouse from my slumber
For he is just a dream
*Ainsley Feyock, Grade 8*
*Centerville Middle School*

## What a Soccer Player Knows

What does a soccer player know?
Scoring goals,
Touching toes,
Screaming fans,
Making plans,
Lots of practice,
Learning new tactics,
Getting muddy,
Don't fuddy duddy!
Staying in shape,
Using medical tape,
Win a ton,
Having fun,
Until the season is
Finally done.
*Breanna Micolupo, Grade 7*
*Easton Area Middle School 7-8*

## I Don't Understand...

What's the matter?
What's the joke?
Aren't I important?
Has our friendship broke?

Was it something I did?
Was it something I said?
I don't understand,
Is it all in my head?

This doesn't make sense,
We have always been friends!
But now of course,
You like her instead.

Don't worry, I get it
You've moved on,
But I still have to say
I don't get why you're gone.
*Elizabeth Fastman, Grade 8*
*Paxon Hollow Middle School*

## Your Big Sister

No one will hurt you.
I won't let them break you.
You'll grow up to be strong,
And sometimes you'll be wrong.

But know I'll be here
To hold you and be sincere.
I love you little bro,
But sometimes I have to go.

Just don't forget me.
Don't forget all our memories.
I'll always be here
Although I may not be near.

I will always love you.
I know you love me to.
You will always be my little brother,
And I will always be your big sister.
*Elizabeth Anderson, Grade 9*
*Bishop McCort High School*

## Happiness

Happiness is a flower.
What bright colors it has.
Where it sways in the meadows.
Why does winter have to come?
Why must it take my happiness away?
All my questions unanswered.
As I wait for the day,
When my happiness comes back to stay.
*Alexis Soifer, Grade 8*
*Lake-Lehman Jr High School*

## Yankees

New York is home to the New York Yankees
A New York Yankee is such a proud man
The men that they face will drop to their knees
Yes, I do consider myself a fan

With pinstripes and grey, they do often play
Green grass, tan dirt, and a strong will to win
The Yankees impress even Tina Fey!
Sharing New York fans with Jeremy Lin

The Yankees are best in the A.L. East
Fighting and winning as they never stop
They will continue to be the best beast
Yankees will cause their opponents to drop

Swinging and fielding, they throw the baseball
As they fight and try, they give it their all

*Patrick George, Grade 8*
*Pocono Mountain East Jr High School*

## Something Truly Special

We come together to make something beautiful.
Music
We all have our own place and role.
Teamwork
Our parts come together as one voice.
Song
We all have excitement and love.
Passion
We wait for the song's peak.
Beautiful
Everyone gets chills.
Pride
We make people smile.
Inspire
We don't want it to end,
But all wonderful things do.
Danville Middle School Band.

*Kailyn Smiley, Grade 8*
*Danville Area Middle School*

## The Dash

My life all started in 1998
I started off with a clean slate
But now I'm 13, and my life is getting shorter
It feels like everything happens in order
I want to accomplish many things in my life
One of those things is I want to be a wife
I want to get a job, and provide
And take a giraffe for a ride
I want to live a good life filled with adventures
but sadly later on I'll have to get dentures
I'll have such a good time in my dash
It will all end with a bash.

*Brooke Senft, Grade 8*
*Spring Grove Middle School*

## Rejoined Love

She stood upon the hillside all alone;
Her golden hair flowing around her face.
A prince below wandering on his own;
Looking up at the maiden full of grace.

She gazes down with wistful eyes at him;
He returns the look with adoring eyes.
Climbing up to meet her while the lights dim;
The girl awaits the prince she'll idolize.

Together they gaze into the sunset.
The love between them too strong to deny,
Rejoined at last there is nothing to fret.
Always be together until they die.

Maiden and prince together forever;
And their undying love will end never.

*Alexandra Spallek, Grade 8*
*Pine-Richland Middle School*

## It's Now or Never

I get ready to start, nervous and scared
We need one more run to win the game
I step up to the plate, the pitch is released
CRACK!
And I hit the ground running,
As the ball flies over the heads of the outfielders
I am running as fast as a cheetah.
I hit first but don't slow down,
As the dirt whispers me to keep going,
As I round second I see my coaches waving me on,
I hit third I'm almost there,
There is just one more base to go
I can hear my teammate telling me to slide,
Next thing I know I black out…
Next thing I know I hear screaming then the umpire calling
SAFE!
We had won the game.

*Kara Whitman, Grade 9*
*Pennbrook Middle School*

## Signs of Spring

Flowers popping, leaves growing,
The farmers in the field plowing,
The oars on the boats rowing as fisherman are fishing,
The planes crossing up above in the shinning sunlight,
The birds singing lullabies as they fly high in the sky,
Bikes riding down the street going to the store,
Tourists going on a tour,
Clouds flying by while a person is saying bye to
The snow,
Snow melting quickly leaving no trace as spring springs in
Winter not knowing what trouble it's in,
Spring finally comes making people happy and full of joy!

*Mikayla Hofer, Grade 7*
*Cambria Heights Middle School*

## The Last Goodbye

He pushed her on a tire swing
Hung from the old oak tree
She giggled and laughed, as tears came to his eyes
So much he could barely see.
He looked into her baby-blue eyes
She could tell something was wrong
He couldn't help but walk away,
Because he knew he didn't have long.
The next morning she was awakened
And put in the car
She didn't know where they were going
But she hoped it wasn't far.
Standing outside the airport
In his uniform, proud and tall
He whispered "I'll be back soon baby girl
No later then next fall."
He picked up his bags
Looking in to her eyes,
He said "Just think about our memories,
You can hold on to them forever and never have to say goodbye"

*Brittney Fisher, Grade 7*
*Pequea Valley Intermediate School*

## What I Learned

Ever since I was born, I have always loved skeletons.
Their smiling faces, their gleaming bones
Have always been welcoming to me.
However the reason why has always been a mystery.

But when I was afraid most
And I believed that I was toast,
I noticed what they are to me,
And that they define me.

Skeletons are not death, they are not sadness or pain.
They are to me freedom, not what has been slain.
Like silver in a clay pot, and your talent in your soul,
Your body a skeleton holds.

It is white and bright and beautiful just like you truly are,
To me a skeleton is not loss, by far.
It is freedom from this world and pain and sorrow.
A skeleton is my hopeful tomorrow.

*Nathan Dietz, Grade 8*
*Redeemer Lutheran School*

## Blue

Happiness is blue
It smells like a warm, sunny day
It tastes like blue raspberry ice cream
It sounds like birds chirping on a cool afternoon
It feels like laying in the grass, looking at the sky
It looks like family and friends meeting again
Happiness is blue

*Lucas Smith, Grade 8*
*Saegertown Jr/Sr High School*

## The Edge

There I stand
Only a few feet away, but it feels like miles
I know I'm going forward, but I feel like I'm falling back
There's a tingling in my feet
A chill crawling down my spine
Goosebumps overwhelm me
I feel the darkness closing in
As day turns to night
I know that I have to trust,
I have to have confidence
Knowing that when I take that leap of faith
Someone will be there to catch me
I pick up my speed
My feet grinding on the hard, rocky ground
Finally, I've reached the edge
The edge between comfort and insanity
between life and death
I must decide, quickly
But there I stand,
Watching and waiting
Ready to take the leap of faith

*Shayna Bashore, Grade 7*
*Tulpehocken Jr/Sr High School*

## Motorcross

We unhitch the trailer and unload the gear
We've traveled so far, but we're finally here
We wait in the line, my dad pays the fee
I'm registered now with the head referee
Now back to the trailer, it's quite a long walk
On the way I'm thinking much more than I talk
My practice is done, I know what the track's like
I ride to the trailer and clean up my bike
The starting lines full and I'm ready to race
My goggles are fogged from the sweat on my face
Just now the gate drops and I follow my plan
I fly to the corner as fast as I can
We're driving towards home, and I don't want to speak
I'm imagining crossing the line first next week

*Noah Brennan, Grade 7*
*Bellwood Antis Middle School*

## Bluebird's Melancholy

I am the bluebird.
To most, I am a symbol of peace and happiness,
But there are others who know my pain.
The light blue of the sky, I am the same.
Just waiting,
Waiting to be noticed.
Too afraid to take action, I soar over the world
And watch,
Watch as the people walk, but do not see.
I am the bluebird.
A symbol of peace, but a hurting heart.

*Nina Pauciulo, Grade 7*
*Villa Maria Academy Lower School*

### The Plunge

I take the giant step off the boat
Enter an underwater world
The water is as clear as glass
Salty water seeps into my mask
Warm water streams into my wet suit
The bright neon fish circle around me
Like a whirlpool of colors
Colorful coral sways in the current
The sand is whiter than snow
Rough with coral pieces
As if sandpaper rubs my skin
The waves lap calmly overhead
I am submerged in an underwater world

*Amanda Wertz, Grade 7*
*Bellwood Antis Middle School*

### Soldier Boy

I look into his eyes,
so filled with hope.
His voice is a firecracker
overflowing with excitement.
His smile is like a fire,
bold, bright and brilliant.
But those eyes,
his magnificent eyes,
his perfectly painted,
beautiful, peridot green, heart-racing eyes,
are filled with hunger and longing.
They're large and filled with bravery;
bravery, like the soldier he dreams to be.

*Lizzy Kirkpatrick, Grade 8*
*Bellwood Antis Middle School*

### A Flower's World

Flowers
   flow   in
the      wind
like a butterfly   or a bird might
   soar      and
fly, it grows   and sometimes
   doesn't   want
to stop, they   wind and climb,
   soar      and
bury. They    are free to be
   just   themselves.
Flowers have   their own
   worlds.

*Brooke Martin, Grade 8*
*Northern Lebanon Middle School*

### Clock

"Tick" goes the hours
"Tock" goes the passing minutes
As I watch the day die

*David Tilli, Grade 7*
*Sandburg Middle School*

### Fear

Recounting,
Recollecting my spirit.
Connecting together what I have left.

The community of the vile creatures,
No benediction will be offered.
Restricted, we must verify of no opposition.
Malnourished, we hide in desperation, as if we were a submerged submarine.
Stringent in these small quarters, needing air and confidence.
Feeling claustrophobic stuck in my own mindset.

There must be more to life than fear.

Screaming whispers,
Quiet stomps,
The burning fire so cold in my heart,

There must be more than fear!

Hear me out!
Take a stand!
Join me in succession to this pity life,
Or forever live in misery!
We just need to start.
Join me, before our chance parts.

Oh there must be more to life than fear!

*Tyler Prah, Grade 8*
*Elizabeth Forward Middle School*

### The Cycle of My Life

When winter is thriving, I will be standing upon fresh blankets of huddled snow,
Gusting winds smudging themselves on my cheeks,
Rosy pink, like a five-year-old girl who just got a hold of Mommy's blush,
Flurries of snowflakes clasp my chocolate hair,
I am the Ice Princess, serene in my kingdom.

When the peak of night lurks upon us,
The changing of the guard between the sun and moon,
Stars sprinkle light gingerly, illuminating anything it touches,
Me and my pretty self are tucked away in my house,
Lost in the entertaining, enlightening, engaging maze we call a book,
Drifting away to the realm of my fantasies, dreams, and imagination,
Dreading the time when the sun awakens,
And rings the bells to a new morning.

Curiosity about my nature interests motivates me to reflect upon myself.
Le Penseur, the thinker,
Intelligent student, absolutely.
Gracious friend to others, always.
Irish dancer, definitely forever.
Fair-skinned Irish girl, passionately.
My personality defines me,
Katie Gannon.

*Katie Gannon, Grade 7*
*Mellon Middle School*

### The Evil Cell
My own worst enemy is my cell phone.
It always forces me to text someone,
Even when I don't want to.
I try to fight it,
But there is no use.
The phone always prevails over my self-control.
When I wish to go to bed at night,
As if on cue,
I hear that evil vibration from my dresser.
This sound lifts me from my bed,
As if I'm in a trance,
And keeps me up all night long.
But then miraculously the tapping stops,
As I pull myself from the trance,
And force my finger onto the power button.
I have won tonight's battle…
But tomorrow is another day.
*Dominic Coconcelli, Grade 8*
*Penn Middle School*

### Advice
This piece of paper I have in my hand
Will soon hold my poetic masterpiece.
My thoughts are sometimes hard to understand;
My devotion to sonnets will not cease.

To all my friends I will give this advice:
To write this sonnet just follow the rules.
Write fourteen lines, always being precise.
The pattern is simple, just use the tools.

I have been thinking what must be written:
Every other line needs to have a rhyme.
Take my advice, avoid being smitten.
The work you do turns out to be sublime.

I finished the sonnet, a great hurray!
So I think this paper deserves an A.
*Alexander Greissinger, Grade 8*
*St Luke School*

### Deception
At the beginning euphoric elation
Living in a fantasy, a frivolous relation
Nothing in my world ever did quite feel
So sublime, defining unmistakably real
With faith like a child's my outlook was jolly
One false step I slipped into a chaos of folly
Like George through the jungle flailing aimlessly
Without such a warning to watch out for that tree
Discovering your feelings had begun to wane
A curve ball, its power brought an end to our game
World War One, like Britain, your actions caught my attention
So naive, fell into your trap of deception
*Joely Lorenzen, Grade 8*
*Centerville Middle School*

### What Should I Write About?
Today in school, I was asked to write a poem.
I'm not good at poems, I thought to myself,
I will never be able to do this.

What should I write about?
Should I write about a season, like winter?
No, that's not creative enough.

I need a topic that is unique,
Something that no one else will write about.
Hmm…this is harder than it seems.

Should this poem be funny, sad, or happy?
Should it be about me or someone else?
There are so many things it could be about!

Oh I think I will just give up!
I cannot think of anything good.
Maybe someday, when I'm older, I'll be a better poet.

Wait a second; I think I know what I'll write about!
I will write about how I don't know what to write about.
I hope this is okay, because I can't think of anything else!
*Braylee McIlwain, Grade 8*
*Redeemer Lutheran School*

### Softball
From the loud smelly ump
To the crack of the ball
the next batter's up and sweating a pound
by the focusing of the pitcher
making the batter uncomfortable
to the crowd that's waiting
then "woshhh" the pitch comes in
the ball spreads its wings and soars across the sky
and the next thing you know the ump says "YOU'RE OUT"
but she's still running
and the crowd's cheering
and our team's jumping in joy
while the other team is weeping in sorrow
the ump comes over, hands us the trophy
and we walk off the field with smilies a mile long
*Rylee Salaki, Grade 8*
*Centerville Middle School*

### School
Walk through the hallways
Dragging my feet
The sound of kids chatting inbetween classes
And teachers yelling
A sight most kids wouldn't enjoy
But for me I just laugh
Not every day you get to come to a wonderful place
Called school
*Kerry Deeb, Grade 7*
*Strath Haven Middle School*

### The Storm

Emergency warnings flashing across the news,
People panic.
The chances of safety are very few.
Why did this have to happen here, now, today?
Hope begins to vanish, as the rain washes it away.
Terror strikes, as we begin our fight,
Against this terrible storm.
Clouds take their ugly, shapeless form.
The chaos continues,
As people frantically try to escape,
Their gloomy, unknown and possible deadly fate.
Will we make it? Will we not?
The rain pounds harder, unrelentlessly,
The streets begin to flood and the wind picks up.
Hopefully the hurricane won't hurt us here
Everybody has a growing fear.
Hopefully the storm will let up soon.
So we can be happy once more.
Maybe this hurricane opened up a door,
To clean up the mess that this danger left behind.
As a community, to come together,
To help each other, to make a difference.

*Haley Liebenberg, Grade 7*
*Indian Valley Middle School*

### Truths of Life

My heart is livid, a melting quaggy heap
The smells of sadness and hate fill my soul
I shall never mend, never ease up
The world is cruel
It twists its evil corrupt branches into the depths of my life
Giving me no rest, no hope
But still I shall live on in pain and misery
Never to see the true light of day
Ash billows around me causing hacking and choking
The feeling of death returns rapping on my door
My conscience staggers away never to return
I will never truly live, my body will stay a hollow home
Phantoms screeching through my ears
Leaving me with the sense of foreboding
The never ending torment of life

*Kayla Mason, Grade 9*
*State College High School South*

### Music

Thoughts are often described in a song,
whether it is short or long.
It could be about love, or someone up above.
Music is a way to bring everything together,
and sometimes make things better.
If you're feeling down,
instead of just moping around,
listen to your favorite song
and your life will carry on.

*Emily Sillaman, Grade 8*
*Donegal Middle School*

### Fun in the Spring

**S** apphire blue flowers everywhere you see
**P** etunias are blooming every day now
**R** ainbows soon to be everywhere
**I** rises soon to be everywhere
**N** ew ways to enjoy yourself every day now
**G** orgeous sun flowers bloom

**T** he sweet smell of flowers in the air
**I** 'm sad to see spring leave
**M** ore and more flowers are blooming
**E** njoy the little things in spring

**F** abulous lilacs that fill the air of sweetness
**U** nique different plants everywhere you look
**N** ew activities to try

**A** lways time to try new things
**L** ots and lots of fun to enjoy
**W** onderful looking flower beds in front yards
**A** dorable baby bunnies hop around
**Y** ellow flowers everywhere you look
**S** weet, sweet smell of roses

*Alexis Niebauer, Grade 7*
*Cambria Heights Middle School*

### The Match

Rising into the air on my broom,
The whistle's shrill shriek filling my ears.
The game has begun.
The chasers are flying around the pitch like eagles.
The beater's bats are banging the bludgers beyond our team.
I've only one job,
Catching the golden snitch.
This little golden ball is the needle in the haystack during a match.
I fly high above the pitch, looking for the ball that wins the game.
I see it, but the other seeker does too.
We both dive for it.
At the very last second, the other seeker pulls up to avoid injury.
I steady my broom and stand up, my hand reaching out.
I caught the snitch.
Gryffindor wins!

*Allie Bausinger, Grade 7*
*William Penn Middle School*

### You Can Do It

"You can do it, you can do it," I chant
While like a dog I pant
Mile after mile
I finally can't help but smile
In the last leg of the race
Beet-red is my face
And even though my legs feel anything but fine
I bet you can see my pride shine
Because pain is temporary, pride will last forever!

*Maura Janoski, Grade 7*
*Pennbrook Middle School*

## Spring

Is beautiful,
Brings out allergies,
Days get much longer,
Spring showers brings new life,
Spring is a special rebirth season.

*Ian Smith, Grade 8*
*Holy Sepulcher School*

## A Piece of Cake

There once was a girl with a cake
She sat down and started to bake.
It was put on a plate,
And tasted real great.
Too bad there was not more to take.

*Emily Scheppner, Grade 7*
*St Luke School*

## Creatures*

Women and men (both little and small)
They come in all sizes (big and tall)
We are all different, as you can see
We are both special, you and me

*Sarah Gu, Grade 8*
*Arcola Intermediate School*
*\*Inspired by E. E. Cummings*

## Spring

Very bright,
Flowers are blooming,
Sometimes it is rainy,
It brightens up gloomy days,
Spring is the best season ever!

*Rebekah Benkart, Grade 8*
*Holy Sepulcher School*

## Dude Named Jay

There was once a dude named Jay
Who had Mexican the other day
He went to work
Felt the need to burp
Oops!  Came out the other way

*Annabella Puizzo, Grade 7*
*Easton Area Middle School 7-8*

## Red

Red is as bright as anger
Red is as hot as big fiery flames
Red is as cute as love on Valentine's Day
Red is as shinny as gleaming blood
Red is as pretty as fresh new roses

*Raysa Perez, Grade 7*
*Pequea Valley Intermediate School*

## Miles and Miles

I started to run,
I could feel the earth beneath my feet,
For me this is fun,
I had no demands to meet,
Running miles and miles,
Over rock, roads, and tiles,
Through ponds and lakes,
I was raising my stakes,
Then all of a sudden I came to a halt,
I could hear a soft cheering in the background it was getting louder and louder,
The reporters wanted a quote,
I said "I feel as rhythm-less as the sea,"
It finally came over me,
I had won the race,
I was in first place,
"Hooray" yelled the crowd,
I was so proud,
Someone hoisted me in the air,
But I didn't really care,
For I had won,
My hard work was finally done.

*Jenna Whitman, Grade 7*
*Pennbrook Middle School*

## Cupcakes Galore

I follow the scent of the sweet devilish treat
That sits on the window of Bakery Street
Every day so perfectly
I just can't pass by that 300 calorie treat
Without peering in for 10 minutes so intensively
My lips start smacking against each other as I walk in the store
While a burst of warm air layer my body, from my head to my toe
I walk over to the cupcake display
And my head starts spinning as I get stuck trying to decide between 20
Little cupcakes all asking for me to buy them and eat them all day
I'm already imagining the delicate folded pieces of the wrapper pressed against my palm
While I sink my teeth into the soft core
Happiness rushes through my body as if I got electrocuted
Oh how I love that feeling
Ooh how I love cupcakes,
Cupcakes galore!

*Ezoza Ismailova, Grade 7*
*Towanda Jr/Sr High School*

## Life Is a Blessing

Life is a blessing;
But life can be taken away just as soon as it is given.
Life is pure and honest;
And yet our own deceit can tarnish that truth.
Life is deep and full of meaning;
But that meaning can be spoiled in the blink of an eye by an unsavory comment.
Life is forgiving;
For time does heal all wounds.
Life is a blessing.

*Ryan S., Grade 9*
*AGHS*

## The Optimist

I have eyes but I cannot see.
I have ears but I cannot hear.
I touch but I do not feel.
Nothing is the way they think.
I am not the same.

They say the glass is half-empty
It's half-full.
They say he died and he's gone.
I say he's in a better place; he's happy.
I am not the same.

However, I do not want to be like them.
Gloomy, dispirited, downcast, grim
Why act that way?  Like an engine that doesn't want to run?
Cheerful, upbeat, sanguine, happy.
I am not the same

But I know they envy me.
Because my perception paints the world.
They wish they could dream like me.
They wish they could aspire, fantasize like me.
I am not the same…but I am satisfied.

*Michael Thomas Behanan, Grade 7*
*C. C. A. Baldi Middle School*

## The Falcon

The falcon proudly stands atop the tree.
Strong.  Bold.  Powerful.
He flies with ease.
He soars high above the clouds and mocks me.

For I do not soar
or fly,
I patiently sit alone, ignored, and wait
for the moment that is sure to come.

Then, suddenly!
One day
the titan lord comes and strikes him down
and he falls
hard.

He shall never mock me again.
Like a slug he moves
slowly, sadly, remorsefully.
I go to him
and help him to his feet

He thanks me
as he watches
the young eagle soar.

*Akshan Shah, Grade 7*
*C C A Baldi Middle School*

## We Can

We turn our heads
Act like we don't see
But they need us

We know what's happening
We know they're in their darkest hour
They work, and work for nothing at all

When we sit down to eat
Do we think of them? Starving?
Do we really deserve this food?

We hear their silent cries
We know their bodies die
Skin and bones
We can't help but think what we could have done

Can we help?
We can.
There's a better day on the way

Reach out a hand
Hold their hand
They need you
They need you more than ever.

*Shannon Ball, Grade 8*
*Indian Valley Middle School*

## If I Were in Charge of the World*

If I were in charge of the world,
I'd cancel disease,
Having to say please,
Drugs and also
Annoying bugs.

If I were in charge of the world,
There'd be world peace,
Geese and
No snuggies made of fleece.

If I were in charge of the world,
You wouldn't have obesity.
You wouldn't have cecity.
You couldn't have dictators.
Or "Mexican haters."
You wouldn't even have traitors.

If I were in charge of the world,
A New York Style Cheesecake would be a vegetable.
And a person who sometimes forgot work,
And sometimes forgot to smirk,
Would still be allowed to be
In charge of the world.

*Daniel Arnabar, Grade 8*
*Danville Area Middle School*
*\*Patterned after "If I Were in Charge of the World" by Judith Viorst*

## Temptation
In life there are so many twists and turns;
I'm just trying to resist all these temptations;
If I can't I may just crash and burn;
So I am pushing away all these sensations;
I can endure this life no longer;
To these feelings I cannot yield;
And every day these feelings are growing stronger;
So now I am praying for a shield;
Every day it's getting harder;
For my feelings I do not want to die;
But I am just a simple martyr;
So now I'm looking to the sky;
And asking you to help me through;
All the trials I go to.

*Zac Dykas, Grade 8*
*Penn-Kidder Campus*

## Football
Another perfect day to go play some football,
It is the best sport ever created,
Our football team will be perfect and not fall.
It is not possible for our team to be defeated.
From the snap of the ball to the last whistle,
Our team will triple their score,
Our defense is the best; we will come at you like missiles.
Before they score, they will be in pain on the floor.
Our defense and offense were perfect today,
The quarterback was throwing first downs,
We will continue our love for the game every day.
And over time, our effort results in touchdowns.
Football is about having intensity and heart,
And my love for the game will never split apart.

*Kevin Vitti, Grade 8*
*Jim Thorpe, Penn-Kidder Campus*

## Rusty Gold
Rusty gold, sitting in the weeds.
The right person is all it needs.
May just seem like a pile of scrap,
But it is an American treasure, wanting to be unwrapped.
It is waiting for someone to rescue it.
And to be taken care of a bit.
Oil cans, porcelain signs, and antique tractors are rusty gold.
If rescued and taken care of, they can be kept or sold.
Every day, people overlook rusty gold.
They scrap it or let it sit there to rot under mold.
It is all American history.
With just a little care,
You will see,
What a treasure rusty gold can be.

*Bradley Turner, Grade 8*
*Wattsburg Area Middle School*

## Speak Up!
Can you imagine
Making a person come undone
At something you think is fun?
They're hit, they're bit, they're hurt,
Because of something simple
"That's an ugly and stupid shirt."
BANG!
They're punched, then they scrunch
To the ground in pain
With a moan, and a groan
You laugh with satisfaction
At their reaction
Then you walk away
Leaving *them* to pay

But it doesn't have to be that way!

If only you knew
What you, the bystander, could do
Just use *your* voice, it's your choice, Speak up!
The tiniest action can and *WILL* cause a chain reaction
Save a life, save a mind
Together we can overcome bullying!

*Amber Clemens, Grade 7*
*Indian Valley Middle School*

## Putting the Broken Pieces Together
Bullying is a problem, it happens every day,
To kids who can't stand up for what they want to say
They drown in tears of sorrow,
Never able to let hate leave
Feeling abandoned and shattered,
Trying to put the broken pieces together
Knowing no matter what your size, skin, or religion,
You cannot be changed

They try to let it go, but they can't bare the pain
They need your help
You walk by them every day, but you don't know what to say
They are there, but you don't hear their cries of fear
They wait for the end to come, but it never stops haunting them.

Stand beside them, stick up for them,
One move and you can change the life of one victim
But there are still millions more,
Waiting, wishing, hoping,
For all of the pain to come to an end
And find the missing piece of their life
They can solve the puzzle,
All you need to do is stand up for them.

*Avani Pandya, Grade 7*
*Indian Valley Middle School*

### The Trial of the Humans

Do you not think my time is short due to you?
Do you not think, I, Mother Nature, know I am dying for the faults you committed?
Do you think I don't weep for the bears of the Poles who lose their homes as your Global Warming seeps into my veins?
Do you not think that I do not scream out in hate and despair,
When you cut down my trees and my skin is dug under for your constant search for oil?
Do you think that I just don't care about how my admirers are shoved into reservations and you label them tree huggers?
Did you even deserve the title of "The Masters of Earth?"
Do you know I shiver to think of the lives that are lost in your "holy wars?"
Do you think that I don't fear what will happen if the gas blanket gets covered in carbon dioxide?
Do you think that your four wheeled polluters that drive in my hair like ticks are there by my choice?
Do you not know that when I die, you die too?
And finally what do you think is the thing holding the rest of the animals back from feasting on your flesh?
Perhaps one day, my grip will slip and then as you humans say...
"Lions and tigers and bears, oh my."

*Joseph Gorman, Grade 8*
*Strayer Middle School*

### August

...Heat. Beating like a wild bass drum,
Rays so defiant, simple gravity takes a hold,
Lush, flowing grass, the most vibrant shade,
Even the trees must watch the scene.
Such a beautiful breeze, yet so silent;
it seems as if the trees are whispering.
Air light as a feather, smooth as silk.
When the rolling hills sway, it seems an ocean appears.
With the lightest waves of certainty, I walk these smooth graves
and pull just one touch.
One touch to a tiny blade, where it all feels it is just a dream.
But, this one doesn't seem to fade. The smooth sun hits my face, as with the light scent of sweet cream.
It isn't a dream. In fact, it is August; where even the blue jays stay intact...

*Sophia Balmer, Grade 8*
*Ephrata Middle School*

### Grandpa

Peanut
Funny, nice, loving, and generous
Son of Stella and Ralph
Who feels happy with friends, confident he never made a bad call, and patient when fishing
Who gives love, patience, and encouragement
Who fears being outbid, family birthday singing, and a bad Phillies season
Who would like to see the ultimate garage sale, Grace 2 winning the bowling season, and his family some day
Who lives in Heaven
Grandpa

*Nathan Becker, Grade 8*
*Ephrata Middle School*

### Am I Different?

Am I really that different? Is my reflection not the same as yours? Just because my hair is not the same color, my teeth are not the straightest, my skin may be darker or lighter, or my family may not have the beautiful things your family does. So what! Who says you can treat me differently than you treat the ones like yourself! How would it feel if I would go up to you and put you down? What if I walk up to you and make your soul drag on the ground. I am who I am. I may be fat, black, poor, ugly, dumb, or have a different religion, but you who make the rest of us feel different... STOP! Know that no one will ever be the same. No two people will ever be alike. So... Get over the differences!

*Chastidy Gilbert, Grade 7*
*Cambria Heights Middle School*

## Lanterns

Lanterns dangling in the wind
From the shops up and down the street

They dance around the night sky
With the warm yellow glow

All I see is the lanterns
Swinging in the wind
From outside the shop windows
As I catch the sight
Of the growing yellow flamed lantern
Dangling from the shop hook

The night sky
Bringing the darkness
As it tries to engulf
The yellow flame but can't
*Logan McHenry, Grade 8*
*Spring Grove Middle School*

## A New Season Buds

The bees buzz by,
Flowers start to bloom,
Piles of snow sigh,
A melting heap of gloom.

The sun fills our world,
Clouds take a back seat,
As the dancing rays swirled,
To a fun, springtime beat.

The lilacs, the roses,
All budding in spring,
Lilies sprout in poses,
They're wonderful things.

Lovely sounds, beautiful sights,
All thanks to springtime's endless delights.
*Rachel Malak, Grade 8*
*Lake-Lehman Jr High School*

## Rain

It's cold and wet
and usually falls,
I have to go inside
and stare at my walls.
But sometimes
I pull out my umbrella,
And jam out to songs
by Rihanna.
To farmers and crops
it is a gain,
yes everyone,
it's called rain.
*Erin LeConey, Grade 7*
*Pennbrook Middle School*

## What Does a Baseball Player Know?

Hits and runs
Not always fun
Swing a bat
Wear a protective hat
Cleats on bases
Looks out at many faces
Bunt the ball
Run, slide, and
Maybe fall
Pretzels, burgers and hot-dogs
Sometimes leaping like frogs
Soft glove made of leather
Bats and balls all a tether
Dugout is home
Players can't roam
America's pastime
*Zachary Gittins, Grade 7*
*Easton Area Middle School 7-8*

## Composing Tomorrow

If I were music,
I would dance through the air,
And twirl through time.

My melodies would fly,
Filling the souls of the hopeless,

My rhythms would match,
The heartbeats of the brave,

And I'd crescendo,
Into a patchwork of harmonies,
Until the world
Could dance with me,

If I were music.
*Kylie Brown, Grade 7*
*Schuylkill Valley Middle School*

## The American Way

War raged in 1944.
Our rights and freedoms, gone astray.
A soldier smiles, the child fears no more.
Protect the American way.

Attacked again on 9/11.
Planes exploded on that fateful day.
People joined hands with eyes to heaven.
Protect the American way.

A grateful kid, a small town school.
Great friends and family that stay
In a country where freedoms rule.
Protect the American way.
*Anthony Deppas, Grade 8*
*Beaty-Warren Middle School*

## Pirates

Yo Ho Ho! It's a pirates life for me!
Gold, Diamonds and Pearls
All waiting for me to claim as I sail
Across the vast ocean,
Mysteries waiting to be seen

The cannons go off,
Boom!
Oh, no! The ship is sinking!
Everybody screaming,
"Yo Ho Ho! A pirates life for me!"

My mother shakes me one last time,
Gently saying my name,
I wake screaming
"Yo Ho Ho… It's a pirates life for me!"
*Kaitlyn Davis, Grade 7*
*Elizabeth Forward Middle School*

## Blackberries

Hard, thick seeds jolt you
As they connect with your teeth
Reminding you
Of the mischief
Of the blackberry
Deep staining
On all that touch it
Rich purple with flecks of black
Released when in danger
Like an octopus and its ink.
Soft, but rough,
Like the coarse fur
Of a bear.
The blackberry
Will always be
The bear's fruit
*Shannon Smith, Grade 8*
*Shipley School*

## Friends

My friends are great
They keep my secrets
They're always there for me
They lead me down a good path
When there is something wrong
They know how to make me smile
When I am having a bad day
They are very funny
They see from my point of view
They are my best friends
There isn't much to say
But I love them
They comfort me
And that's why they are my friends
*Alexis Brown, Grade 8*
*Wattsburg Area Middle School*

### The Beach

I watch as the waves crash onto the sand
I see the seashells being pushed onto land
There are little kids laughing and playing
Digging for the crabs or shoveling sand
It makes me smile to see such cheer
To see the joy, the happiness so near
Off in the distance there's a couple holding hands
Oh the innocence, so pure and true
Their hands never parting, as if stuck by glue
I watch as the lifeguard, high on his throne
Inspects the scene with his keen eyes
Ready to run if danger occurs
No one needs worry with him so near
If something's to happen he'll be here
Ready to save a life, no matter what age
I watch all the people with adoring eyes
Oh how cheerful and calming it is!

*Abigail Boutiller, Grade 7*
*Bellwood Antis Middle School*

### Dear Grandma

Dear grandma, may I ask you a question?
Why are you always so sad?
Why is every time you see me, you start to cry?
I asked before, but you shunned me away.
Is the reason you won't tell me is because I am so young?
You may say it's nothing, but we all know it's something.
Are you scared of me knowing?
Do I remind you of someone?
Or is the reason you cry something I did?
Dear grandma, may I ask you a question?
Please just tell me the truth?
I can handle it, I swear!
Dear grandma, why are you so sad?
Not telling me makes the world stand still.
Just always remember, who I am.
And who you are.
I love you!!

*Megan Todd, Grade 8*
*Wattsburg Area Middle School*

### Summer Plea

The snow falls heavy
As I watch cold and still
Weighing down the branches of every tree
They say silence is golden
But I wonder if it is weighing down on me
I close my eyes and drift away
Feeling the warmth of the sun on my cheeks
Imagining the palm trees as I slightly sway
I open my eyes only to feel weak
The blizzard seems to have no end
A bottle with a plea for summer into the icy ocean I will now send

*Madeline Payne, Grade 7*
*Pennbrook Middle School*

### The Seasons

Silver ice
chilling winds blow
hard grey skies
unyielding

Green leaves
warm breezes flow
clear blue skies
rejuvenating

Browning grass
hot gusts rush
hazy air shimmers
oppressive

Orange leaves
cool trickles play
soft air caresses
comforting

*Sarah Knox, Grade 7*
*Lancaster Mennonite School - Locust Grove*

### Fighting

The bombs have fallen,
Saving the powers,
The ones who fought then
Are raising their towers, again.

The sirens sound,
Planes high and proud,
Peace has left our faithful ground,
Held hostage by lights bright and loud, again.

Before the soldiers,
Stand their lifelong purpose,
All know the cause on up high fliers,
They die fighting this screwed up chorus, again.

Flying death up above,
Pulling us out of our houses,
They lie to us, "It's all for love."
War, in the end, is all it rouses, again.

*Mike Kampas, Grade 8*
*Pine-Richland Middle School*

### Swimming Fantasy

When I swim I feel like a dolphin,
Gliding through the water without a care
I don't care if I win
Only that I have fun
Once I'm in the water
I feel like there's nothing I can't do
There's a chance I could be Poseidon's daughter.

*Devni Jobanputra, Grade 7*
*Pennbrook Middle School*

## Maturity

Even though we are teenagers
Curious children lurk within
They are deathly monsters
Animals filled with rage far from thin
The kids spill out undesirable mistakes
Howl words of colossal hate
Happiness and excitement mine takes
Highlighting every imperfection irate
And for them to finally leave us,
We wait
We wait
We wait
Still the entanglement to them constricts our brains
Deception devours our souls
Our minds scream with endless pain
Theirs just clutches still, dark as coal
Soon I notice they will never retire
Maturity will aid their desire

*Crystal Wong, Grade 8*
*First Philadelphia Charter School for Literacy*

## My German Shepherd

Waiting for him to come by my side
My German Shepherd has nothing to hide
He drops the ball at my feet
Playing fetch, to him, is like a treat
I grab the ball and clean it off, all nice and neat
Playing with him is like my getaway
My retreat
I throw the ball
For it to fall
Into a lake
The ball is all he wants to take
He likes to swim
But the light is getting dim
We have to go home
For we can no longer roam
My German Shepherd looks up to me
Now I can see
He is extremely happy

*Summer Howard, Grade 8*
*Wattsburg Area Middle School*

## My 13th Birthday

My birthday was great, never ever better.
Had fun in the sun because of the beautiful weather.
It was my friends Gavin, Jacob and me which made three.
We all climbed up the tallest trees.
For me it was a wonderful time,
Because my two best friends devoted all of their time.
My friend Jason came, and that made us four,
So we played and played till we could play no more.
So that is what happened on my 13th birthday,
Unfortunately I have to wait 365 more days.

*Matt Milanesi, Grade 7*
*Cambria Heights Middle School*

## The Question

I have been asking myself a question lately
Why have I been sad
I have been sad because I lost a friend
I have lost a best friend.

I have been spending time with the girl of my dreams
You have been standing on the side looking at me
I have ignored you, stepped on you, and spit on you
I have to say I'm sorry for what I have done.

Now the final question is here
Do you forgive me or do you not forgive me
I want to be your best friend again no matter what you say.

*Brayden Black, Grade 7*
*Greencastle-Antrim Middle School*

## The Heart of Soccer

Soccer is like ballet;
it is graceful but can be filled with tragedy.
If you know all the right moves you can glide,
the ball never stopping.
But, even if you are graceful,
you can fall and break a bone.
Soccer is a heart attack;
you never know when you will get hurt, it just happens.
Soccer is filled with mixed feelings.
You can be having fun the one minute,
but the next frustrated because the other team scored.
Soccer takes a real heart,
and I enjoy every minute of it.

*Abigail Lapp, Grade 8*
*Ephrata Middle School*

## Things That Remind Me of Home

Eating a homemade pie,
Sleeping in a comfy bed,
Drinking warm milk,
Seeing my family,
Watching people play outside,
Seeing a pine tree,
Having a dog,
Watching a favorite show,
The smell of happiness,
The scent of a candle,
Those are some things that remind me of home.

*PJ Fraker, Grade 7*
*Big Spring Middle School*

## Kitten

Kitten
Playful, joyous
Jabbing, throwing, scratching
Always getting in trouble
Feline

*Nathan Pauls, Grade 7*
*Lancaster Mennonite School - Locust Grove*

## When the Pencil Goes Down

Bottle it down deep
Hold it in, no emotions
Brain twisting stomach aching
Cannot speak of all these feelings

Nauseatingly moving through the day
but when I get home
The cracks begin to show

When the pencil goes down
The storm of thoughts begins
The raindrops of emotion plump and full
Appear as tears tracing my cheeks as they fall

Electric words travel
through dark crevices of my mind
Finding their way to my fingers
Landing poetically in shocks on the paper

These sentences of words
words of letters
fix the me I thought was her

Writing is the rain
To end the drought
To quench to thirst inside to fix my doubt
*Taylor Rhoades, Grade 8*
*Derry Area Middle School*

## The Future Needs Hope

Hope,
This is the word of love.
The word of peace, the word of joy.
Is this the word we need to come true?
Is this the word we must make?
Is this the word for people in need?
It's now or never

Believe, believe that this is the time.
Not tomorrow, but today
Believe the children will get the medicine they need
Believe that the parents will no longer need to suffer
Believe in the future, and make it shine TODAY!
Believe that the stars will twinkle in the starry night,
Believe that the eagle will soar to the greatest heights.

Let the world hear you out "WE NEED HELP!"
Preach to the heavens that this is not what is meant to be.
Let the waves calm the scenes that haunt us today,
Empty the world of waste, together we unite!

There are two paths to take
War or hope, you decide
Choose wisely
*Brandon Nelson, Grade 7*
*Indian Valley Middle School*

## Weedwockey*

'Twas Sunday, and the slimy worms
Did chew and digest in the soil;
All tired were the kids,
And the early onions grew.

"Beware the weeds, my son!
The roots that break, the seeds that spread!
Beware the deer and shun
The smart groundhog!"

He took his deadly weeder in hand;
Long time annoying weed he sought
So rested he by the tomato plant, and stood awhile in thought.

And, as in deep thought he stood,
The weed with roots of steel,
Came slowly through the fertile soil,
And screamed as it came!

One, two! One, tow! And through and through
The deadly weeder went snicker-snack!
He left it dead, and with its head he went hopping back.

"And has thou slain the weed? Come to my arms, my gardener boy!
O fabulous day! Hurray, Hullay!" He smiled in his joy.
*Katsuaki Yoshimizu, Grade 8*
*Danville Area Middle School*
*Inspired by Louis Carroll's "The Jabberwockey"*

## Two Brothers, Two Sides

Once upon a time in history,
Were two brothers, and this is their story;.
Now, one of the brothers was kind to slaves
Even helped one or two sharpen the plow blades.

He soon grew up tall and brawny,
While the other was short and scrawny.
The short brother was lazy and fat.
He had his slaves going crazy doing this and that.

Those Southerners decided, "Hey, let's separate!"
Those no longer United were called the Confederates!
They said, "We'll keep our slaves if you don't mind,"
But Lincoln stopped them just in time!

Now good ole Abe got up and decreed,
"Those slaves are free. Let them go if you please!"
The North, the Union; the Confederates, the South,
Kept getting together and fighting it out.

The taller brother fought for the north, the other for the south,
The tall one lived, the other died when shot in the mouth.
The North prevailed, and for the slaves, justice had been served,
And in the South, the call for freedom had finally been answered!
*Reilly Lauffer, Grade 7*
*Redeemer Lutheran School*

**A Dream I Dream That I Dream**

In this dream I dream that I dream, all is not exactly as it seems. Though the time comes and goes, there are just some things we'll never know. Though I move to where I am to be, sometimes I do not feel like me. It must then appear, as it seems, a dream I dream that I dream. It must be.

Though my presence means to be sane, all I sense is that I am lame. I do not disturb the craziest of man, but myself is who I am. Nor shall I be this or that, but only an image of me in this dream I dream that I dream which yearns to be.

And entwined in these weak, ever so fragile, dreams I dream, lies the one thing that actually matters. But if I dare to even spatter a whisper, my desire shall shatter. So trapped in a box it appears, but that does not exclude my fear. But it is within a box, so what's the purpose? Me, thyself, myself, the only me, does not know. But that is fine because time comes and goes in this dream I dream that I dream.

Though a voice men have! But thyself, what do I contain? Perhaps the remains of unknown evolution, or maybe a song of a chime. This, indeed, has changed within time, so what does that leave me with? A pencil to scribble down a cheap rhyme? All exist, manifests fully, to be unknown. However, evolution changed. Our resolution will too. But that is fine, because time comes and goes in this dream I dream that I dream.

*Anthony Vecchio, Grade 9*
*Hempfield Area High School*

**City**

Walking down the city street,
The buildings so high that I felt sick below them,
Imagine them crumbling down at my feet,
Just thinking about it would turn my legs numb,
I turned my thoughts away toward the juicy food that the vendors sold,
Picking me off the ground when the hot dogs floated off the shelves,
The outside air made air turn cold,
But the magnificent skyline with the shining bright colors made me feel like I was three foot twelve!

The streets were thick with people visiting from here and there,
Crowding around to see the spectacular sights to be seen,
The subways heavily crowded as I paid my fare,
The intricate system and speed made me lean,
Heading home wasn't easy in the place that will never sleep,
Manhattan, the place that always makes a peep!

*Tommy Rowe, Grade 7*
*William Penn Middle School*

**A Baseball Game**

I know a baseball game...
People screaming, popcorn popping, the ball hitting the bat, the ball hitting the catcher's glove
I know a baseball game...
People sliding into base, teams shaking hands,
players jumping on the wall to make amazing catches, coaches' tempers throbbing and throwing their hats
I know a baseball game...
The smell of popcorn is heaven, fresh peanuts, newly cut grass, adrenaline of the players, hot dogs roasting
I know a baseball game...
"Strike three"
"Peanuts, peanuts, get your fresh peanuts"
"He's stealing, he's stealing"
"Good game, good game, good game"
"That ball is out of here"
"I got it, I got it"
I do know a baseball game!

*Nick Auker, Grade 8*
*Ephrata Middle School*

### Grief on the Island

A path with no purpose is what I will travel,
brave face on as I fall into the gravel.
Pain in my tears pours from my face;
lost time comes to haunt me as I stand in this place.
I hear my voice echo across the sea,
rebounding from between you and me.
All this time I waited and grew,
expecting the truth to bleed from you.
I waited too long,
from across the sea.
Shrouding my feelings with hope and misery.
And know I'm certain you've sailed on,
still standing here but already gone.
Joy,
where is it,
come pay me a visit!
I'll be waiting here on my island of hope.
You've moved on,
and I'm drowning to cope.
A path with no purpose on what I will travel,
brave face on as I fall in the gravel...

*Maria Sofish, Grade 7*
*Greencastle-Antrim Middle School*

### The Stillness in the Water

Far below the water deep
A creature so evil does creep
Its monstrous size and hulking girth
Sends chills up the spine of the Earth
Near the bottom of the sea it lies
With a heart as black as a doll's eyes
It's prey of which walks
Has no clue of when it stalks
If only the victims had the might
Try to escape the creature's bite
With sudden rise and rushing swell
Will send any man straight to Hell
A tale of horrors that cannot begin
Until you see the evil fin
Right in the water underneath
You can just see the rows of teeth
People start to scream and shout
Once they see the terrible snout
Even if you are on the safety of an ark
You can't get away from the terrible dark
Because you can never escape the killer shark

*Paul Stainbrook, Grade 8*
*Trinity Middle School*

### The Winter Season

Stunning
Snow glistens like diamonds
When the sun shines down on it
Snowflakes fall gently
And sparkle like stars
They hit the ground with no sound
Houses are under a blanket of snow
With wisps of smoke coming out of the chimney
Curling like snakes around the sky
The sound of the snow crunching
Beneath my feet
A gentle breeze blowing
Soft and sweet
Sticking out my tongue
To catch a snowflake
Or two

*Megan Watchey, Grade 7*
*Bellwood Antis Middle School*

### Volleyball

It was a life or death situation whether or not we won our game
We got to our state competition
We all stretched, practiced and warmed up
Then we got in our positions on the court
SMACK!
The ball bulleted over the net
It came straight towards me
I hit it hard back over the net
This went on for about 3 minutes
The one girl on my team spiked it over the net
And we scored the last point we needed to win the match
So far we had won the 1st and 2nd match
One more match to go and we would be champions
We started off losing the match but made a comeback
And won the game
We were so thrilled and we got a huge trophy

*Adoria Kline, Grade 7*
*Bellwood Antis Middle School*

### What a Hurt Person Knows

how to cry,
How to hurt,
How to ask for help
How to want to be alone,
How to not want to talk to someone,
How to take their anger out on other people,
but instead to find a friend
That's what a hurt person knows :(

*Kianna Riley, Grade 7*
*Easton Area Middle School 7-8*

### Fall

The leaves change from green to orange to red to yellow to brown.
I can smell the crisp air and feel the crispy leaves beneath my feet.
The weather gets cooler as we move closer and closer to winter.
I see my breath when I breathe.
Pinecones fall from the trees.
Soccer balls kicked into goals.
Going trick or treating on Halloween.
Fall.

*Max Memeger, Grade 7*
*Strath Haven Middle School*

## The Rainstorm

The raindrops come down big and fat, and plenteous, too, I'm sure of that.
They come down quickly, quicker than I can run through them, unattacked by sky.

Umbrellas; oh, they'll keep you dry, unless the wind whispers, "Bye-bye!"
It blows the metal sticks straight up, up, up; turning it into a giant rain cup.

You'd have to be fast as the wind and skinny as a stick, to make it through this! Oh, quick, quick, quick!
Running between the raindrops; running between the raindrops.

So stay inside, I warn you now, let it do its job, to feed the cow.
Let it wash the cars, and water the plants, let it pour and shower, and call the ants.

If you're in a car, down it will come pattering down, and not just some.
Thud, thud, thud, thud, down they go; swish, swish, swish, swish, the wipers echo.

You'd have to be fast as the wind and skinny as a stick, to make it through this! Oh, quick, quick, quick!
Running between the raindrops; running between the raindrops.

The trees are soaked, the ground is damp, the sun is shining better than a lamp.
Now here's one thing you'll hate, I bet; all your clothes on the line are soaking wet!

Just wait a day to let them dry, and hope there's not a cloud in the sky.
There's just one last thing I must confess; dirt plus water, equals a mess!

You'd have to be fast as the wind and skinny as a stick, to make it through this! Oh, quick, quick, quick!
Running between the raindrops; running between the raindrops.

*Nicole Sekol, Grade 8*
*Commonwealth Connections Academy*

## A Shining Figure

In this darkness I see nothing, I look left, I look right.
I look up and down, I see nothing, everything is black, even the ground.
There is no light here, none that I can see at least.

Will I survive? Should I try and get out?
I don't know. I'm not sure if there is danger out there or not. Wait!

I feel something moving. It's engulfing me. It's the darkness.
There go my legs, my midsection, and lastly my arms. I can't move now.
I should have moved when I had the chance. I try to call for help. Sadly it doesn't work. I start to cry.
The darkness begins eating the rest of me. I'm about to die.
I feel my life force growing dimmer and dimmer. I get scared.

Stop! The darkness is vanishing.
It's disintegrating. I can feel my whole body again.
The darkness drops me hard on the ground. I get up and look around for what has saved me.
I see a bright glowing light. I run to the bright figure. I see that it is human.
I hug it and thank it repeatedly. For it has saved my life yet again. I ask for it's name…it does not answer.
Instead it says, "I am here when you need me. I will always be here to help you.
Especially when things look bleak, and you turn to the darkness for relief."
I say, "You have shined light into this dark abyss. I thank and commend you for that."
It says, "No problem," and vanishes into my subconscious.
I feel better now for I know that it is always there for me.

*Amy Flyte, Grade 8*
*Nazareth Area Middle School*

**A Little Girl's Broken Heart**
She was a daddy's girl
Always by your side
You did everything together
You carried her to bed and kissed her goodnight
Those little things
Meant the world to her
But then you changed
Not for the better
She didn't know you anymore
You came home
Angry and unhappy
She tried to make you happy
But you pushed her away
She doesn't know you, and she doesn't care too
I hope you're happy you ruined her childhood
And I hope you're happy you pushed away
Those who
Loved
You
Most.

*MaKayla Winders, Grade 8*
*Danville Area Middle School*

**Who Am I?**
As I lay looking at the sky,
I wonder,
I question myself.
Who am I?
Am I like the stars that twinkle in a blink?
Or am I the sun that is fearless and in charge?
So I question myself again,
Who am I?
Am I that famous person on the front of a magazine?
Or just another person on Earth?
But no…
From day to weeks, to month and years,
I know who I am, I am simply light.
I am what everyone needs, I am something special.
Nothing can destroy me or create me.
I am beautiful, bright and unique.
Now that I know who I am,
I will never question myself again.
Because it's hard to forget that I am important to my
World!

*Lindy Arzola-Velez, Grade 8*
*Blue Ridge Middle School*

**School**
Sharpened pencils for writing essays in English
Challenged by the RC goal every marking period
Have to study for tests in geography
Outstanding efforts will be rewarded in the future
Over your head the ball goes in gym class
Leaving school makes all kids happy

*Shane Sever, Grade 7*
*Cambria Heights Middle School*

**Motor City State of Mind**
The Detroit Lions sprouted a team
That brought Detroit a sort of gleam.
The team thrived, so did the city.
Then a century later, both filled with pity.

The auto industry had surely fallen,
Like the Lions, the players were all bawlin'.
Nobody was good, nobody was great,
And the city of Detroit was full of hate.

But now you see, after losing time after time,
They made the playoffs for the first time since 1999.
The team is ready on the Super Bowl route,
But now don't count the Big 3 out.

Chrysler, Ford, GM, all part of the auto industry,
Will be their best, since 2003.
The cars are running, big, small, and tall.
Then every Sunday, workers go to Ford Field,
All painted, pumped, and proud to watch some football.

*Jack Jeter, Grade 8*
*Pine-Richland Middle School*

**She Rode into His Life on Her Bike**
I was told of that very special April night,
When my mom rode into my dad's life on her bike.
He felt a connection and knew something was right,
When he saw her beautiful face and something he liked.
She would become the inspiration of his life,
By becoming his true love and grasping his heart.
No doubt that one day she would become his wife.
Forever from then nothing could take them apart.
They stand on the Lord's alter of love,
By becoming as one united under "his" grace.
They honor those blessings from high above,
Joined as man and wife here in the human race.
Hand in hand with their daughter they follow God's way.
Together we shall live walking in that glorious light.
This earthly love will grow night and day,
Be coming so pure with joy and so blessingly bright.
It all started on that night they met,
She rode into his life on her ten-speed bike.
It is love so strong, so real…you can bet!
So get ready world — here comes Amanda and Mike!!!

*Autumn Wayman, Grade 8*
*Blue Ridge Middle School*

**Someday I'll Get to See Him**
Someday I'll hear him say you got tall
Someday we'll watch TV and he'll make jokes
Someday he'll help me up when I fall
Someday we'll laugh about the funny circus folks
Someday he will let me style his hair
Someday I will be so glad to see my grandpa again

*Brittnee Steen, Grade 7*
*Pequea Valley Intermediate School*

## 100% Me!

While I write this I am not going to cry, you know why,
Because I am not going to waste my tears, on you,
I am not going to waste my tears on something,
That's not worth crying for, you see,
People don't understand the fact that
I hate when they say…I look like you,
I'm not like you, I am not you,
Was never you, and never will be you,
Yeah, I might have your anger,
But we handle it 2 totally different ways,
You're this boy who pretends to be a man,
You will never be a man, as much as I dislike you,
I thank you for showing me that I have to be independent,
That I have to trust no one,
That I have to look up to myself,
I will be successful in life, unlike you,
I am not you, never was you, never will be you,
Just a fraction, a portion, a piece,
I am only 10% of you, 40% my mom,
And 50% me, which equals my own person,
100% me!

*Elika Lantigua, Grade 8*
*First Philadelphia Charter School for Literacy*

## Performance in Arts

Wake up and find my prize
Knowing and wanting my prize
Hoping and dreaming and thinking
I want to be someone famous someday
I learn I pray and I try
Standing and acting in front of strange men
Waiting and thinking and wondering
Hoping they pick me oh please pick me
Callbacks and excitement through my body
Friends and family excited for me
I'm in and ready and determined to be the best
Clothing and suits are for me
Practicing and rehearsing are troubled things
Learning and learning and getting back up
I hope I can stay and become the best
Bright lights and wood floor
Colored lights and an audience roar
Clapping and bowing and whistling
Cheers from an audience who are pleased
I've done it
I've been the best I could be!

*Sarthak Patel, Grade 8*
*Blue Ridge Middle School*

## When!

If you are not here, it is white and black
But when you walk into the room, all the colors are clear
Thank you for lighting my path as I grew up
I love you!!

*Kaylee Sexton, Grade 8*
*Wattsburg Area Middle School*

## Success: The Best Goal to Achieve

Success is something big,
A dream, waiting to be done.
You must work hard to uncover it,
To have the task won.

Success is something large.
Doing, completing, achieving,
Not giving up, quitting, or leaving.

Success is something huge.
Pushing out 'til the end,
Running the final stretch,
Completing that final bend.

Success is something gigantic.
Winning the match, getting good grades,
Then, the success has been made.

Success is something humongous.
Living happy and healthy,
Living free and spiritually wealthy.

Success is something wonderful!
Going to bed accomplished,
Waking up recharged, ready for the next day,
Having your life go just the right way.

*Madelyn Dolinsky, Grade 9*
*Tamaqua Area Sr High School*

## My Wishes

I wish I could fly
Like a butterfly or bird.
I wish I was famous
So I would be known and be heard.

I wish I could be free
To dance in the rain.
I wish I could actually be myself
And not worry about life's suffering and pain.

I wish I could go to space
And walk on the moon.
I wish I could travel the world
By journeying on cruise ships, gondolas, and hot air balloons.

I wish I could help
Everyone I know.
I wish that there was peace
That no one had an enemy or foe.

Although my dreams and wishes
Might not all come true,
If I think positively and do my best,
My life will never be dull or blue.

*Annu Suresh, Grade 9*
*Bishop McCort High School*

### Finding Your Gift

Barry the frog,
Had a happy life.
He lived on a log,
With his son and his wife.

He went out to find food,
As Mr. Dove cooed,
And David the deer trotted by.

Barry said, "My oh my,
All animals have a gift,"
He thought with a sigh.

"Oh you'll see someday,"
Said Mrs. Frog to her love,
"You have gifts just like a deer and a dove."

As Barry the Frog went out to catch flies,
A sly sneaky fox slowly stalked by.
The fox lunged at Barry, making him his prey,
But Barry's strong legs just got him out of the way.

Barry hopped home,
And said to his wife,
"I have found my gift,
My legs saved my life."

*David Fohner, Grade 7*
*St Dorothy Elementary School*

### Making a Difference

Waves of oceans, filthy and gray
Where is the crystal blue?
There is much concern today.
It is not something new.

Careless people dumping oil;
Discarding choking toxic waste and rotten trash.
Plastic rings strangling ducks necks make my blood boil;
The color of the water has become dark ash.

Dead zones in the ocean that used to be alive;
Fish and oxygen are disappearing, there's no fish to eat.
Endless debris when we dive,
Can this pollution be beat?

Extinction of marine-life makes me sad;
Many plants that are not growing back.
Carelessness of people makes me mad,
It it time to react!

Recycle your plastic bottles and aluminum,
Don't let anybody dump anything in the sea.
Save the oceans by following these rules at a minimum.
The future of our planet is up to you and me!

*Nicholas Blessing, Grade 7*
*Indian Valley Middle School*

### Unfamiliar Waters

The recognizable fish.
The clear water.
The brown pebbles.
The glass bowl.
Everything, everyone, is so familiar.
I will never get lost.
I am free to be who I am, because everyone knows who I am.
How could I ever leave this place I call home?

But I have to leave.

Leave everything and everyone that is so familiar.
Go to the ocean that's so BIG.
I don't know those things.
Those different fish.
That salty water.
That dark seaweed.
That vast ocean.

But I have to go.

I will begin to learn, and find my way.
I will meet new fish, and they'll discover who I am.
So, I will leave the familiar,

Because the unfamiliar is my new home.

*Madeline Mast, Grade 8*
*Lancaster Mennonite School - Locust Grove*

### Red Lion House

Upon the hill, a small house abides
Where weary eyes and feet reside
It's grass of green and walls of gray
Hold sure to all its promise to stay

Outstretched with hand, the door stood wide
With hope of forgiveness tucked inside
And yet with all its glory be
A secret still that held the key

For years before, a life once thrived
Then taken young and future deprived
For stripped from he was hope anew
Of flowers bright and skies of blue

Until the day dark that cast before
The red of blood, which stained the door
A casket opened with marigolds bloomed
Entwined as one in the earthly tomb

So albeit either kiss of death
Or life reborn of godly breath
A heart once torn heals not the same
And pristine scars will still remain

*Charity Huggins, Grade 9*
*21st Century Cyber Charter School*

## Second Chance

Thinking about it excites me
Moving on leaving a place that I've been so long
Seeing new faces
Going to different places
Exploring what's out there to see
Choosing the best for me
But some people aren't as excited
Some people don't have that choice
Some people think it's torture
Pointless and a waste of time.
I assure you those are the people who hate their lives
The people who talk about doing big things but don't
The people who talk about 'when I hit the lottery' but shortly stop
And get ready for work Monday
Because they know it won't happen
The person that wants a second chance
The person who tells you to always try your best in school
But their words go right through your ears
Because they say it all the time…
But there's a reason for that and you should listen
Because you may be your own second chance.

*Nathan Vazquez, Grade 8*
*First Philadelphia Charter School for Literacy*

## Animal Cruelty

Animals needlessly tortured
Animals whimpering and suffering
Animals close to death
But we can change that for good.
We can save the animals
We can make stricter laws
We can volunteer to help them
We can nurse an animal that is suffering
We can treat the animals with love and respect
We see animals healthy rather than bony and weak
We see animals walking rather than limping
We see animals wagging their tails instead of cowering in a corner
We see animals smile rather than frown
We see animals back to their life
Happy and free

*Aaron Steinhauer, Grade 7*
*Indian Valley Middle School*

## So-called Friends

So tired of all these lies
So-called friends come just to say goodbye
These lies are tearing me apart
From the inside out
You say you are my friend
But I know you are building me up just to knock me back down
And family
What kind of family does the same as these so-called friends
Some I admit are actually there for me when I need them
But others are so-called friends

*Ronnie Harkless, Grade 8*
*Wattsburg Area Middle School*

## Waiting Just Waiting

I am standing alone in the dark,
Waiting, not sure what for,
Because nothing is happening,
No one is coming nothing is there but air to surround you,
So you wait just wait…
I thought you said you loved me forever and you'd never leave me,
You broke a promise to me and you took my heart,
But you played with it instead of cared for it…
I don't know why I am surprised,
It happens every time,
I give you another chance but I don't know why,
Because you always hurt me and leave me standing alone,
Waiting just waiting for you to say sorry but that never happens,
To answer my calls my cries for help,
You leave me waiting…
But I have found my strength again,
I am strong and you cannot hurt me anymore,
Because I believe in myself now,
And I don't need you to lean on,
I no longer have to wait for you because I have moved on,
Now you can wait for me…

*Lianne Covington, Grade 8*
*Fred S Engle Middle School*

## Home Run

I hit a home run.
I hit a home run.
The sound of the bat filled the air,
as the wind went through my hair.
I saw the ball flying by,
as it almost touched the sky.
I ran around the bases with cheer,
as all the laughter filled my ear.
When I landed on home base
I was faced with my team's embrace.
I ran into the dugout and the coaches greeted me
as if I was a celebrity.
We won the game that day
with little dismay,
if only we could do it every day.

*John Paul Grabowski, Grade 8*
*Bellwood Antis Middle School*

## Three Things

Three things that never happen,
The family I never had time with
Like the puppy I never hugged
Like the father who never stuck around
Pain is like a bullet going through me
Like bulls running after me
Like bullies running trying to hurt me
But I run fearing for my life
My heart is racing like a rapper rapping a sag
Like a boom box beating to the words…of this poem.

*Fabian Torres, Grade 8*
*First Philadelphia Charter School for Literacy*

### Times Square

I walk through the crowd of people, all hustling and bustling down the busy crosswalk. Giant objects and advertisements surround me, giving the vibrant square a more real and an unreal look at the same time. If you decide to take it in all at once, you'll be overwhelmed, so just do everything one at a time. There is so much to do, so much to see…

The moon and the stars are high in the sky, but are merely the second attraction when covered by exuberant glowing fireworks, each different colors, each one more exciting and lit up than the previous one. Choppers and floats of dogs and nutcracker soldiers add to the brilliant lighting of everything, as all shines down from above, as if it was a scene set by God himself…

Screaming, yelling, a request for money, a firework exploding, so many conversations and talking with the entire city yelling with excitement. Another firework explodes, and even more people are captivated by sound and enjoyment that you couldn't find at the cinemas. So many noises and people from so many different places…

When will the show start? How long must we wait? Thousands of impossible questions with thousands of impossible answers hurtle through my brain, frying it and enhancing it at the same time. When will the show start? What will happen next? Will the suspense kill us all?

The shows starts, my highest expectations matched. I'm amazed, full of wonder, wonder of what will happen next in the greatest city on Earth. It wows, it amazes, it does everything possible and more. The excitement never stops, oh, this is so amazing…

This is so amazing…
This is so amazing…
This is so amazing.

*Kiran Pandey, Grade 7*
*Saucon Valley Middle School*

### Little Sailor

So our little sailor pulled up his sail, white as a sheet, thus beginning his tale.
He readied his ship, called on his crew, telling them to get ready, for the voyage on the ocean blue.
So they set off, out to the sea. To catch a terrible monster, so a hero he will be.
On the ocean they traveled, for days upon weeks, focused on their prize, far from land's mountain peaks.
But the monster remained elusive, and Sailor's anger began to pent, on catching the creature, our little Sailor became intent.
He ordered his crew, "Throw over our water, blankets, and food." His crew began to protest, so he threw them over too.
"Speed is the key!" He thought to himself. "With speed I'll catch this monster, and I will display his head on my shelf!"
Finally our little Sailor caught him! This gave him great glee, he approached the great creature, just as the sun set over the deep blue sea.
Upon closer inspection, the monster was dead, dead as a door and Sailor hit his little head.
"What have I done?" He cried in great pain. "I have done nothing at all! Why in the world was I ever so vain?"
With no food and no water, no help from his crew, our little Sailor was all alone, on the great big blue.
Our little Sailor, is not a little Sailor, anymore.

*Lindsey Jacks, Grade 8*
*Pine-Richland Middle School*

### The Big Sister I Should Have Been

The big sister I should have been has the height of a mother
She wears long jeans and T-shirts.
The big sister I should have been protects and teaches her underling.
She shows her little sis how the world works.
The big sister I should have been always remarks, "Come on, Tyler, there is nothing to be scared of."
The big sister I should have been always babysits her sis.
She could not even begin to imagine the world of trouble she would get in if her sister got hurt.
The big sister I should have been was always annoyed that she had to take care of her little sister instead of hanging out with friends.
But now, she realized that those little memories of protection that always made her feel warm can never come back, because her big little sister no longer needs help.

*Olivia Serafini, Grade 7*
*Strath Haven Middle School*

## Spring in Bloom

Everywhere you look
New life is growing
Pastel flowers poke their heads out of crumbling black dirt

Trees begin to blossom
Leaves sprout from branches
Splashing barked limbs with streaks of color

Animals come out from hiding
From the cold and storms that chased them away
So many months before

The world seems to begin again
You can see it all around you

Baby animals come out to play
They stumble as they gain their footing for the first time

The animals may fall but they get back up again

Spring showers feed the growth
They bring heavily perfumed air
And a freshness to the atmosphere

What was once lost is found after snow melts away
To reveal pastures that seem greener than the new sprouted growth

The plants come bearing good tidings
And a chance to begin again

*Julia Zenkevich, Grade 8*
*Sacred Heart Elementary School*

## The Broken Hand

On the way to the hospital,
It is raining and cold.
He holds onto his hand
To keep it from hurting even more.

The drive is endless.
The pain is ridiculous.
Ice balls hit the windshield with force.

The hospital is in sight.
His hand is throbbing
As he fights the blinding snow storm
On the way into the emergency room.

Finally, the doctor arrives.
He looks out the window at the slowing storm,
While the doctor gives him a shot for the pain.

The cast is now on his hand.
He leaves the hospital to go home
In the sunshine after the storm.

*Elizabeth McMurry, Grade 8*
*Pine-Richland Middle School*

## curse of war

why must there be so much war
people dying
people crying
mothers waiting alone
for their little boys to come home
but in the war they're men
the enemy sprays lead
this danger is not pretend
they are on the front lines
fighting people that commit terror crimes
as the enemy bathes in a blood bath of our soldiers
we fall forth to the doom of our world
war has been going on forever
our country was built on war
through the revolutionary war
to a genocide of natives
even fighting ourselves
we can never stop fighting
for that is the curse of war

*Marcos Corchado, Grade 8*
*First Philadelphia Charter School for Literacy*

## What Is Life?

What is life?
Is it the chirp of a cricket on a warm, summer night?
Or the sight of a bird about to take flight?
Is it the steady beat of drums?
Or the continual tap of texting thumbs?
Is it the strength of the ocean pure and clean?
Or looking through a scope, magnified an keen?
Is it the flow of a river cutting through rocks?
Or the constant washing of dirty socks?
Is it the whoosh of wind against a window pane?
Or the tapping of an old person's lonely cane?
Is it the turning color of an unsuspecting leaf?
Or the constant broad strokes of Georgia O'Keefe?
Some say we are merely motion picture
For a crowd upstairs in gigantic bleachers
Or perhaps each one of us see different colors
When you point at brown, I point to another
The point is we truly know nothing about this world
And someday what we think we know, might be swirled

*Luke Deasy, Grade 8*
*Sacred Heart Elementary School*

## Summer Strawberry

It's a warm summer evening as I sit on my porch,
Looking up at the pink-orange sky
I've got a bowl of sweet red strawberries,
And whipped cream piled up high
There's a little breeze as I take my first bite,
And the world stops from this simple pleasure
I save this memory of the summer strawberry,
Because it is a treasure

*Alizeh Khan, Grade 7*
*Pennbrook Middle School*

### Soon It Will Be Spring!

Soon it will be Spring
And the church bells will still ring
Soon we will be changing seasons
But there are many reasons
The animals in hibernation must come out
They sure are rested without a doubt
And the groundhog will show its shadow in the snow
But my answer to snow is NO
The flowers will grow, oh many kinds
But they will grow at different times
The Easter bunny will come around
And lay Easter eggs on the ground
And the snow will melt all day
For it's time to put the shovels away
There are many reasons why the seasons change
The seasons will change all around the range
Soon it will be Spring and it comes with a bound
As Spring enters the world all over your town!

*Jonathan Kirk, Grade 7*
*Cambria Heights Middle School*

### The Beach

Warm, soft sand of the beach between my toes
Shimmering blue waves crash along the shore
Songs being played by old shiny stereos
The sea and the sand cannot be a bore

The bright hot sun like a ball of gold fire
Colorful umbrellas and towels set up
The blue sea shimmers like a bright sapphire
Fruit smoothies dance at the tip of the cup

Sweet taste of ice cream dripping down the cone
Seeing people surfing in the ocean
A guy played fetch with his dog and a bone
Everyone danced to the Loco Motion

I think the beach is a fun place to be
Staring at the sunset over the black sea

*Madison Moretti, Grade 8*
*Pocono Mountain East Jr High School*

### If Rage Was A...

If rage was a color,
It would be as black as a new moon night,
As dark as a never-ending nightmare.
If rage was a taste,
It would be just like a burnt marshmallow.
If rage was a feeling,
It would be as painful as a bullet wound.
If rage was a smell,
It would be as rank as a dumpster in the sun.
If rage was a sound, it would be as loud as
A gunshot.

*Terry Disanto, Grade 7*
*Pequea Valley Intermediate School*

### Her Reflection

Her reflection says
That she doesn't even know her, anymore
Standing in the only light of the dark
She's been wishing that one day
She'd wake up and realize
She lost sight years ago, of who she even was
Perfect family, perfect life
She couldn't ask for much else
Says everyone else
Fights and arguments litter the clean air
So many times he came back, just to leave again
Did he even give a second thought
When he walked back the road alone
Or did her reflection scare him off
She sits prisoned
Cursed with no escape
Those scars aren't hers either
Slowly but surely
She desperately tries to find her way back
But her past is holding her back
But how, that reflection isn't even her.

*Ashley Hade, Grade 8*
*Greencastle-Antrim Middle School*

### Sunny Days

Water rushing in and out,
Watching the birds fly about.
Wind and sand flying through my hair,
Jumping in the water without a care.

The blue sky is an endless ceiling.
The heat from the sun, my shoulders are stealing.
A cool breeze blows around,
Like a whisper, that makes a whistling sound.

Walking on the sand and leaving a trace,
Salty water sprays in my face.
This happens on sunny days,
When I'm on the beach by the waves.

*Carla Anderson, Grade 7*
*Garnet Valley Middle School*

### Later Gator

The undemanding blueprint of green-brown scales
No longer reflect the daylight as they would sodden
They are now coarse like arid cracked land
The aroma of stagnant pond water was over and done
Replaced with scentless sand

He was ensnared in a mistake
A mistake done by something that was beyond his power to prevent
But it was not otherworldly, just complex
It was a drought, an abundance of dehydrated earth
Later gator

*Brenden Bruce, Grade 7*
*South Side Middle School*

## Smile

A smile
They seem innocent and pure
Don't they?
I should know this
I see them every day
But behind every smile lies a lurking past,
An unknown secret
One that wants to go away
The darkness behind that smile only wants to seek light
To be set free
So the smile isn't fake
So it isn't just a mask of happiness
So it can be pure once again
Next time you see someone, anyone.
Think about the smile they have on
Try to look past it
And see what's really inside
Who knows,
Maybe you could shine the light they need
Maybe you can free them.

*Jeanette Gonzalez, Grade 8*
*First Philadelphia Charter School for Literacy*

## The Strongest Things in Life

Everything in life is balanced and even,
Because the elements are something to believe in.
It's the warmth from the dazzling light.
It's the sparks that fly late at night.
The thing that you seek as your burning desire,
Is the logs of wood and the blazing fire.
The gentle breeze that stirs the grass,
It soars and floats as you feel it pass.
You stand back to look at the tent that you pinned,
Then a blast goes by and it's gone with the wind.
It's the luscious greens and the buzzing bees,
From the growing herbs to the healthy trees.
You may eat fruits and berries not knowing of their worth,
Because they are priceless, just like our mother Earth.
The chilling blue tides that come in and out,
Make up the streams that run about.
The home of the fish and the home of the otter,
Is the aqua-blue sea with the shimmering water.
Nothing is stronger than the elements and what they may bring,
Except for the love of nature, for it's the same thing.

*Brenna Ryabin, Grade 7*
*Pennbrook Middle School*

## Peace and Serenity

Peace and serenity is what I'd like to have.
Peace and serenity is what my grandparents had.
Peace and serenity is what you need.
Peace and serenity will answer anybody's plea.
Peace and serenity is what I've come to desire.
Peace and serenity is the ignition to every fire.

*Luke Scioscia, Grade 7*
*Northgate Middle/High School*

## The World

Wars Hate Death
Where is God? The truth is lost
All we feel is despair
Life becomes death
This needs to change
Change! Change the world
Small acts of kindness change the world
Rain still falls, the rain of death and hate
But we have our umbrellas
Umbrellas of hope and love
People abused
We can change that
People hurt
We can change that
Please Help
Love, hope
Have faith
Faith in a better future
God is there if we feel him or not
So start today
Because it's a gift that's why it is called the present

*T.J. Malanga, Grade 8*
*Indian Valley Middle School*

## Have You Ever…?

Have you ever sensed the breeze on your face?
The way it runs its fingers through your hair.
Smelled the aroma of food on the wind?
It comes to you and waves it under your nose.
Have you ever heard the sounds of laughter?
Shrieks of pure joy and happiness,
Carried from over yonder.
Have you ever thought of sitting in a tree,
A book in your lap and a sunset on the horizon?
Leaves jingle a soft lullaby over your head.
When the breeze shifts,
And consumes you in a bear hug,
You laugh with joy at the feeling.
Have you ever longed to have a feeling?
A feeling so sweet…so pure,
You never want it to end.

*Jolene Snodderly, Grade 8*
*Ephrata Middle School*

## For Stenciling, Sharpening, and Other Stuff Too

Only writes in one color, that color is gray,
It will help you finish the PSSA.
It sells in numbers 1, 2, and 3,
0.5 and 0.7 it can also be.
When sharpened it can be like the point on a knife,
And if you collect them, well, you have no life.
It helps you trace those lovely stencils,
Now what was it called?
Oh, yes! It's a pencil!

*Katie McKenna, Grade 7*
*Pennbrook Middle School*

## What Love Is

I never
Never
Knew that feeling
I never had butterflies
Never.
Then, I met you.
Butterflies
Butterflies when I see you.
My heart races, faster, faster.
When you come closer
I catch my breath
And
My heart races, faster, faster.
That feeling I get,
I never knew
That feeling
And now that
I've met you
I know what
Love
Is.

*Gabby Davis, Grade 7*
*Garnet Valley Middle School*

## What I Found in My Room

What I found in my room was
a rusty old broom
a pile of tar
and a small race car.

A
Big snare drum
an old piece of gum
a big torn book
and a small wooden hook.

A
Pencil that's broken
an arcade token
a movie that's scary
and an old man named Gary.

I found all these things
but the one thing that's missing
that bothers me more
was my nice wooden floor.

*Matt Buczynski, Grade 7*
*Pequea Valley Intermediate School*

## Snowflakes

Snowflakes fall so wonderfully,
Crystals sent from above.
The children watch so happily,
We all show lots of love.

*Allie Snider, Grade 7*
*St. Luke School*

## Spread

The bug bites
The pain burns
Darkness spreads with one touch
No retreat
No relief
People dying
Loved ones weep
But as the light
Fades away
Salvation comes
No more pain
No more crying
Life is back
Humanity is saved
From its death
We wear masks
To hide ourselves
But the storm has passed
The land was scorched
But plants will grow
And we will live

*Erik Thele, Grade 7*
*Indian Valley Middle School*

## Life

walking down a road with a friend
walking uphill laughing
sun shines down upon us
as we walk up the hill

walking down a road with a friend
walking downhill crying
rain falls and mixes with tears
as we walk downhill

walking down a road with a friend
walking through ruts of tire tracks
fog covers the land
as we walk through ruts of tire tracks

walking down a road with a friend
walking around twists and turns
over logs and ditches
pausing at crossroads
doubling back at dead ends
walking down a road with a friend

*Kate Deitch, Grade 7*
*William Penn Middle School*

## Where Have You Gone?

I really miss the weather so sunny and nice,
When I could drink water with ice.
Now it's all snowy and gloom,
And I just wish flowers would bloom.

*Maximilian Wieczorek, Grade 8*
*St Luke School*

## Things a Sister Knows

What does a sister know?
Tears and cheers.
Hiding places
Teases
Tortures
Fights and yelling
A home with quiet
Moments
Chasing
Brothers
Upset mothers
Through
Good times
And bad,
All the things a
Sister knows.

*Paige Haycock, Grade 7*
*Easton Area Middle School 7-8*

## Dreams

Dreams are the hope of the future,
The goal of life,
The one thing to keep you going,
When nothing seems right.

Having a dream
Is having a purpose,
Something to work for,
Or simply fall into place.

A magical experience
That grows with excitement,
Twinkling so bright,
Shining like a star,
In the darkest
Of nights.

*Jillian Franko, Grade 9*
*Tamaqua Area Sr High School*

## The Beach Is What Awaits

Slather on the sunscreen,
Put on your cool shades,
Don't forget your towel,
The beach is what awaits.

Hear the sandals flip-flop,
Find shells as sharp as blades,
As ice-cream drips onto your hands,
The beach is what awaits.

Get suntanned as you lie there,
Listen to the crashing waves,
As your thoughts slowly melt away,
The beach is what awaits.

*Ally Rothman, Grade 7*
*Pennbrook Middle School*

**Lost and Found**

I am lost and need to be found,
This is not what I planned; not what I wanted.
I wonder when I will be discovered, found, uncovered.
These words I say now are the truth; no lie.
This could be the end, the final stand; the final hour.

I see birds in the east, and a mountain towering in the west.
How free they are; their ability to fly in the sky, seeing their surroundings.
But I'm not a bird. I'm a helpless human being, stuck on the ground, with no wings to carry me home.
I want to just survive another day, another hour; to enjoy these final moments of life as it is.

I pretend I can fly away; see the world again.
I am not a creature who thrives in the wild, but more of a leaf who gets blown wherever the wind takes it.
Oh, how I've messed up this world I once loved.

I understand I am lost, I fear death, starvation, the dark days to come.
I pray, God, help me; I can't do this alone.
I dream of having my old life back; the life I once loved, cherished and endured.
I try to stay calm and realistic, but I am going insane,
My mind turns different ways;  the dawning of disgrace.
I will find my way, I am lost and need to be found.

*Jacob Miaczynski, Grade 8*
*Wattsburg Area Middle School*

**Embracing Aging**

Glimmering pale oceans melt softly, Spring blissfully arrives.
Tinkling chortles float along the sweet breeze.
Dewdrops glow golden, managing to hug emerald grass blades
Resisting gravity's enthralling grasp.
Thick, sticky fingers hungrily lunge at sunny dandelions, reaching for the swaying stems,
Petals nodding to melodic rhythms of delighted shouts.
But spring grows quieter, older.
No longer the young child it used to be.
Summer, busy with long days, cool nights.
Just enough time to sit and rest and drink thirstily from an almost empty well.
Reflecting quietly on peaceful summer days from the past.
And summer cannot last forever.
Neither will young adulthood, for Autumn is here.
Crisp leaves, the color of dying embers tumble down,
Drifting ever so slowly towards the packed brown earth.
She watches as young children jump about, carefree and grinning, piles of leaves to be no more.
She gently traces an aged hand along the ridged trunk, skeletal branches faintly baring a trace of orange.
Then Autumn feels a shiver creep down her spine, knowing her time is up.
Repetition; not dying, but embracing.
Eyelids close soothingly, her last breath coaxed out by frigid air.
Winter.

*Alexa Silverman, Grade 7*
*Mellon Middle School*

**The Great Sorrow**

Not knowing what to do or how to do it. Telling myself I will and I won't. My brain reaches out but my heart pulls back. My feet go numb all is still. Time passes from minutes to days to years. Waiting for someone to dry up the tears. The Pain stayed, the Joy never came out to play. My mouth screamed at Hate, but Hate never stayed away. All the words are slurred. I'm confused how they come so close together. The great sorrow cast a cloud over me. The rain made it hard to see.

*Noreaga Wells, Grade 8*
*Northern Lebanon Middle School*

### Getting Down on One Knee

Getting down on one knee before the big game!
No quarterback in history has ever been the same.
Tebow thanks God without shame.
He's so filled with faith.

Getting down on one knee, to God he prays
On every single one of his big game days!
Although he's mocked, his strength and faith don't ever sway.
He is steadfast in his faith.

Getting down on one knee to show the world his trust
In God, who's always there for every one of us.
He stands up with much courage
To those who make a fuss
When he gives his thanks and shows his faith.

Tim Tebow is the person who ignores those poking fun.
He gives praise inside the end zone to the Father and the Son.
Tim Tebow is a world awakener.
He is a key change-maker,
All by getting down on one knee.

*Madeline Link, Grade 8*
*St John Vianney Regional School*

### In the Line of Duty

Gone in an instant
Or so we hope
We hope that it was not long,
Long nor painful.
We hope it was as peaceful as can be.

In our prayers we remember
The ultimate sacrifice they made
Brave, honored, and helpful,
They are already missed, one young and one old.

We salute you, all of you
Deep in the dark, devoted
To keeping the people safe
Gone but definitely not forgotten

*Jacob Trombley, Grade 8*
*Daniel Boone Middle School*

### Never Lose Your Pen!

If you lose your pen, you can't take notes.
If you can't take notes, you can't study.
If you can't study you will fail.
If you fail, you will drop out of school.
If you drop out of school, you can't get a job.
If you can't get a job, you won't make money.
If you don't make money, you can't buy food.
If you can't buy food, you will starve.
If you starve, you will die.
Therefore, don't lose your pen, or you will die.

*Brandon Jacobs, Grade 7*
*Elizabeth Forward Middle School*

### One World

Pain, Poverty, Suffering
Fires of hate burn throughout…all the world.
Some people stand up to the hate and are united.
Most people fuel the flames and remain broken.
The whole world is flooded with pain…
Prejudice and hate
People are killing,
people are dying
Skies are fiery and gray
Filled with ash and smoke
More and more the hate builds up.
There is death,
There is hunger,
There is darkness
One person stands and speaks up…
A light of hope pierces through the hate and darkness
It wraps around the whole world and unites it again, making it one
One World
It only takes one person to make a difference
That one person…
Could be you.

*Alex D'Annunzio, Grade 8*
*Indian Valley Middle School*

### Enchanted Forest

Enchanted forest
The breeze sighs
Dew drops glisten on the meadow
Humid, serene, and content
The birds chirrup in a melodious chorus
Come, young child, rest your soul in the wood
A safe haven you have found, dear one
Receive all its exquisite facets
For you are welcomed as the guest of honor
Fairies shall bow before you
Unicorns admire your bravery
You have opposed the demons, now you live in peace
As ruler of our realm
Breathe easily again
Enchanted forest

*Sarah Cain, Grade 7*
*South Side Middle School*

### His

His eyes they shine like the sun shining from above.
His walk is as smooth as a flying dove.
His hugs give me warmth like a summer day.
I know this boy is here to stay.
His laugh is like a ringing bell,
He brought me out of my built up shell.
He showed me how to be myself.
He makes me laugh,
He makes me smile,
I want this boy to stay for awhile.

*Samantha Rutland, Grade 8*
*Centerville Middle School*

### Atlantis

Atlantis is lost to the sea
But its memories and fantasies live on

The Market Place,
Loud and bustling,
Stall owners shout their wares in languages lost
Fruit is bought for the little ones
Who hungrily devour it at home

The Temple,
Quiet, with monks' voices echoing from the bowels
Worshippers praise their God, giving thanks
The walls are smooth with intricate and simple designs

The Council,
The councilors are old yet strong,
Their gray hair and blue eyes
Blaze with intelligence and ingenuity

The Simple Home,
The smell of homemade cooking
Wafts through the house
The soft silk sheets of the beds
Are just one of the amazing things
Of this civilization lost to the sea

*Jacob Uccellini, Grade 7*
*Northgate Middle/High School*

### Ode to the Beach

The visit to the beach,
can be a reach,
if you don't have a ride,
you can stick to the tide.

The waves can hit you like a brick wall.
Which can cause you to have a great fall.
Whoosh they go —
such a great blow.

The sand is a million degrees,
but once in a while you can get a good breeze.
The surf zone is a great rush,
watch out you might just get crushed!

The dolphins soar in the air,
even though they are rare.
Great whites lurk below,
looking for prey who are too slow.

The shells are as sharp as knives.
The scuba divers are careful on the dives.
The lighthouse was protecting,
as the swimmers were unsuspecting,
while the lifeguards were directing.

*Torie Wang, Grade 8*
*Centerville Middle School*

### The Jennie Wade House

Cold
Chills ran down my spine
As I stood waiting
To enter the house of Jennie Wade
Poor Jennie
Had met an unhappy ending
While baking bread for Union soldiers
When a stray bullet ended her life
They carried her body to safety
In the basement of the family's home
She was the only civilian casualty
Of the Battle of Gettysburg
A truly tragic piece of history
She haunts the Jennie Wade House
And when I entered through the doors
I felt the presence of Jennie
Watching my every step
And all throughout the tour
I felt like someone was following me
Then I felt a hand cold as ice on my shoulder
I turned and saw the face of Jennie Wade

*Hannah Watchey, Grade 7*
*Bellwood Antis Middle School*

### My Angel

I think of the start of our adventure
When the days remained forever brand new
You smiled on the day I became a dancer
I remember my first bright pink tutu
I treasure you playing the piano
I loved hearing you play my favorite song
You sang, "do. re. mi. fa. sol. la. ti. do"
With your beautiful voice, my days seemed long
We traveled together around the world
Walking side by side, creating memories
Every memory we had is impearled
All events in our lives have been created into stories
Many girls love to remember their prom,
But, there's one thing that matters more, my mom.

*Jennifer Ra, Grade 9*
*Linden Hall School*

### A Free Spirit

I always knew you were the one,
From the instant our eyes met in the shop window
I made a promise then and I keep that promise now
You will not suffer from pain that won't heal
You brought me joy and pure laughter
And now the sad pain is excruciating
Tears stream down like a waterfall of sorrow
I must be willing to let you go
So go easily now,
Go quickly now, your spirit is free to soar
So rest easy now, your pain will soon be gone

*William Borishkevich, Grade 8*
*Ephrata Middle School*

### The Darkness Project

Violence and rage
have set the stage;
the show is about to begin.

Back out from the light
and into the fright;
the show is about to begin.

There is no hope
in this never-ending slope,
of this queer and mysterious night;
the show is about to begin.

But out of this hole
comes one newborn soul;
the show has been void
our project destroyed
to another soul, darkness begins.

*Ethan Gingrich, Grade 7*
*Lancaster Mennonite School - Locust Grove*

### Image of Soccer

The smell of grass in the air
Fans are cheering everywhere
The ball is zooming through the sky
The losing team screams out why
The feeling of running through the grass
Fans are cheering as I pass
The opponent rushing to you in a hurry
You get it then he starts to worry
You are heading straight for the goal
You're almost there until tripped by a hole
With a mouth full of dirt and in a rush
You hear the fans they start to hush
Don't wonder, don't care, and don't worry how
You need to get the ball right now
You run, you rush, and kick the ball
The goalie jumps but starts to fall
The ball has made it you have won
And truly this game was so much fun

*Devin Haefner, Grade 8*
*Ephrata Middle School*

### The Lake

As I watched the oh, so dreaded,
shining silver crescent moon
descend upon the horizon of the lake,
it drifted lower and lower toward its pure, calm, untouched waters,
until finally, it met the horizon
creating a ripple effect upon the beauty held before me
sending sheathing water to cover my feet
and bury my toes in the sand at the lake's shore
and I became
sad.

*Drake Jacobs, Grade 8*
*Ephrata Middle School*

### My Dream Place

The stone benches are rotting as I seek
The air is warm and moist
As the wind pushes the small wooden swing,
It glides gently back and forth until it stops
Dirt shuffles as I walk silently upon it
Sunlight is trying to peek through,
But is blocked by white clouds
It makes light purples and pinks
As my feet crunch the leaves,
Wind blows them across the ground
Birds are chirping softly in the trees
I wonder why I feel warmth when I'm here?
I wonder why there are no shadows of the past?
I wonder why it feels different here?
Happy is just a word that describes it
Calm is what I feel
Peaceful is what it's like
My dream place
My dream place
My dream place

*Athena Nugent, Grade 7*
*William Penn Middle School*

### Writing a Poem

Writing a poem is immensely bothersome,
It takes a person who is the opposite of dumb.
You need to wait and be patient,
And your mind will often be vacant.

Writing a poem takes time and effort.
You have to think hard about every word and letter.
Concentration and focus are the necessary parts.
Poem writing requires mastery of the Language Arts.

A poet also needs creativity.
The best poems often have originality
To make it a unique poem, include your own personality.
Everybody loves individuality.

Finally, all you need is a nice beat,
And trust me, that is no easy feat.
Hard work and labor are a must
It took me forever to write this, just
Don't give up!

*Andrew Jia, Grade 7*
*Pennbrook Middle School*

### Fall

Fall tiptoes in
Hands shaking, lips quivering, she changes the colors
On the trees
Slow as a turtle
She prances away
Leaving all that is left to stay

*Erin Stoops, Grade 7*
*Garnet Valley Middle School*

### It Can't Be the End
I heard the angles calling my name
I guess they heard my cries of pain
I want it all to go away
But it stays with me every day

It causes a hole in my chest
I have tears in my eyes
I don't know what to do
Does this mean anything to you?

How do I keep being me,
When nothing makes sense?
I feel sick to my stomach
I feel the pounding in my head

But I have to keep going
For my family and friends
Though it seems hard now
I know it can't be the end
*Holly Bruns, Grade 7*
*Salisbury Middle School*

### Power in Your Words
Secrets have their way of slipping
Slithering off the tongue
And gossip grows
From secrets told
Like whispers down the lane

Lies are monsters
Terrible things
They eat you up inside
They grow and grow
Until they pop
Leaving a mess behind

They build you up
They take you down
They happen to be all around
But what matters most
Are the ones you choose
As your shield and your sword
*Abby Loftin, Grade 8*
*Centerville Middle School*

### Music
**M** usic is playing all around me
**N** ow it starts to fade
**O** h no! I
**P** roclaim
**Q** uieter now, as it
**R** uns away from my ears
**S** tarting
**T** o fade into nothingness
*Jonathan Lausch, Grade 8*
*Ephrata Middle School*

### Never Go Away
I am from tears coming
Down my face
From trying to find my way

I am from fake smiles,
To trying to fake a life,
From mistakes to forget

I am from losing no meaning to,
Face happiness,
From waking up, remembering,
The tears of yesterday.

I am from losing friends and family,
From, having no one at all.

I am from long walks by myself,
To find a future of sorrow.
From, day to nights my life is going away,
From tear to rain it's
All the same way, it will
Never go away!
*Rachel Murphy, Grade 8*
*Ephrata Middle School*

### Toast
Bread
In the dragon's nose
Roar
Toast is done
Melted gold
Running on the toast
Sprinkle
The fairy dust on the toast
Fall
In love with the golden brownness
Eat
The toasty toast
*Kalieb Mielnik, Grade 8*
*Bellwood Antis Middle School*

### Dance
Dance flows like water on the
Stage and through me.
Dance decorates delicate movements
That makes me feel free.
Dance is the sun to my summer
Day, need in every way
And I dance to all music
Every day.
Dancing to take away the pain,
I forget about the world,
Working hard for skills to gain,
I leaped, jumped, and twirled
*Ashley Monaco, Grade 8*
*Pine-Richland Middle School*

### Fire Fire!
Fire, fire!
Inmates crying and sparks flying,
Sirens as loud as the fire is high;
Smoke is in the air.

Fire, fire!
The death toll was taken,
It was the most horrible one in a century;
Destruction is in the air.

Fire, fire!
Cries and sobs rose from the crowd,
As the smoke slowly thinned from the air;
Death is in the air.

Fire, fire!
Many have died but memories will not,
Who can forget this tragic event?
Tragedy is in the air.
*Sarah Hahn, Grade 8*
*Conestoga Christian School*

### Change Will Come
Natural disasters
Terrible
Tornadoes shred
Tsunamis crush
Earthquakes tumble
Complete destruction
So much injustice
Many ignore the cries of innocent people
Some choose to leave them to suffer
Isolated and alone
We must pitch in when we can
Then change will come
Tears
Will turn to smiles
Sadness
Will turn to joy
Happiness
Will flourish
The world will be a better place
*Evan Bozek, Grade 7*
*Indian Valley Middle School*

### The Garden
After a long hard winter full of snow,
Always comes a sun that will brightly glow,
It brings a spring full of rain,
That will wash away everyone's pain,
Flowers are beginning to bloom,
Underneath the vibrant moon,
And every day the sun will rise,
As newborn flowers open their eyes.
*Kaley Egan, Grade 8*
*Lake-Lehman Jr High School*

### Spring's Return

Birds sing in the wind
Horses gallop through the snow
Wind whistling fast

*Alliyah Bode, Grade 7*
*Shippensburg Area Middle School*

### October

October leaves fall
Falling all over the ground
Beautiful gold tones.

*Alaina Auell, Grade 8*
*Saegertown Jr/Sr High School*

### Snowflakes

Snowflakes are crystals
Shining in the morning sun.
They are beautiful.

*Chris Mattern-Gilchrist, Grade 8*
*Saegertown Jr/Sr High School*

### Roses

The bright and fair rose
Which grows on a bush with thorns
As red as rubies

*Jasmine Samek, Grade 8*
*Redeemer Lutheran School*

### Scary Night

Spirits haunt my dreams
Skeletons muffle my scream
Night as black as death

*Michaela Mattson, Grade 8*
*Ephrata Middle School*

### Clear Water

Crystal stream flowing
Fish swish back and forth shining
My face reflecting

*Amber Brill, Grade 7*
*Pequea Valley Intermediate School*

### Flowers

Petals are growing
Sun beating on the soil
Water falls gently

*Shaela Marsh, Grade 7*
*Moravian Academy Middle School*

### Summertime

Strolling on the beach
Gazing at the crashing waves
Walking hand in hand.

*Nicole Kreiser, Grade 8*
*Northern Lebanon Middle School*

### Firewocky

'Twas Reaping Day, and the frightened children did worry and wait in the streets:
All commanding were the peacekeepers, and the anxious parents did stand.

"Beware the Careers, my child! The swords that swing, the knives that pierce!
Beware the elements, and shun the deadly Tracker Jackers!"

She took her magnificent bow in hand; Long time the ominous foe she sought —
So rested she by the pine tree and stood awhile in thought.

And, as in defiant thought she stood, the tributes, with eyes of flame,
Came hacking through the dense wood, and mocked as they came!

One, two! One, two! And through and through, the deadly bow went snicker-snack!
She left them dead, and with her friend, she went triumphing back.

"And has thou won the Hunger Games? Come to my arms, my courageous girl!
Oh victorious day! Hooray, Mockingjay!" She beamed in her joy.

*Amanda Zhang, Grade 8*
*Danville Area Middle School*

### It's Funny What the Sun Can Do to a Person

As I watched the rain trickle down the window,
my mind began to wander.
It went immediately to my favorite things,
The Hunger Games, gumdrops, and soccer.
It bothered me when the sky wasn't clear blue.
I felt like it would never show its face again.
I looked back up to the dreary sky,
and I couldn't keep the sad thoughts from flying by.
Dying, crying, and depression,
put a damper on my mood that could not be lifted.

When our car pulled in to our driveway,
My heart sank down to my stomach as I dragged myself inside.
A few hours later I saw a mouse run outside into the rain,
So I chased after it, all the way outside and I couldn't stop smiling at what I found.
The sun was in full bloom
And didn't seem like it was coming down any time soon.

*Allison McFarland, Grade 7*
*Pennbrook Middle School*

### The Forest of Deep Greens

As a peacock wanders through a forest of deep greens
It gazes around
The light hits its pavonated blue head
In a way that every color sparkles
And all of a sudden
Its train of feathers fan open —
Beautiful, bright, and vibrant colors are revealed
The eye upon every feather
Stares back with midnight blue and emerald
And with a final glimpse of its gold, turquoise, and chartreuse feathers
The peacock vanished
Its beauty lost in the forest of deep greens

*Paige Meily, Grade 9*
*State College High School South*

**Things a Skier Knows**
What does a skier know?
Snow and ice,
Heavy boots,
Poles,
Cold,
Hard falls,
Speed,
Trees and fees,
Mountains,
Ski lifts,
Crashes,
Heavy clothes,
Goggles,
Gloves,
What's not to love?
　　　　*Lexus Holton, Grade 7*
　*Easton Area Middle School 7-8*


**The Walk Toward the Podium**
The goal
The ultimate goal
Which many dream
The pride, the joy
The knowledge you've succeeded
The road, the journey
That got you there
The failures, the anguish
You had battled through
The friends, the family
There every step of the way
All comes to this one moment
The anthem being played
When you get to stand
On the podium
　　　　*Jennifer Strine, Grade 9*
　*Spring Grove Area Sr High School*


**What Am I**
Who am I
I help you remember
I am very helpful in school
I go over and on top of stuff
Do you know what I am
Think outside the box.

I come in many different colors
But after I get used a lot
I run out
they throw me away
I am helpless
What am I?

I am a highlighter.
　　　　*Tyke Shubert, Grade 8*
　*Spring Grove Middle School*


**Butterfly**
High in the blue sky.
There goes a pink butterfly.
Fly butterfly, fly.
　*Rebecca Peterman, Grade 7*
*Cambria Heights Middle School*

# Index

*Author Autograph Page*

*Author Autograph Page*

*Author Autograph Page*

*Author Autograph Page*

*Author Autograph Page*

*Author Autograph Page*

*Author Autograph Page*

*Author Autograph Page*

*Author Autograph Page*

*Author Autograph Page*

*Author Autograph Page*

*Author Autograph Page*